Great Depression and New Deal
Biographies

7/04

Great Depression and New Deal Biographies

Sharon M. Hanes
and
Richard C. Hanes

Allison McNeill,
Project Editor

Detroit • New York • San Diego • San Francisco • Cleveland • New Haven, Conn. • Waterville, Maine • London • Munich

THOMSON

GALE

Great Depression and New Deal: Biographies

Sharon M. Hanes and Richard C. Hanes

Project Editor
Allison McNeill

Permissions
Lori Hines

Imaging and Multimedia
Dean Dauphinais, Robert Duncan

Product Design
Pamela Galbreath, Cynthia Baldwin

Composition
Evi Seoud

Manufacturing
Rita Wimberley

LIBRARY OF CONGRESS CONTROL NUMBER 2002015353

Printed in the United States of America
10 9 8 7 6 5 4 3 2 1

Contents

Introduction

Embedded within the timeline of a nation's history are certain extraordinary events that spur rapid change within the society and impact the political life and thinking of the people for decades thereafter. In the timeline of the United States, such events include the American Revolution (1775–83), the Civil War (1861–65), World War II (1939–45), and perhaps the Vietnam War (1954–75). Aside from wars, other momentous and highly influential events include the industrial revolution (roughly nineteenth century), the civil rights movement of the 1950s and 1960s, and the Great Depression (1929–41). The Great Depression was the longest and worst economic crisis in U.S. history. It was not only economically devastating for millions, but was a personal tragedy for Americans from the very young to the very old.

What could cause such a dramatic economic downturn in the United States? To most Americans it seemed the prosperity of the "roaring" 1920s would go on forever. Yet, throughout the 1920s economic difficulties in certain segments of the American economy began to surface. Industrialization, that is, the development of industries that mass-produced consumer goods such as washing machines and automobiles, dramatically affected the United States. Rolling off assembly lines at ever increasing rates, goods were touted by advertisers who encouraged consumers to borrow money to buy the goods, a practice known as buying on credit. In the 1920s American values of thrift and saving money increasingly gave way to accumulating debt as Americans bought the latest products on "credit" just as soon as the products appeared in the stores. Banks eagerly made loan after loan. However, by 1929 this buying had slowed. It seemed consumers could only buy so much.

The major share of wealth in the nation rested in the hands of a tiny percentage of individual families. The very wealthy could not sustain enough buying power to make up for the slowdown in buying by the rest of the population. Goods began to accumulate on store shelves forcing factories to slow down production and lay off workers.

Another sector of the U.S. economy experiencing difficulty was the agriculture sector. Farmers had been overproducing since the end of World War I (1914–18), even after the drop in overseas demand for their products. The glut of farm products had driven farm prices so low that farmers could barely earn a living much less buy consumer goods. Farm families still accounted for 25 to 30 percent of the U.S. population, so a significant number of Americans were already struggling.

Although these various signs of economic trouble began emerging in the 1920s, hardly anyone paid attention. The majority of Americans were enjoying prosperity as never before. So, when in October 1929 the U.S. stock market crashed, the American public was shocked. They suddenly realized the economic health of the nation was not as good as it had seemed. Billions of dollars were lost and small investors were wiped out. Although the stock market crash was only one of a number of factors leading to the Great Depression of the 1930s, in the public's mind it has always marked the start of the worst economic crisis in U.S. history. By 1932 twelve million workers, amounting to over 25 percent of the workforce, were jobless. Industrial production had dropped to 44 percent of the average in the 1920s. For those who kept their jobs, incomes dropped an average of 40 percent between 1929 and 1932.

For the first time many citizens questioned the U.S. system of democracy and capitalism (an economic system in which goods are owned by private businesses and price and production is decided privately). They also questioned the notion of individualism, the American belief that people can successfully make their own way in society without government intervention. The prevailing mood of the nation moved from opportunity to despair; from progress to survival. A philosophical tug of war raged between big business, who wanted to work out the country's economic woes voluntarily, and those who wanted government to begin regulating business. President Herbert Hoover (served 1929–1933) was unable to halt the economic slide.

The inauguration of Franklin D. Roosevelt as the thirty-second president of the United States in March 1933 signaled the beginning of a new relationship between Americans and their government. For the first time in U.S. history the people began to look to the government to aid in their economic well-being. For many Americans, President Roosevelt's introduction of an incredible variety of social and economic programs, known as the New Deal, brought hope again. People believed they had a leader who actually cared about their welfare and establishing economic safety nets. The New Deal programs were designed to first bring relief (food, clothing, monetary payments) to Americans hardest hit by the Depression. Next came the recovery and reform programs to stimulate the economy and put into place plans that would lessen the danger of future depressions. Government became intricately involved in business regulation, labor organizations, public support of the arts, social security, resource conservation, development of inexpensive and plentiful energy sources, stock market reform, farming reform, photodocumentary journalism, housing reform, public health programs, and increasing the number of minorities and women in public life. Business leaders and the well-to-do despaired that the atmosphere of *laissez-faire* (les-a-fair) government (in which industries operated free of government restraint) was over. Government regulations and higher taxes ended the long tradition of industry voluntarily regulating itself.

As the Depression lingered on through the 1930s, various segments of American society were affected differently. Those in the middle classes learned to "make do," creating meals from simple ingredients, making their own clothes, finding entertainment at home with board games and listening to the radio, and helping other family members who had lost their jobs. The extreme competitiveness and consumption-oriented values of the 1920s gave way to cooperativeness and neighborly help. Those Americans already considered poor or part of a minority group suffered mightily during the Depression. In contrast America's wealthiest families, for the most part, seemingly ignored the Depression and continued their luxurious lifestyle.

Roosevelt's New Deal did not lead directly to major economic recovery for the United States. By the mid to late 1930s President Roosevelt hesitated to spend the amount of money necessary to push the economy into complete recovery. While the New Deal programs did not stop the Depression, they did end the dramatic plunge in the economy and gave food and shelter to those most in need. The Great Depression did not fully end until 1941, as the United States prepared for World War II. The mobilization of industry to manufacture massive quantities of war materials and the growth of the armed forces at last ended the Great Depression.

The extraordinary event of the Great Depression brought major change in how Americans view government. Historically the federal government was viewed as detached from the everyday activities of Americans. The severity of the Depression made Americans consider, even demand, that the federal government act to enhance and insure the well-being of its citizens. At the beginning of the twenty-first century debate continues over how far the government should go in guaranteeing the financial security of its citizens. Debates still rage over government regulation of business, individualism versus cooperation for the common good, and over specific issues such as the Social Security system, the role of labor unions in business, and the welfare system providing aid to the nation's poorest.

Sharon M. Hanes and Richard C. Hanes

Reader's Guide

The Great Depression, which took place between 1929 and 1941, was the deepest and most prolonged economic crisis in United States history. It is a story of great human suffering for many and the inspiring rise of some to meet the challenge. President Franklin D. Roosevelt introduced a diverse series of new federal programs, known collectively as the New Deal, that revamped the nation's governmental system. From the strife came the modern bureaucratic state providing economic safeguards for its citizens. America emerged as a profoundly different nation by 1941 than it had been in 1929. The New Deal did not end the Great Depression and lead to full economic recovery, but it did end the dramatic economic plunge, gave those most affected food and shelter, and reestablished hope in the future and faith in the U.S. economic system.

Great Depression and New Deal: Biographies presents the life stories of twenty-nine individuals who played key roles in the governmental and social responses to the economic crisis. Individuals were selected to give readers a wide perspective on this era of American history. Included are presidents, a senator, cabinet members, government administrators, photographers, an educator, a musician, industrialists, intellectuals, a journalist, a priest, activists, and a labor leader. *Great Depression and New Deal: Biographies* includes well-known figures such as Franklin D. Roosevelt, Eleanor Roosevelt, Will Rogers, Herbert Hoover, J. Edgar Hoover, and Woody Guthrie, as well as lesser-known individuals such as Hallie Flanagan, head of the Federal Theatre Project, and Mary McLeod Bethune, educator and the first black American to head a federal agency.

Features

The entries in *Great Depression and New Deal: Biographies* contain sidebar boxes that highlight topics of special interest related to the individual; each entry also offers a list of additional sources students can go to for more information, including sources used in writing the chapter. Fifty-seven black-and-white photographs illustrate the material. The volume begins with a timeline of important events in the history of the Great Depression and a "Words to Know" section that introduces students to difficult or unfamiliar terms (terms are also defined within the text). The volume concludes with a general bibliography and a subject index so students can easily find the people, places, and events discussed throughout *Great Depression and New Deal: Biographies*.

Great Depression and New Deal Reference Library

Great Depression and New Deal: Biographies is only one component of the three-part U•X•L Great Depression and New Deal Reference Library. The other two titles in this set are:

- *Great Depression and New Deal: Almanac* (one volume) presents a comprehensive overview of the period in American history known as the Great Depression in sixteen chapters, each geared toward offering an understanding of a single element of the crisis; from the crash of the U.S. stock market in October 1929 to the end of the Depression in 1941 that came as a result of mobilization for World War II (1939–45).

- *Great Depression and New Deal: Primary Sources* (one volume) tells the story of the Great Depression in the words of the people who lived it. Thirty full or excerpted documents provide a wide range of perspectives on this period in history. Included are excerpts from presidential press conferences, inaugural speeches, addresses to Congress, and radio addresses; later reflections by key government leaders; oral histories of those who experienced the economic crisis, including youth who rode the rails; lyrics of songs derived from the Great Depression experience; and reflections by photographers who recorded the poverty and desperation of the time.

- A cumulative index of all three titles in the U•X•L Great Depression and New Deal Reference Library is also available.

Advisors

A note of appreciation is extended to the *Great Depression and New Deal: Biographies* advisors who provided invaluable suggestions when the work was in its formative stages:

Frances Bryant Bradburn
Director of Educational Technologies
North Carolina Public Schools
Raleigh, North Carolina

Elaine Ezell
Media Specialist
Bowling Green Junior High School
Bowling Green, Ohio

Dedication

To our son, Dustin, who endured numerous discussions and debates of New Deal policy and Great Depression issues over dinner and during car trips.

Special Thanks

Catherine Filip typed much of the manuscript. Much gratitude also goes to the advisors who guided the project throughout its course.

Comments and Suggestions

We welcome your comments on *Great Depression and New Deal: Biographies* and suggestions for other topics to consider. Please write: Editors, *Great Depression and New Deal:*

Biographies, U•X•L, 27500 Drake Rd., Farmington Hills, Michigan 48331-3535; call toll-free: 1-800-877-4253; fax to (248) 699-8097; or send e-mail via http://www.gale.com.

Great Depression Timeline

January 17, 1920 The Eighteenth Amendment, known as Prohibition, goes into effect, banning the sale and manufacture of all alcoholic beverages in the United States.

1921–1932 With every passing year, Prohibition is ignored more and more while the gangsters of organized crime become immensely wealthy from "bootlegging" illegal alcohol.

1923 The value of stocks on the U.S. stock market begins a six-year upward climb.

1928 "Amos 'n' Andy," a radio program, premieres and becomes the most popular radio show through the 1930s.

November 1928 Republican Herbert Hoover is elected president of the United States. His policies would prove ineffective in fighting the Great Depression that strikes in October 1929.

February 23, 1929 The Brotherhood of Sleeping Car Porters, headed by A. Philip Randolph, is the first African American union to be chartered by the American Federation of Labor (AFL).

A. Philip Randolph (right).
©Joseph Schwartz Collection/CORBIS.

October 24, 1929 Known as "Black Thursday," a record-breaking crash on the New York Stock Exchange begins several weeks of market panics. Many investors lose vast sums of money when the value of stocks plummets. Approximately 12.8 million shares of stock are sold in one day, most at prices far below their values only a few days earlier.

October 29, 1929 Known as "Black Tuesday," the value of stocks on the New York Stock Market continues its dramatic decline. Approximately 16,410,000 shares, a record number, are sold. The nation's economy steadily erodes into the Great Depression, the worst economic crisis in U.S. history.

1930–1932 Gangster movies are at their height of popularity.

1930 Hostess food manufacturer creates the Twinkie, an inexpensive treat for economy-minded Americans.

1930 Congress authorizes construction of Hoover Dam, known as Boulder Dam during the New Deal, on the Colorado River. Construction begins in 1930 and is completed in 1936. The project provides thousands of jobs.

1931–1932 More than 3,600 banks suspend operations as the Depression deepens and thousands lose their jobs and incomes.

1931 Sales of glass jars for preserving food at home increases dramatically. Preserving food decreases a family's food expenses.

1931 A drought begins in the Eastern states during the summer and quickly spreads to the Midwest and Great Plains. The drought will continue throughout the decade resulting in "dust bowl" conditions.

1931 New York City reports ninety-five cases of death by starvation as the number of unemployed and those going hungry increases.

October 24, 1931 Alphonse Capone, the nation's most notorious gangster, receives an eleven-year prison sentence for income tax evasion.

1932   Franklin D. Roosevelt forms a group of political advisors during his presidential campaign. This group, known as the Brain Trust, is composed of Rexford Tugwell, Adolf Berle Jr, and Raymond Moley.

1932   Jigsaw puzzles are mass-produced for the first time and provide inexpensive entertainment.

1932   Molly Dewson develops key campaign literature for Franklin D. Roosevelt: distinctive, brightly-colored, one-page fact sheets known as Rainbow Flyers.

1932   Prices for farm produce hit bottom as farmer unrest rises.

1932   Sixty percent of the U.S. population still faithfully pay the few cents it costs to attend movies.

1932   The Depression spawns cuts in educational budgets affecting teacher salaries and programs offered and leads to school closures, especially in rural areas.

1932   Father Charles Coughlin, "the radio priest," becomes a supporter of Franklin D. Roosevelt and coins the slogan, "Roosevelt or Ruin." By 1934, Coughlin's radical political views cause Roosevelt to distance himself from Coughlin.

January 22, 1932 Congress establishes the Reconstruction Finance Corporation to provide federal financial support to the banking system.

July 2, 1932 Franklin Delano Roosevelt delivers a speech accepting the Democratic nomination for president pledging "a new deal for the American people."

July 28, 1932 Thousands of unemployed and financially strapped World War I veterans and their families, known as the Bonus Army, march on Washington, DC, seeking early payment of previously promised bonus pay, but are denied by Congress. Violence erupts, reflecting badly on the Hoover administration.

November 1932 Roosevelt handily wins the presidential election over incumbent Republican Herbert Hoover but will not be inaugurated until March 4, 1933.

1933–1935 Midwestern outlaws rob banks and kills citizens on wild rampages through the nation's heartland.

Rexford Tugwell. *UPI/Corbis Bettmann.*

Charles Coughlin. *AP/Wide World Photo.*

Franklin D. Roosevelt. *©Bettmann/Corbis.*

Herbert Hoover (left) and Franklin D. Roosevelt. *Hulton Archive/Getty Images.*

Frances Perkins. *AP/Wide World Photo.*

1933 Unemployment reaches 25 percent of the nation's workforce.

1933 Actor and humorist Will Rogers ranks among the most popular and highest-paid celebrities of the day.

1933 Estimates reveal that well over one million Americans are homeless and almost one-fourth are riding the railroads in search of work or aimlessly drifting. Youth comprise 40 percent of that number on the rails.

1933 The number of marriages declines 40 percent from the 1920s level as couples, unable to earn a living wage, postpone marriage.

1933 The number of lynchings of black Americans in the United States during the Great Depression peaks at twenty-eight.

1933 Membership in teachers' unions such as the American Federation of Teachers (AFT) increases rapidly in reaction to budget and staff cuts due to the Depression.

1933 Big, splashy musicals become hit movies taking Americans' minds off the hard economic times.

1933 Child actress Shirley Temple is introduced to movie audiences.

1933 The Chicago World's Fair opens.

1933 Harold Ickes serves as secretary of the interior for thirteen years, from 1933 to 1946; longer than anyone else in U.S. history.

March 4, 1933 With the U.S. banking system all but paralyzed, Franklin D. Roosevelt is inaugurated as president declaring "there is nothing to fear but fear itself."

March 4, 1933 Franklin D. Roosevelt appoints Frances Perkins secretary of labor. The first woman in a U.S. president's cabinet, she stayed at the post until July 1, 1945.

March 4 1933 Franklin D. Roosevelt appoints Henry Wallace as secretary of agriculture. He holds the position until 1940, when Roosevelt names him as his vice presidential nominee.

March 6, 1933 At 1:00 A.M. President Roosevelt orders a nationwide "bank holiday" from Monday, March 6 through Thursday, March 9, and then extends it through March 12.

March 6, 1933 First Lady Eleanor Roosevelt begins her weekly news conferences open only to women journalists.

March 9, 1933 Congress begins a special session to approve legislation aimed at economic relief and recovery. Congress passes the Emergency Bank Act in a successful effort to restore public confidence in the banking system.

March 12, 1933 President Roosevelt delivers his first radio "fireside chat," explaining to the American people what has happened in the U.S. banking system.

March 13, 1933 Most U.S. banks successfully reopen.

Mid-March 1933 President Roosevelt begins the first of his informal and informative presidential news conferences.

March 31, 1933 The Civilian Conservation Corps (CCC) is established providing jobs in conservation activities for young Americans replanting forests, soil conservation, and flood control.

April 5, 1933 Robert Fechner is appointed head of the Civilian Conservation Corps. He holds the position until his death in 1939.

May 1, 1933 Dorothy Day publishes the first edition of her newspaper, the *Catholic Worker*.

May 12, 1933 Congress passes the Agricultural Adjustment Act (AAA), designed to raise farm prices by encouraging farmers to reduce production.

May 12, 1933 Congress passes the Emergency Farm Mortgage Act to provide loans to farmers in heavy debt.

May 12, 1933 Congress passes the Federal Emergency Relief Act (FERA), providing funds to assist state relief programs helping the unemployed, aged, and ill.

May 17, 1933 The Tennessee Valley Authority (TVA) is created to bring economic development to the Southeast

Eleanor Roosevelt. *AP/Wide World Photo.*

Dorothy Day. *©Bettmann/CORBIS.*

Harry Hopkins. *AP/Wide World Photo.*

through construction of numerous dams and hydropower plants.

May 22, 1933 Harry Hopkins is appointed administrator of the newly created Federal Emergency Relief Administration (FERA).

May 27, 1933 Congress passes the Federal Securities Act, requiring companies and stockbrokers to provide full information about new stocks to potential investors.

June 1933 Ellen Woodward is appointed director of the Women's Division of the Federal Emergency Relief Administration (FERA). She remains in this position until 1935.

June 1933 Lorena Hickok begins working for FERA administrator Harry Hopkins as chief investigator of New Deal relief programs. Hickok serves in the same investigative capacity when Hopkins takes over administration of the Civil Works Administration (CWA) in the winter of 1933–34 and the Works Progress Administration (WPA) starting in 1935.

June 13, 1933 Congress passes the Home Owners' Refinancing Act, which creates the Home Owners'Loan Corporation (HOLC) to provide loans to homeowners facing the loss of their homes because they cannot make payments.

June 16, 1933 Congress passes the Farm Credit Act. It formalizes the earlier-created Farm Credit Administration, which established a system of banking institutions for farmers.

June 16, 1933 Congress passes the Banking Act, also known as the Glass-Steagall Act, establishing the Federal Deposit Insurance Corporation (FDIC) insuring individual bank accounts against loss.

June 16, 1933 Congress passes the National Industrial Recovery Act establishing codes of fair practice for industry and business and creating the National Recovery Administration (NRA).

June 16, 1933 The Public Works Administration (PWA) is created to distribute almost $6 billion between 1933 and 1939 for public works projects, including construction of roads, tunnels, bridges, dams, power plants, and hospitals.

June 16, 1933 Congress finishes the special session, an intensive period of lawmaking that becomes known as the First Hundred Days.

November 9, 1933 Roosevelt establishes the Civil Works Administration (CWA) to assist unemployed workers through the winter months.

December 5, 1933 The thirtieth state ratifies the Twenty-first Amendment ending Prohibition, which banned the sale of all alcoholic beverages.

1934–1935 J. Edgar Hoover's Special Agents of the Federal Bureau of Investigation (FBI) capture or kill all of the famous Midwest outlaws and restore confidence in U.S. law enforcement.

1934 Horace Bond publishes *The Education of the Negro in the American Social Order.* The book is considered a major contribution to the study of black education in America and influences black educators for decades.

J. Edgar Hoover (right).
©*Bettmann/CORBIS.*

1934 Lammot, Irénée, and Raskob du Pont, along with other leading industrialists and financiers in the nation, establish the American Liberty League (ALL). The league is dedicated to defeating Roosevelt in his 1936 reelection bid and stopping his New Deal programs.

1934 Molly Dewson establishes the Reporter Plan, a network of women who volunteer to study the impact of Roosevelt's New Deal programs and monitor the progress of government agencies in their communities. Five thousand women join the network in 1934; by 1940 thirty thousand have joined.

January 1, 1934 Franklin D. Roosevelt appoints Henry Morgenthau secretary of the treasury. Morgenthau remains in the position for the next eleven years.

January 31, 1934 Congress passes the Farm Mortgage Refinancing Act providing $2 billion in loans to refinance farm loans.

Franklin D. Roosevelt (left) and Henry Morgenthau.
©*Bettmann/CORBIS.*

June 6, 1934 Congress passes the Securities Exchange Act that prohibits certain activities in stock market trading, sets penalties and establishes the Securities Exchange Commission (SEC) to oversee stock market trading.

June 18, 1934 Congress passes the Indian Reorganization Act (Wheeler-Howard Act) establishing the cornerstone of New Deal Indian policy.

June 19, 1934 Congress passes the Communications Act that creates the Federal Communications Commission (FCC) to oversee the nation's mass-communications industry.

June 28, 1934 Congress passes the National Housing Act, creating the Federal Housing Administration (FHA) to assist homeowners in buying a new house in hopes of spurring the construction industry. This act is the last piece of legislation passed under the First New Deal that began with legislation in March 1933.

November 15, 1934 Marriner Eccles is appointed governor of the Federal Reserve Board by Franklin D. Roosevelt.

1935 Eleanor Roosevelt continues her support of women, young people, and black Americans during the Depression. She is determined that no group who needs New Deal projects be left out.

1935 Warner Brothers' sensational hit movie *G-Men* immortalizes J. Edgar Hoover as America's number one cop, made his "government men," later known as FBI agents, famous, and helped restore a general respect for law enforcement.

1935 In one week people buy twenty million Monopoly games, providing inexpensive entertainment.

1935 More than 500,000 men are enrolled in 2,600 Civilian Conservation Corps camps across the United States.

1935 Du Pont researchers develop nylon, and it is unveiled to the public at the 1939 New York World's Fair. Nylon became the hottest-selling product in Du Pont history and was used to make new consumer goods such as nylon hosiery.

April 8, 1935 Congress passes the Emergency Relief Appropriation Act creating the Works Progress Administration (WPA) and providing almost $5 billion for work relief for the unemployed for such projects as construction of airports, schools, hospitals, roads, and public buildings. This act marks the beginning of the Second New Deal

April 9, 1935 Ellen Woodward is appointed assistant administrator for the Works Progress Administration (WPA).

April 27, 1935 Congress passes the Soil Conservation Act establishing the Soil Conservation Service (SCS) to aid farmers suffering drought and massive soil erosion.

April 30, 1935 Roosevelt creates the Resettlement Administration (RA) to help poor farmers either improve the use of their lands or move to better lands. The agency's Historical Section begins a major photodocumentary project of the Depression.

May 1935 Roy Stryker is named administrator of the Historical Section within the RA's Division of Information. He gathers many talented photographers, including Dorothea Lange and Arthur Rothstein.

May 11, 1935 Roosevelt creates the Rural Electrification Administration (REA) to bring inexpensive electricity to rural areas.

May 27, 1935 In one of several rulings against New Deal programs, the U.S. Supreme Court in *Schechter Poultry Corporation v. United States* rules the National Industrial Recovery Act is unconstitutional thus removing legal protections for labor unions. This day becomes known as "Black Monday."

June 26, 1935 Roosevelt creates the National Youth Administration (NYA) to provide part-time jobs to high school and college students and other unemployed youth.

June 26, 1935 Roosevelt appoints Aubrey Williams director of the National Youth Administration (NYA). Williams remains in the position until the program ends in 1943.

July 1, 1935 The Federal Deposit Insurance Corporation (FDIC) begins operation providing stability to the banking system by insuring bank deposits.

Ellen Woodward. *AP/Wide World Photo.*

Hallie Flanagan. *AP/Wide World Photo.*

July 5, 1935 Congress passes the National Labor Relations Act, better known as the Wagner Act (named after Senator Robert Wagner who drafted the legislation), to support the right of workers to organize and bargain collectively with employers over working conditions, benefits, and wages. The act also bans certain unfair business practices.

August 2, 1935 Created as part of the WPA, the Federal One program is established to provide jobs for the unemployed in music, theater, writing, and art.

August 1935 Hallie Flanagan is appointed director of the Federal Theatre Project (FTP), a program for unemployed actors and artists established under the Works Progress Administration.

August 14, 1935 Congress passes the Social Security Act establishing a program of social insurance to aid the unemployed, the elderly in retirement, needy children and mothers, and the blind.

August 23, 1935 Congress passes the Banking Act strengthening the Federal Reserve System.

August 30, 1935 Congress passes the Wealth Tax Act creating higher tax rates for the wealthy and corporate and inheritance taxes.

November 1935 The Federal Surplus Commodities Corporation is established to continue distributing food to the needy.

November 9, 1935 Labor leader John L. Lewis establishes the Committee of Industrial Organizations to represent semi-skilled and unskilled laborers of the mass production industries.

1936 Mary McLeod Bethune is named head of the Division of Negro Affairs of the National Youth Administration becoming the first black American to head a government agency.

1936 Horace Bond publishes *Negro Education in Alabama: A Study in Cotton and Steel*. It provides a detailed look at the economic, political, and social factors influencing black public school education in the South.

Mary McLeod Bethune. *UPI/Bettmann.*

1936 Songwriter Woody Guthrie begins to write his "Dust Bowl Ballads." One of the earliest ballads is "Dust Storm Disaster." Between 1936 and 1941 Guthrie writes approximately twenty ballads about the dust storms, the farmers, and the farmers turned migrants.

January 6, 1936 The U.S. Supreme Court in *United States v. Butler* rules the Agricultural Adjustment Act is unconstitutional.

March 1936 FSA photographer Dorothea Lange photographs a migrant woman and her children in a pea pickers' camp in Nipomo, California. Known as the "Migrant Mother," the photograph becomes a lasting symbol of hard times during the 1930s Depression era.

June 16, 1936 Congress passes the Flood Control Act in response to massive floods in the Ohio and Mississippi River areas.

November 1936 Franklin D. Roosevelt wins a landslide re-election capturing a record 61 percent of the vote.

December 30, 1936 Sit-down strikes shutdown seven General Motors plants in Flint, Michigan. The company will give in to worker demands by February 11, 1937.

1937 Roosevelt appoints attorney William Hastie as the first black American federal judge in U.S. history.

1937 Author Erskine Caldwell and photographer Margaret Bourke-White publish *You Have Seen Their Faces.*

1937 Kraft introduces the "instant" macaroni and cheese dinner and Hormel introduces Spam meat. The low cost of both items helps feed families who are on a tight budget.

February 1937 Arthur Altmeyer is appointed head of the Social Security Adminstration, a position he holds until 1953.

February 5, 1937 Roosevelt introduces a proposal, known as the "court packing plan," to reorganize the U.S. Supreme Court. The plan attracts substantial public opposition.

May 24, 1937 The U.S. Supreme Court upholds the constitutionality of the Social Security Act.

Dorothea Lange. *Library of Congress.*

Arthur Altmeyer. *AP/Wide World Photo.*

Robert F. Wagner.
©Bettmann/CORBIS.

July 22, 1937 Congress passes the Bankhead-Jones Farm Tenancy Act making low interest loans available to tenant farmers, farm laborers, and small landowners, many of whom are victims of the Dust Bowl, to purchase or expand their own lands.

August 20, 1937 The Bonneville Power Act establishes the Bonneville Power Administration to market public power in the Pacific Northwest.

September 1, 1937 Roosevelt creates the Farm Security Administration, absorbing the Resettlement Administration including the photography project.

September 3, 1937 Congress passes the National Housing Act, known as the Wagner-Steagall Housing Act, creating the U.S. Housing Authority to oversee construction of low-cost housing.

October 1937 An economic "recession" begins as industrial production and farm prices fall and unemployment rises. In hopes of never again using the term "depression," President Roosevelt coins the term "recession."

February 16, 1938 Congress passes the new Agricultural Adjustment Act providing new price supports for farmers and promoting conservation practices.

June 24, 1938 Congress passes the Food, Drug, and Cosmetic Act.

June 25, 1938 The Fair Labor Standards Act places legal protections over child labor, minimum wages, and maximum hours. This act is the last legislation of the Second New Deal.

October 30, 1938 Orson Welles' *Mercury Theatre of the Air* broadcasts a radio adaptation of H.G. Wells' 1898 novel *The War of the Worlds* causing widespread panic.

1939 Eighty percent of American households own radios.

1939 The Golden Gate International Exposition opens in San Francisco and the New York World's Fair opens in New York City.

1939 The Federal Writers Project publishes *These Are Our Lives* and John Steinbeck publishes *The Grapes of Wrath*.

1939   Drought comes to an end as rains return to the Great Plains in the fall.

1939   Reporter Edward R. Murrow broadcasts from London, England, during the German bombing raids on the city shifting public concerns away from domestic economic issues to foreign issues.

1939   World famous American opera singer Marian Anderson is denied the opportunity to perform in a private concert hall in Washington, DC, because she is black, leading to a major public backlash against racism.

May 16, 1939 The Food Stamp program begins.

August 10, 1939 Congress passes the Social Security Act Amendments adding old age and survivors' insurance benefits for dependents and survivors.

1941   Roosevelt signs an executive order prohibiting racial discrimination in the defense industry, the first such proclamation since Reconstruction in the 1870s.

1941   Author James Agee and photographer Walker Evans publish *Let Us Now Praise Famous Men*.

1941   Woody Guthrie writes twenty-six songs in thirty days—including "Roll On, Columbia," and "Pastures of Plenty"—while employed by the Bonneville Power Administration (BPA), a New Deal agency.

Woody Guthrie. *Archive Photos.*

July 9, 1941 President Roosevelt announces extensive preparations in case of U.S. entrance into World War II.

December 7, 1941 Japan bombs U.S. military installations at Pearl Harbor, Hawaii, leading the United States to enter World War II in both Europe and the Pacific.

January 16, 1942 The War Production Board is established to direct war mobilization.

April 1942 The War Manpower Commission is created to help allocate manpower to industries and military services.

April 12, 1945 Franklin D. Roosevelt suddenly dies at sixty-three years of age from a cerebral hemorrhage.

Words to Know

A

abstinence: A voluntary decision not to drink alcoholic beverages.

activist: One who aggressively promotes a cause such as seeking change in certain social, economic, or political conditions in society.

amortize: To allow a loan to be repaid with stable monthly payments that include both principal and interest; amortizing mortgages allow buyers to gradually repay the principal balance until the loan is paid back in full.

appraisal: The set value of a property as determined by the estimate of an authorized person.

appropriations: Money authorized by Congress to an agency for a special purpose.

atomic bomb: A bomb whose explosive force comes from a nuclear splitting-apart of atoms releasing a large amount of energy.

attorney general: The chief law officer of a state or country and head of the legal department. In the United States, the person is head of the U.S. Department of Justice and is a member of the president's cabinet.

B

bank holiday: The legal suspension of bank operation for a period of time.

bank run: A sudden demand to withdraw deposits from a bank; bank runs occurred after the stock market crash of 1929, when depositors feared that their banks were unstable.

benefits: Financial aid (such as insurance or retirement pension) in time of sickness, old age, or unemployment. Also holidays, vacations, and other privileges provided by an employer in addition to hourly wages or salary.

big business: Large and influential businesses such as industries or financial institutions.

Black Cabinet: An informal organization of black Americans serving in various federal positions that advised President Franklin Roosevelt on black issues through the late 1930s.

bootlegger: A person who illegally transports liquor.

boycott: A refusal by a group of persons to buy goods or services from a business until the business meets their demands.

breadlines: During the Depression, long lines of unemployed people waiting to receive a free meal of soup and a chunk of bread from a charity or soup kitchen.

broker: One who buys or sells a stock for an investor and charges a fee for the service.

budget: The amount of money a person or family has to spend on food, clothing, shelter, and other necessities.

buying on margin: The purchase of stock by paying some cash down and borrowing the rest of the purchase price.

C

cabinet: An official group of advisors to the U.S. president including the heads of the various major governmental departments such as Department of Commerce.

capital: Money invested in a business and used to operate that business. Capital is the amount banks owe their owners.

capitalism: An economic system in which goods are privately owned and prices, production, and distribution of goods are determined by competition in a free market.

chain gangs: Groups of convicts chained together while working outside the prison.

collective bargaining: Negotiation between representatives of an employer and representatives of labor, with both sides working to reach agreement on wages, job benefits, and working conditions.

collectivism: Shared ownership of goods by all members of a group; a political or economic system in which production and distribution are controlled by all members of a group.

commercial bank: A bank that offers checking accounts, savings accounts, and personal and business loans.

communism: A theory calling for the elimination of private property so that goods are owned in common and available to all; a system of government in which a single party controls all aspects of society, as in the Union of Soviet Socialist Republics (U.S.S.R.) from 1917 until 1990.

conservation: The planned management of natural resources, such as soil and forests.

conservative: A person who holds traditional views and who seeks to preserve established institutions; a conservative approach to education, for example, stresses traditional basic subject matter and traditional methods of teaching.

cooperative: A private, nonprofit enterprise, locally owned and managed by the members it serves and incorporated (established as a legal entity that can hold property or be subject to lawsuits) under state law.

corporate volunteerism: To encourage business to support a public program or goal through voluntary actions rather than by government regulation.

craft union: A type of union that represents workers having a particular skill, regardless of their workplace.

cutting lever: The device on rail cars that can uncouple or detach rail cars from each other.

D

default: Failure to meet the payment terms of a legal contract, such as failure to make payments to repay a home loan; in cases of default, lenders may begin foreclosure proceedings to regain their losses.

dependents: People who must rely on another person for their livelihood; generally applied to children age eighteen and younger.

deportation: The removal of immigrant noncitizens from a country.

desegregation: To stop the practice of separating the races in public places such as public schools.

direct relief: Money, food, or vouchers given to needy people by the government for support. This term is not commonly used in the United States anymore; the current term is "welfare."

dividend: A payment made from a corporation's profits to its stockholders.

documentary literature: Articles or books describing actual events or real persons in a factual way.

documentary photograph: A photographic image in black and white or color that is realistic, factual, and useful as a historical document.

domestic goods: Goods related to home life; also, goods produced within the nation as opposed to foreign-made goods.

drought: A long period of little or no rainfall.

drug trafficking: Buying or selling illegal drugs; drug dealing.

E

electrification: The process or event in which a house, farm, industry, or locality is connected to an electric power source.

entrepreneur: An individual willing to take a risk in developing a new business.

eviction: To force a tenant from their home by legal process.

executive order: A statement written and issued by the president that uses some part of an existing law or the U.S. Constitution to enforce an action.

exposure: Being unsheltered and unprotected from the harsh weather elements, such as wind, rain, or cold, to an extent leading to illness or death.

F

foreclosure: A legal proceeding begun by a lender, usually a bank, to take possession of property when the property owner fails to make payments; in a home or farm foreclosure the lender seizes and auctions off the borrower's property to pay off the mortgage.

G

genre: A category of entertainment, such as radio comedy, drama, news, or soap operas.

H

hobo: A tramp, vagrant, or migratory worker.

holding companies: A company that controls one or more other companies through stock ownership.

Hoovervilles: "Towns" of shacks and other crude shelters put up by homeless people; sarcastically named after President Herbert Hoover, whom many felt did nothing to help Americans devastated by the Great Depression.

hopper cars: Rail cars that can readily dump their loads out the bottom.

humanitarian: One who helps others improve their welfare.

hydroelectric power: Electricity generated from the energy of swift-flowing streams or waterfalls.

I

immigration: Legal or illegal entry into a country by foreigners who intend to become permanent residents.

incentives: Something that encourages people to take action such as a guarantee of substantial profits for business leaders.

industrial mobilization: To rapidly transform or change an industry from one manufacturing household or peace-time goods to production of war materials in the time of war for government service.

industrial union: A union that represents all workers, skilled and unskilled, in a particular workplace.

infrastructure: Basic facilities and developments that form a foundation of an economic system including roads, airports, power plants, and military installations.

installment buying: Purchasing items on credit; making a down payment and, after taking possession of the item, paying off the rest of the cost with monthly payments.

interest: Money paid to a lender (in addition to the principal amount borrowed) for use of the lender's money.

L

labor leader: An individual who encourages workers to formally organize so as to more effectively negotiate better working conditions and wages from the employer.

labor movement: The collective effort by workers and labor organizations to seek better working conditions.

labor unions: Employee organizations established to seek improved working conditions and wages from employers.

laissez-faire (les-a-fair): A French term that describes the general philosophy of a government that chooses not to intervene in economic or social affairs; in French the term means "let people do as they choose."

leftist: A person promoting radical or socialistic politics in the form of liberal reform or revolutionary change.

lobby: A group of persons attempting to influence lawmakers.

lynching: The murder of an individual, most commonly a black American by a mob of white Americans, with no legal authority, usually by hanging.

M

making do: Using items on hand to stretch a budget. For example, sewing one's own clothes instead of buying them at a store, or using leftovers and other simple ingredients to spread meals over several days.

maldistribution: An uneven distribution of income or wealth; if the distribution is too unbalanced, it can cause general economic problems.

mass media: Various means of communication such as radio, movies, newspapers, and magazines that reach large numbers of people.

migrant workers: Laborers who travel from place to place to harvest farm crops for various farmers as the crops mature through the seasons.

missions: A place to aid the needy and preach the gospel, often located in poorer city areas.

mobilization: Preparations for war, including assembling of materials and military personnel.

mortgage: A legal document by which property is pledged as security for the repayment of a debt; when a buyer takes out a loan from the bank to purchase a home, the buyer pledges the home as security; if the buyer defaults on the loan, the bank takes the home to pay the debt.

municipal: A local government of a town or city.

mural: A painting applied directly onto a permanent wall.

N

New Dealers: Influential members of President Roosevelt's administration who promoted economic and social programs designed to lead the nation to economic recovery.

newsreels: Short films presenting current events.

O

old-age insurance: Assurance of cash payments, generally made monthly, to retired workers; also called a pension plan.

oral history: The memories of an event or time, captured in the words of the person who lived it.

organized crime: A specialized form of crime carried out by loosely or rigidly structured networks of gangs with certain territorial boundaries.

P

principal: The original amount of money loaned; a buyer must repay the principal and also pay the lender interest for the use of the money.

private sector: Businesses not subsidized or directed by the government but owned and operated by private citizens.

productivity: The rate at which goods are produced.

progressive tax: Taxing the income of wealthy individuals at a higher rate than those with lower incomes.

Prohibition: The period from 1920 to 1933 during which a legal restriction against the manufacture, sale, or distribution of alcoholic beverages was in effect in the United States. Officially known as the Eighteenth Amendment.

proletarian literature: Writing about the working class largely for working class consumption.

public utility: A government-regulated business that provides an essential public service, such as electric power.

public works projects: Government funded projects often for providing jobs for the unemployed such as construction of roads, bridges, airfields, and public buildings.

pump priming: Federal government spending designed to encourage consumer purchases; during the Depression the federal government spent money to create jobs through work relief programs, reasoning that if enough people received wages and began buying goods and services, the economy would improve.

R

racketeering: A person who obtains money through fraud or bribery. In the 1930s, gangsters worked their way into positions of authority in regular labor unions and then stole money from the union's pension and health funds.

recession: A slump in the economy; another term for "depression."

reclamation: A program of converting land unsuited for farming to agricultural production by providing water through irrigation systems.

refinance: To set up new terms for repayment of a loan that are beneficial to the borrower.

relief: Easing the strife of the needy by providing food, money, shelter, or jobs. (See also direct relief and work relief.)

reservations: Tracts of public land formally set aside for exclusive use by American Indians.

retrenchment: Cutbacks in school budgets, including cuts in teacher salaries, number of classes, and number of teachers.

run: Unexpected numerous withdrawals from a bank by depositors fearful of the soundness of the bank.

S

scab: A person who refuses to join a strike and fills the job of a striking worker.

school board: A local committee in charge of public education in their area.

school district: A region or locality within which the public schools share an overall budget and common leadership through a school board.

securities: Stocks or bonds.

sharecroppers: Farmers who rent the land that they work and who use the landowner's tools; sharecroppers give part of the harvest to the landowner.

shysters: Lawyers who use questionable or unprofessional methods.

sit-down strike: A refusal to work conducted by laborers who stay at their workstations and block employers from replacing them with other workers.

slum: An overcrowded urban area characterized by poverty and run-down housing.

social insurance: A broad term referring to government-sponsored social well-being programs, such as old-age pensions, unemployment support, workers' compensation for those injured on the job, and health care programs.

social legislation: Laws that address social needs such as assistance for the elderly, retirement payments, unemployment support, workers' compensation, and health care programs.

social reconstructionism: A radical philosophy in education that calls for a new, more equitable social order to be established through classroom instruction in public schools.

soup kitchen: A place where food is offered free or at a very low cost to the needy.

speakeasy: A place where alcoholic beverages were sold illegally during Prohibition.

speculation: Buying stocks and/or other high-risk investments with the assumption that they can always be sold at a higher price.

standard of living: The level of consumption by individuals or a society as reflected by the quality of goods and services available.

strike: An organized effort by workers to gain official recognition, better working conditions, or higher wages by refusing to work.

suburb: A community on the outskirts of a city.

suffrage: The right to vote.

survivor benefits: Monthly cash benefits paid to the surviving family members of a worker who has died. Survivors may include a spouse, dependent children under eighteen years of age, and a dependent parent age sixty-two or older.

syndicate: An association or network of groups that cooperate to carry out certain business or criminal activities.

syndication: An agency that buys articles or photographs and sells them for publication at the same time in numerous newspapers.

T

temperance: Moderation or abstinence in the use of alcoholic beverages.

tenant farmers: Farmers who rent the land they work but who use their own tools; tenant farmers give part of the harvested crops to the landowner.

tenement: A large housing structure containing apartment dwellings that barely meet minimum standards of sanitation, safety, and comfort.

trade unions: Labor unions in which the workers share a common craft in contrast to general labor unions in which workers share a common employment in a common industry.

transient: A person traveling around, usually in search of work.

U

underworld: The world of organized crime.

unemployment insurance: Cash payments made for a limited period of time to workers who involuntarily lose their job; workers must be able and willing to work when a new job is available.

union: An organized group of workers joined together for a common purpose, such as negotiating with management for better working conditions or higher wages.

U.S. Mint: The place where U.S. money is produced.

V

vocational education: Providing instruction or training for a particular trade.

W

welfare: The health and prosperity of an individual or group; also financial assistance to those in need.

white-collar workers: Professional workers whose jobs do not normally involve manual labor.

work relief: A government assistance program that provides a needy person with a paying job instead of money, food, or vouchers (known as direct relief). Different from the twenty-first-century welfare-to-work program, work relief involves government-sponsored projects; the "work" in welfare-to-work is in the private sector. The term "work relief" is not commonly used anymore in the United States.

workers' compensation: A system of insurance designed to provide cash benefits and medical care to workers who sustain a work-related illness or injury.

Great Depression and New Deal
Biographies

James Agee

Born November 27, 1909
Knoxville, Tennessee

Died May 16, 1955
New York, New York

Poet, novelist, movie critic,
movie scriptwriter

Although a relatively young man when he died at age forty-five, James Agee filled his years with a variety of literary pursuits. He wrote poetry, movie scripts, movie critiques, short prose, and novels. His best-known works are a documentary on white tenant farmers in the Deep South, *Let Us Now Praise Famous Men,* first published in 1941; a short novel called *The Morning Watch,* published in 1951; and a longer novel, *A Death in the Family,* published in 1957, after his death. Agee's literary themes were strongly influenced by his childhood experiences: growing up in a Christian family in Knoxville, Tennessee; suffering the loss of his father; and attending an Episcopalian grammar school, where he was taught various social and religious philosophies.

"The talk, in the end, was his great distinguishing feature. He talked his prose, Agee prose…. It rolled just as it reads; but he made it sound natural…."

Walker Evans, in the introduction to Let Us Now Praise Famous Men

James Agee. *Courtesy of the Library of Congress.*

Early life

Born and raised in Knoxville, Tennessee, Agee attended grammar school with his sister Emma at Saint Andrews. Saint Andrews was run by members of the Order of the Holy Cross of the Episcopal Church. Agee became friends with Father Flye, a member of the St. Andrews community. For years after leaving Saint Andrews he kept up correspondence with Father Flye, with whom he shared many intellectual interests.

Agee entered the prestigious Phillips Exeter Academy in New Hampshire in the fall of 1925 and told Father Flye that he felt his literary career would take root there. Literature and writing were already Agee's only real love. By 1927 he was editor of the school magazine, the *Monthly,* and president of the literary club, the Lantern. His attempts at poetry had come to the attention of famous poets such as Robert Frost (1874–1963). With his talent already apparent, Agee was accepted into Harvard University, where his determination to become a writer intensified. However, Agee was often sidetracked by uncertainty, and his spirits would plummet so low that he sometimes considered suicide, only to be in a much improved mood the next day. These emotional extremes would continue throughout his life. Despite this internal conflict, while at Harvard he wrote for, then became president of the Harvard *Advocate.*

At *Fortune* magazine

After graduation from Harvard, Agee went to work for *Fortune* magazine in 1932 as a reporter and later an editor. While at *Fortune* Agee enhanced his skills as a writer. He wrote about various businesses and about the Tennessee Valley Authority, a massive New Deal project that brought jobs and electricity to the Southeast. ("New Deal" was the name given to the many programs the administration of President **Franklin D. Roosevelt** [1882–1945; served 1933–45; see entry] initiated to help America recover from the Depression.)

In 1934 he published his first and only volume of poems, *Permit Me Voyage.* The poems were highly personal, some written as early as his high school days at Exeter. Agee would continue writing poetry but did not collect it into another book. His poems were eventually published in 1968 in *The Collected Poems of James Agee,* edited by Robert Fitzgerald.

In 1936, in the middle of the Great Depression, the worst economic crisis in U.S. history, *Fortune* sent Agee to Alabama. His assignment was to study the Southern farm economy and write a series of documentary articles on the daily life of a sharecropping family. Sharecroppers were farmers who did not own the land they worked. Instead, the landowners supplied them with land and tools and then took part of the crop in exchange. In the 1930s sharecroppers rarely earned more than a few hundred dollars in cash for their crops, and once bills were paid for expenses such as food and medical care, almost nothing was left to live on for the rest of the year. Walker Evans (1903–1975), a photographer on leave from the Resettlement Administration's Historical Section (a federal agency), accompanied Agee. The assignment was to last one month, but Agee and Evans ended up staying two months. In writing and pictures Agee and Evans attempted to honestly relate the lives of three families called the Ricketts, Gudgers, and Woods. Rather than write the articles from the viewpoint that the families were "social problems," Agee showed the great human dignity the families possessed. The material was rejected by *Fortune,* but Agee continued to work on it, and in 1941 Houghton Mifflin Company published Agee's writing and Evans's photographs in a book titled *Let Us Now Praise Famous Men.* The book was not well received and sold only a few hundred copies. However, in 1960 Houghton Mifflin reprinted it, and it became an American classic. In *Let Us Now Praise Famous Men* Agee comes to a realization and understanding of the humanity in himself and in others. In the introduction of *Let Us Now Praise Famous Men,* Walker Evans describes Agee's total commitment while researching the book and his joy at leaving behind the New York intellectual scene for a while:

> He could live inside the subject, with no distractions. Back country poor life wasn't really far from him, actually. He had some of it in his blood, through relatives in Tennessee. Anyway, he was in flight from New York magazine editorial offices, from Greenwich Village social-intellectual evenings, and especially from the whole world of high-minded, well-bred, money-hued culture.... In Alabama he sweated and scratched with submerged glee. The families understood what he was down there to do. He'd explained it, in such a way that they were interested in his work.

Movie critic

Ever since his childhood, Agee had relished movies. Combining his interest in movies with his writing ability, Agee became a well-known movie critic in the 1940s. He wrote movie critiques for *Time* magazine from 1941 until 1948. He also wrote a widely read column on movies for the magazine *Nation* from 1942 to 1948.

Not only a critic, Agee also wrote movie scripts, but none of his original scripts were ever filmed. However, he wrote several screenplays based on novels written by other authors, most notably *The African Queen* (1951) and *The Night of the Hunter* (1955). Agee, always vitally involved with how the camera was manipulated during filming, frequently outlined the entire filming process.

Novelist

Agee's best-known novels are *The Morning Watch* and *A Death in the Family*. Published in 1951, *The Morning Watch* is a short novel about a twelve-year-old lad attending an Episcopal school, just as Agee had done as a child. In the book he explores how the child comes to an appreciation and understanding of his real self.

A Death in the Family, published in 1957, two years after Agee's own death, received a 1958 Pulitzer Prize for fiction. It was adapted into the play *All the Way Home,* which was produced in 1960 and 1961 and received a Pulitzer Prize for drama.

Fame after death

Having abused his body with both alcohol and tobacco, Agee died of heart failure in 1955. He achieved his greatest fame after death, with the Pulitzer Prize for *A Death in the Family* and with the successful reprinting of *Let Us Now Praise Famous Men.* In 1958 his film reviews were collected and published in *Agee on Film.* His poetry and prose were published in separate collections in 1968, and *James Agee: Selected Journalism* came out in 1985.

For More Information

Agee, James. *Agee on Film: Reviews and Comments.* New York, NY: McDowell, Obolensky, 1958.

Agee, James. *A Death in the Family.* New York, NY: McDowell, Obolensky, 1957.

Agee, James. *The Morning Watch*. Boston, MA: Houghton Mifflin, 1951.

Agee, James, and Walker Evans. *Let Us Now Praise Famous Men*. Boston, MA: Houghton Mifflin, 1941.

Ashdown, Paul, ed. *James Agee: Selected Journalism*. Knoxville, TN: University of Tennessee, 1985.

Fitzgerald, Robert, ed. *The Collected Poems of James Agee*. Boston, MA: Houghton Mifflin, 1968.

Fitzgerald, Robert, ed. *The Collected Short Prose of James Agee*. Boston, MA: Houghton Mifflin, 1968.

Phelps, Robert. "James Agee." In *The Letters of James Agee to Father Flye*. New York, NY: Braziller, 1962.

Arthur Altmeyer

Born May 8, 1891
De Pere, Wisconsin

Died October 17, 1972
Madison, Wisconsin

Administrator

"Those who worked closely with Mr. Altmeyer knew that besides his superior intellectual and administrative abilities, he was also a man of sensitivity, of compassion, of integrity, and of stubbornness."

Former secretary of health, education, and welfare Wilbur J. Cohen

Arthur Altmeyer. *AP/Wide World Photo. Reproduced by permission.*

Arthur Altmeyer was one of the most influential figures during the development of New Deal social programs. The New Deal was a diverse collection of federal legislation and government-funded programs introduced by the administration of President **Franklin D. Roosevelt** (1882–1945; served 1933–45; see entry). The new laws and programs were designed to bring economic relief and recovery to the U.S. economy, which was suffering its most serious downturn ever, the Great Depression of the 1930s. Altmeyer was one of the leading advocates for social insurance. Social insurance—also called social security—refers to retirement payments to the aged, payments to those injured on the job (workers' compensation), payments to those who become unemployed (unemployment insurance), and health insurance. Altmeyer took a leadership role in drafting the original legislation that was passed as the Social Security Act of 1935, and he served as the head administrator of Social Security from 1937 to 1953.

Early influences

Arthur Altmeyer was born in May 1891 to John Altmeyer and Carrie Smith Altmeyer in the small town of De Pere, Wisconsin, not far from Green Bay. His grandparents had come to America in a wave of German immigration in 1848. Arthur's childhood proved challenging. His parents divorced while he was young, and he began supporting himself by working in his uncle's law office at the age of fourteen. One day while sorting the office mail Altmeyer came across a pamphlet about the newly enacted Wisconsin Workmen's Compensation Act. The act was a landmark piece of legislation, creating the first state insurance plan for workers injured on the job. Reading the pamphlet inspired Altmeyer's lifelong interest in social insurance programs. After saving enough money, Altmeyer entered the University of Wisconsin in 1911 at twenty-one years of age. After only three years he graduated with honors. His first job was teaching school in northern Minnesota. Two years later Altmeyer married Ethel Thomas, who had been his high school history teacher. Four years older than Altmeyer, she served as one of his intellectual mentors in life. They had no children.

Altmeyer served as a high school principal in Kenosha, Wisconsin, from 1916 to 1918. In 1918 he returned to the University of Wisconsin, one of the top public universities in the nation in the social sciences and economics. Enrolling as a graduate student, Altmeyer also became a student research assistant for acclaimed labor economist John R. Commons (1862–1945). Commons stressed that academic figures should play an important role in developing government policy and that government should play a strong role in society. These ideas were new to a nation that traditionally kept government out of everyday life and distant from the common citizen. Commons was the principal author of the landmark Wisconsin Workmen's Compensation Act that had caught Altmeyer's attention years earlier. He became another mentor in Altmeyer's life.

In addition to working for Commons, Altmeyer worked as a statistician for the Wisconsin State Tax Commission and then as the chief statistician for the Wisconsin Industrial Commission in 1920. There he founded a monthly publication, *Wisconsin Labor Market,* that published labor statistics for the state. The publication became a model for other states. In 1922 Altmeyer became secretary of the commission and would remain in that position until 1934. Meanwhile, he completed a master's degree in 1921 and a Ph.D. in 1931 in economics. He and Commons coauthored "The Health Insurance Movement in the United States," a highly influential report, that helped other states create their own social insurance programs.

Mr. Altmeyer goes to Washington

When the Great Depression began in late 1929, Altmeyer started spending a good deal of time in Washington, D.C., looking for federal assistance for the many unemployed Wisconsin laborers. He soon was a well-known figure around the U.S. Department of Labor. At home Altmeyer pushed the Wisconsin Unemployment Reserves and Compensation Act through the state legislature in January 1932. It was the first unemployment insurance law in the United States. The new U.S. secretary of labor, **Frances Perkins** (1882–1965; see entry), and President Roosevelt were both impressed with Altmeyer's work on the Wisconsin legislation and with his reputation as an exceptional administrator. In early 1933 Perkins asked Altmeyer to take temporary leave from his Wisconsin post and lead the reorganization of the U.S. Labor Department. She also wanted him to help establish better working relations between the federal government and the various state labor departments. As the year progressed, Altmeyer also served as a compliance officer. In this role his job was to enforce standards for working conditions, wages, and product prices in various industries. (These standards were developed by the National Recovery Administration, or NRA.) The goal was to help industry recover from the Depression and to save workers' jobs. Altmeyer also assisted in establishing two major public works programs in 1933, the Federal Emergency Relief Administration (FERA) and the Civil Works Administration (CWA).

After six months of temporary service to Perkins, Altmeyer prepared to return to his Wisconsin position. However, Perkins and other New Deal leaders wanted Altmeyer to build a national social insurance program and labor legislation modeled after Wisconsin's. Perkins offered Altmeyer a perma-

nent Washington position as assistant secretary of labor. Accepting the appointment, Altmeyer immediately drafted a key speech that President Roosevelt delivered to Congress on June 8, 1934. The speech promised a major proposal outlining social insurance, or what would become known as economic security programs.

To begin the process of drafting the proposal, Roosevelt created the Committee on Economic Security (CES). Perkins was chairperson of the CES, and Altmeyer was chairman of a technical subcommittee. The CES developed a far-reaching proposal for providing economic relief to the elderly, the poor, the blind, and families with dependent children. It proposed to finance retirement insurance with moneys from payroll deductions collected from employers and employees; create a coordinated unemployment program between the federal and state governments; include provisions for workers' compensation; and expand public health care. The CES crafted this proposal into the comprehensive Social

Security bill. Congress passed the legislation, and President Roosevelt signed it into law on August 14, 1935.

Running Social Security

The Social Security Act established a three-member Social Security Board to oversee the initial operations of the social insurance program, called Social Security. Altmeyer was appointed as one of the board members. With his extensive experience and administrative skills, Altmeyer would function as the primary policy maker for the board and become its chairman in February 1937. Altmeyer was a sensitive and shy but determined person who often had a serious demeanor. He loved figures, tables, and charts. As head of Social Security, Altmeyer constantly had to combat traditional American ideas about self-reliance. Many Americans considered social welfare shameful because they believed people were responsible for their own problems and must therefore be responsible for their own recovery. In 1946 the Social Security Board was replaced by the Social Security Administration (SSA), and Altmeyer became the SSA's first commissioner. He would remain in that role until his retirement in April 1953.

Thanks to Altmeyer's total dedication, the SSA developed a reputation as a highly efficient organization. Altmeyer personally selected and placed many of the regional administrators and established an intensive training program for employees. The SSA's primary goals were to serve the citizens and make sure that they received the maximum benefits for which they qualified. This SSA philosophy marked a significant change in the government's relationship with its citizens. Previously, the federal government had few dealings directly with the common citizen and it was the citizen's responsibility to see that they received the benefits due them. In contrast, Altmeyer directed the SSA to act as an advocate for the common citizen, guaranteeing maximum service and benefits allowable.

Social Security's leading advocate

Throughout the years Altmeyer remained the leading spokesman for the Social Security program. He stressed that

Social Security Start-Up

The Social Security Act, signed into law by President Franklin D. Roosevelt on August 14, 1935, was a landmark piece of legislation introducing national social insurance in the United States. The task of setting up an administrative system was monumental. Employers, employees, and the general public had to be informed on how to report earnings, what kinds of benefits would be available, and how they would receive those benefits. The act stated that in 1937 workers would begin accumulating credits that would entitle them to old-age insurance benefits. Therefore, to put the system in place, all employers and employees had to be officially registered by January 1, 1937. To accomplish this the Social Security Board contracted with the U.S. Postal Service to distribute applications in November 1936. The post offices then collected the completed forms, typed social security number (SSN) cards, and delivered those cards to the applicants. The Social Security Board established a national processing center in Baltimore, Maryland, to register the numbers and maintain employment records. Over thirty-five million cards were issued in late 1936 and 1937.

Monthly benefit payments began in 1940, two years earlier than originally planned. Until 1940 benefits were paid in single, lump-sum payments rather than monthly payments because the benefits were so modest in size (owing to the fact that individuals had not been contributing to the system for very long). The lowest number issued, SSN 001-01-0001, went to Grace Dorothy Owen of Concord, New Hampshire. The first payment went to Earnest Ackerman of Cleveland, Ohio, who retired the day after Social Security went into effect. He had contributed five cents, and his total retirement payment was seventeen cents. The first monthly check went to Ida May Fuller of Ludlow, Vermont, on January 31, 1940. It amounted to $22.54.

aging, illness, and unemployment were disruptions in people's lives and, for the most part, beyond their control. He portrayed the program as an economic safety net protecting the common citizen against these major economic hazards in life.

Through the late 1930s Altmeyer fought hard for expansion of Social Security benefits. Congress passed a key amendment to Social Security in 1939 that added benefits for spouses and dependent children and provided survivor benefits (continued benefits to spouse and dependent children even after the main benefactor's death). Thus Social Security became an economic security program for the whole family.

Other duties

Like most federal administrators during World War II (1939–45), Altmeyer was called upon to serve in other roles. Among other assignments he was executive director of the War Manpower Commission (WMC) from 1942 to 1945 and adviser on social welfare programs to the United Nations Economic and Social Council from 1946 to 1953.

Altmeyer was influential in bringing Social Security to many other nations. He served on various international social insurance commissions. From 1942 to 1952 he was chairman of the Permanent Inter-American Committee on Social Security, which was involved in creating social insurance programs in Central and South America. He was also a social welfare adviser to Iran and Turkey in 1955.

President of the National Conference on Social Work in 1954 and 1955, Altmeyer continued lobbying for social insurance programs such as disability and health insurance in the United States. On occasion he was called upon to fight congressional efforts to significantly change Social Security, usually involving a reduction in benefits, or eliminate it altogether. In addition he taught as a visiting professor at several universities.

Retirement years

In December 1952, not long before his anticipated retirement, Altmeyer received the Distinguished Service Award in recognition of his long-term leadership in creating and nurturing social insurance programs in the United States. Earlier, in 1939, he had received an honorary law degree from the University of Wisconsin. With the new Republican administration of President Dwight Eisenhower (1890–1969; served 1953–61) coming into office, Altmeyer retired in April 1953. Altmeyer and his wife moved back to Madison, Wisconsin. In his retirement Altmeyer became more active in Democratic politics. In 1954 he was cochair of the Democratic campaign organization for the party's candidate for governor and even briefly considered a run for the U.S. Senate in 1956.

Additional changes to Social Security that Altmeyer had promoted did not become reality until after his retirement in 1953. The program was expanded in 1956 to provide disability insurance for permanently injured (disabled) workers. In 1965 health care coverage, known as Medicare, was added. However, the Medicare program provided benefits only for people over sixty-five years of age. It was not the universal coverage for everyone that Altmeyer had recommended. In 1966 Altmeyer published a book called *The Formative Years of Social Security,* which provides an account of the program's early phases. Altmeyer died in October 1972 and the SSA national offices located in Baltimore, Maryland, were named in his honor the following year.

For More Information

Books

Altmeyer, Arthur J. *The Formative Years of Social Security.* Madison, WI: University of Wisconsin Press, 1966.

Perkins, Frances. *The Roosevelt I Knew.* New York, NY: Harper & Row, 1946.

Witte, Edwin E. *The Development of the Social Security Act.* Madison, WI: University of Wisconsin Press, 1962.

Web Sites

Cohen, Wilbur J. "Arthur Altmeyer: Mr. Social Security." *Social Security Administration.* http://www.ssa.gov/history/cohen2.html (accessed on September 4, 2002).

DeWitt, Larry. "Never a Finished Thing: A Biography of Arthur Joseph Altmeyer—The Man FDR Called 'Mr. Social Security.'" *Social Security Administration.* http://www.ssa.gov/history/collectalt.html (accessed on September 4, 2002).

Mary McLeod Bethune

Born July 10, 1875
Mayesville, South Carolina

Died May 18, 1955
Daytona Beach, Florida

Educator, advocate for black Americans and women, administrator

"Colored people all along the eastern seaboard spread a feast whenever Mrs. Bethune passed their way. The chickens went flying off seeking a safe hiding place. They knew some necks would be wrung in her honor to make a heaping platter of southern fried chicken."

Langston Hughes from I Wonder As I Wander: An Autobiographical Journey

Mary McLeod Bethune.
UPI-Bettmann. Reproduced by permission.

Mary McLeod Bethune was an educator, organizer, and activist. She was an advocate and spokeswoman for black Americans and for women in general. Having strong religious faith and a belief in the power of education, Bethune felt that the economic and political power of black women would inevitably increase. Through her confident and dignified behavior, she provided leadership and inspiration to many during a period of legally enforced racial segregation. Appointed by **Aubrey Williams** (1890–1965; see entry) as the director of the National Youth Administration's Negro Affairs Division, Bethune became the highest-ranking black administrator ever to serve in the federal government up to that time. Appointed in 1936 during the Great Depression, she successfully guided desperately needed assistance to thousands of black youths. Representing and promoting black interests inside the federal government, she was often the only black person present at high-level government policy meetings. She was both a role model and mother figure to many.

From humble roots

Bethune was born in 1875 in Mayesville, South Carolina, to former slaves who raised cotton on a 5-acre plot they had purchased. It was only a decade after the American Civil War (1861–65), and antiblack violence was common throughout the South. She was the fifteenth of seventeen children and grew up in a four-room log cabin. Though none of her family could read, Bethune proved to be a gifted student. After attending a one-room Presbyterian mission school in Mayesville, she attended Scotia Seminary for black girls (later Barber-Scotia College) in Concord, North Carolina.

Upon her graduation in 1894, Bethune journeyed to Chicago, Illinois, and attended the Moody Bible Institute for Home Foreign Missions. Bethune had plans to be a missionary in Africa, spreading the Christian religion and educating the young. However, no positions were open for her, so she turned to a career in education. At first Bethune returned to Mayesville to work as an assistant at the Presbyterian mission school she had previously attended. Soon she received an appointment to the Haines Normal and Industrial Institute in Augusta, Georgia, a school for girls. There she sharpened her skills at teaching all levels, from elementary to vocational courses.

From the Haines Institute Bethune moved on to the Kendell Institute in Sumter, South Carolina. In Sumter she met and married clothing salesman Albertus Bethune in 1898. They would have one child, a son. By 1899 she was ready to start a school of her own. Bethune and her family moved to Palatka, Florida, where she started a mission school and taught for five years. In 1904 Bethune was invited by a local reverend to start a school in Daytona Beach, Florida. In an old two-story cottage, Bethune founded the Daytona Literary and Industrial School for Training Negro Girls. While she was busily nurturing the new school, her marriage fell apart. Albertus returned to South Carolina in 1907 and died in 1918. They had never divorced.

Social activist

Bethune's reputation as an organizer and administrator rapidly grew. She became more outspoken on key issues besides education, including women's suffrage (right to vote), black American voter registration, school desegregation (allowing black students and white students to attend the same schools), and access to health care. Bethune campaigned for women's suffrage with the Equal Suffrage League, a branch of the National Association of Colored Women. When women gained the right to vote in 1920, she strongly encouraged black American women to vote.

Bethune served as president of the Florida Federation of Colored Women's Clubs from 1917 to 1925 and organized black women's clubs throughout the Southeast. She also served as president of the Southeastern Federation of Colored Women's Clubs from 1920 to 1925. She became vice president of the National Urban League in 1920 and created a women's section in that organization. Meanwhile, her Daytona Beach school for black girls had grown from a small elementary school to a college. In 1923 the school merged with Cookman Institute, a school for boys, to form the co-educational Bethune-Cookman College. Bethune served as the college's president. From 1924 to 1928 she also served as president for the prestigious National Association of Colored Women, taking on her first national role in promoting issues important to women and black Americans. In this new role Bethune attended the Child Welfare Conference called by President Calvin Coolidge (1872–1933; served 1923–29) and then participated in the National Child Welfare Commission under President **Herbert Hoover** (1874–1964; served 1929–33; see entry).

From 1929 to 1941, the period of severe U.S. economic problems called the Great Depression, Bethune continued her activism. In 1933 and 1934 she served on a federal committee to promote education of black youths. In 1935 she established and became president of the National Council of Negro Women, a coalition of hundreds of black women's organizations in the United States. That same year, the National Association for the Advancement of Colored People (NAACP) awarded Bethune its highest honor in recognition of her efforts to advance the political causes of minorities. In 1936 Bethune also became president of the Association for the Study of Negro Life and History. Through her leadership in women's and education initiatives, Bethune became good friends with First Lady **Eleanor Roosevelt** (1884–1962; see entry).

Mary McLeod Bethune and Eleanor Roosevelt were leaders in women's and education initiatives.
UPI/Corbis-Bettmann. Reproduced by permission.

Life in the government

Bethune's next post was with the National Youth Administration (NYA). President **Franklin D. Roosevelt** (1882–1945; served 1933–45; see entry) created the NYA in June 1935 to help keep young people in school. Roosevelt believed that if students could not contribute to family income during the Depression years of economic hardship, they would likely have to quit school and seek work, so the NYA was designed to provide part-time employment to people ages sixteen to twenty-five.

The president appointed Aubrey Williams, a white native of Alabama, to be executive director of the agency. Greatly disturbed by the poverty and racial injustice he witnessed as a youth, Williams had become a social worker in order to fight poverty; he was a natural fit for Roosevelt's New Deal program. ("New Deal" was the name given to the many programs the Roosevelt administration initiated to help America recover from the Depression.) Determined to bring minorities into the New Deal work relief projects, Williams appointed Bethune first as an adviser and then as director of the NYA's Negro Affairs Division. Due to Bethune's efforts, about three hundred thousand black youths participated in the NYA, making up 10 to 12 percent of all participants. Bethune led the Negro Affairs Division until it was closed in 1943.

As an official member of the New Deal administration, Bethune pursued issues of importance to black Americans. She organized the "Black Cabinet," a small group of black federal officials who advised the White House on such issues. In 1937 Bethune organized the National Conference on the Problems of the Negro and Negro Youth. Held in Washington, D.C., the conference tackled critical issues such as health care, legal protections, and housing needs. In 1939 Bethune organized a second national conference on black American issues. These two conferences were perhaps the high point in Bethune's illustrious public career, confirming her role as a national black leader. Throughout the 1930s Bethune also fought hard, but unsuccessfully, for antilynching laws.

Following the Depression, Bethune maintained an active role inside government. As special assistant to the secretary of war, Bethune recruited black women to the Women's Army Auxiliary Corps; they received officer training for service in World War II (1939–45). She also became head of the Women's Army for National Defense, a black women's organization pressing for greater roles for black women in national defense. After the war, President Harry Truman (1884–1972; served 1945–53) sent Bethune to an United Nations organizational meeting in San Francisco, California. There Bethune met with people of color from other parts of the world.

The Black Cabinet

During his first few years in office, President Roosevelt became increasingly aware of major issues important to black Americans. However, no blacks held high government advisory positions to keep the president apprised on such matters. To fill this void in formal black leadership, in 1936 Mary McLeod Bethune, head of the Negro Division of the National Youth Administration, helped organize a group of black government employees to advise Roosevelt on issues of importance to the black community. It was the first group of its kind. They officially called themselves the Federal Council on Negro Affairs, but they were popularly known as the "Black Cabinet." The group would periodically visit the White House to meet with the president. Besides Bethune, the Black Cabinet included William H. Hastie, an attorney in the Interior Department; Robert C. Weaver, an economist in the Interior Department; Edgar Brown of the Civilian Conservation Corps; Robert L. Vann, editor of the *Pittsburgh Courier* and special assistant in the Justice Department; and Lawrence A. Oxley, a social worker in the Department of Labor.

With the guidance of this advisory group, President Roosevelt began reaching out to black Americans. As a result, the political party Roosevelt represented, the Democrats, gained the support of black Americans across the nation for decades to come. However, despite the Black Cabinet's suggestions, Roosevelt refused to actively promote antilynching bills in Congress and the proposed prohibitions against the poll taxes (fees to vote, which the poor, largely black population, could not afford) charged at election booths. These were two major civil rights goals supported by black Americans during the 1930s. But Roosevelt feared that promoting these goals could cost him the support of white Southern Democrats, support that was critical for his New Deal programs. Still, thanks to Bethune, the Black Cabinet gave black Americans never-before-seen representation in the White House.

Later Life

Always active in education and civil rights, Bethune wrote numerous magazine articles and newspaper columns on the subjects. In addition she used an authoritative voice to give highly inspirational speeches. She continued these activities until her death in 1955. Bethune's social activism helped set the stage for the civil rights movement of the 1950s. She lived long enough to witness the landmark 1954 U.S. Supreme Court decision prohibiting racial segregation in public schools.

Bethune won many awards for her work. In 1930 she was listed among America's greatest women. Nearly six decades later, in 1989, *Ebony* magazine listed her among the fifty most important black figures in U.S. history, along with Frederick Douglass (1817–1895) and Martin Luther King Jr. (1929–1968). While attending the 1949 Haiti Exposition she was given Haiti's highest award, the Medal of Honor and Merit. As a U.S. representative to Liberia in Africa she received Liberia's top award, the Commander of the Order of the Star of Africa. In July 1974 Bethune became the first black and the first woman to have a national monument dedicated to her in Washington, D.C.—the Mary McLeod Bethune Memorial Statue at Lincoln Park.

For More Information

Books

Anderson, LaVere. *Mary McLeod Bethune: Teacher with a Dream.* Champaign, IL: Garrard, 1976.

Holt, Rackham. *Mary McLeod Bethune: A Biography.* Garden City, NY: Doubleday, 1964.

Hughes, Langston. *I Wonder As I Wander.* New York, NY: Rinehart, 1956.

McCluskey, Audrey Thomas, and Elaine M. Smith, eds. *Mary McLeod Bethune: Building a Better World, Essays and Selected Documents.* Bloomington, IN: Indiana University Press, 1999.

Peare, Catherine O. *Mary McLeod Bethune.* New York, NY: Vanguard Press, 1951.

Sterne, Emma G. *Mary McLeod Bethune.* New York, NY: Knopf, 1957.

Web Sites

Bethune-Cookman College. http://www.bethune.cookman.edu (accessed on September 4, 2002).

Horace Bond

Born November 8, 1904
Nashville, Tennessee

Died December 21, 1972
Atlanta, Georgia

College professor, administrator

Horace Bond was an extraordinary black American scholar and college administrator, dedicated to improving education for black Americans. He was determined and brilliant, not afraid to challenge long-held ideas. Bond rose to prominence during the Great Depression. During his career he authored several books and nearly one hundred articles on various black education topics in academic journals and popular magazines. He is most noted for two classic books on black education published during the Great Depression: *The Education of the Negro in the American Social Order* (1934) and *Negro Education in Alabama: A Study in Cotton and Steel* (1936). Both books dealt with the poor condition of black education in public schools and colleges. Besides working for improvement in black education, Bond was also active in the civil rights movement of the 1950s.

An education background

Horace Mann Bond was born in Nashville, Tennessee, to a minister father and a schoolteacher mother. The Bond family placed a high value on education and produced a

"Horace Bond's mother named him in honor of Horace Mann's—the great Massachusetts educational reformer and abolitionist—antislavery activities."

Wayne J. Urban in his 1992 book Black Scholar: Horace Mann Bond, 1904–1972

Horace Bond. *AP/Wide World Photo. Reproduced by permission.*

21

number of scholars as well as civil rights leaders. Bond's grandmother, a former slave, had raised two sons, each of whom earned college degrees. Three of Bond's four siblings also earned college degrees and had professional careers. While he was still very young, Bond's mother would take him to school with her so she could mind him while she taught her classes. He soon began following along with the lessons and learned to read by age three.

While Bond was growing up, black schools were greatly underfunded. The teachers were poorly prepared and poorly supported. Average education spending for black students was considerably less than half of the amount provided for white students. In addition, black schools focused more on vocational training. In general, whites in the United States believed that black Americans were intellectually inferior. Therefore, offering blacks more academic school programs seemed unnecessary.

At an early age Bond began showing he was gifted in academics. He began high school at age nine. After attending a one-room schoolhouse, Bond was educated at secondary schools associated with colleges and universities. He entered college at Lincoln University in 1919 at age fourteen. At that time few blacks had the opportunity for a college education. Established in 1854 in southeastern Pennsylvania, Lincoln was the first black college in the world, but like most black colleges, Lincoln had an all-white faculty. Bond participated in many student activities, and he was the editor of the student literary magazine and president of the school's athletic association. He graduated in 1923 when he was only eighteen years old.

Establishing a career

Bond attended graduate school at the University of Chicago in Illinois, majoring in education. To pay for his school expenses he worked at a series of teaching jobs. He also left school at times to make money and then would return to resume his studies. First he worked as director of the School of Education at Langston University, the black state college for Oklahoma. During this time Bond tackled the issue of educational testing. The common interpretation of the lower scores recorded for blacks on national "intelligence" tests was that black Americans were intellectually inferior to whites. Bond set out to prove that the lower test results were not due to lack of learning ability but to the limited educational opportunities available for black students. In June 1924 Bond published an article titled "Intelligence Tests and Propaganda" in *The Crisis,* the journal of the National Association for the Advancement of Colored People (NAACP). The article emphasized the need for increased funding for education in black communities. After working at Langston, Bond became director of the education extension program for Alabama Agricultural and Mechanical College in Montgomery, the black state college for Alabama. Bond trained Alabama primary and secondary schoolteachers.

In 1928 Bond's developing career in education took him to Fisk University, a highly respected black college in Nashville, Tennessee. There he was an assistant professor and research assistant before becoming chairman of the education department. At Fisk Bond met his future wife, and they married in October 1930. During his time at Fisk, Bond published many articles promoting equality for black education. The articles appeared in leading black publications such as the *Journal of Negro Education* published by Howard University and in nationally circulated magazines such as *Harper's* and the *Nation.* Bond's most important publication during this time was the 1934 book *The Education of the Negro in the American Social Order.* This book continued Bond's theme that poor funding of black schools affected the quality of education for black Americans. In the book Bond also presented recommendations on how to improve black education. The publication was considered a major contribution to the study of black education in America and influenced black educators for decades. While at Fisk, Bond had become a recognized national authority on black education.

During his years at Langston and Fisk, Bond had continued work on his graduate degree program through the University of Chicago. For his research topic Bond focused on the importance of economic and social factors influencing education; he concentrated his study on the development of public education in Alabama. He finally received his doctoral degree in education in 1936. The book that resulted from his doctoral research, *Negro Education in Alabama: A Study in Cotton and Steel,* provided a detailed look at the economic, political, and social factors influencing black public school education in the South. Bond showed that a drop in the number of black schools during the Depression was not because blacks lacked interest, but because school boards dominated by whites had funneled the shrinking school budgets primarily toward white schools. He showed that exceptional black students could be produced by well-financed and well-administered black schools and that poor educational performance was related to poverty, not natural ability. Therefore, he advocated equal funding for black schools and white schools.

An administrator

Owing to the pronounced racial segregation (separation of black Americans and white Americans in public places such as stores, schools, and restaurants) in the United States at the time, Bond, like other noted black scholars, did not receive any offers to teach at white universities upon finishing his graduate work. With scholarly positions closed to him, he followed a path into administration of black colleges. In September 1936 Bond was selected as academic dean at Dillard University in New Orleans, Louisiana. Dillard was a new college created by merging two older ones. Bond worked there for three years before returning to Fisk as chairman of the education department. In 1939 he was selected to be president of Fort Valley State College in Georgia, a training college for rural schoolteachers. Under Bond's leadership this small junior college became a full-fledged four-year college. In 1945 Bond became the first black president at Lincoln University, his alma mater (a school one has attended) and one of the best black colleges in the nation. The prestigious position put Bond in the national spotlight.

Though Bond would spend twelve years at Lincoln, it was not a completely positive experience. Since he was the first black president of the long-established institution, Bond had to break down racial barriers. He enthusiastically built an African studies program at Lincoln, a program that was unpopular with other administrators and faculty at the school. He even journeyed to British West Africa in 1949 and several more times after that, establishing connections with Nigeria, Ghana, and Liberia. Soon, 10 percent of Lincoln's student body was African. In 1956 Bond also organized the American Society of African Culture (AMSAC).

Schooling for Black Americans during the Depression

The United States was racially segregated in the early twentieth century, which meant black students and white students attended separate public schools. Even before the Great Depression began, most black Americans were already living in poverty. Their schools had low-quality facilities, and their teachers received little training and low salaries.

Though many schools in affluent white communities survived the worst years of the Depression with few problems, the Depression all but eliminated budgets for most black schools. Influenced by a belief that black students were incapable of higher learning, school boards, especially those in the Southern states, refused to fund black education. This widespread belief was accepted without question by most whites in the 1930s. As a result, the combined barriers of poverty and racism kept black education at woefully inadequate levels. Annual funding for black education was only 15 to 20 percent of the amount given to white schools. In Alabama, the Alabama State Agricultural and Mechanical Institute, a school for blacks, received only $40,000 a year, whereas Auburn Polytechnic Institute, a white school, received $635,000.

Because of the meager funding for black education, black families had to pool their limited resources to finance and build local schools. Those who did not have any money donated labor, helping build and maintain the tiny schoolhouses. At least half of the schools had no desks, only rickety benches and a wood-burning stove. The typical schoolhouse was a crude shack built out of scrap lumber, with daylight easily visible through the walls. Sometimes newspapers were tacked on the walls to keep the wind out. Rain often poured through the roof. By 1932, more than 3,400 schools had been built in 880 Southern counties. Virtually all the schools were elementary schools.

The few black high schools in the South were in cities. Almost half of black Americans did not go beyond the fifth grade. In 1932, 230 Southern counties had no high school for black students. Most black high schools were vocational. They rarely taught traditional academic subjects such as literature, history, or math. Instead, they taught carpentry, bricklaying, and auto mechanics. Vocational education aimed to prepare black Americans for low-paying positions in the industrial workplace. The Depression, however, soon eliminated even those jobs.

During the early 1950s Bond also served as historian for the NAACP in their legal battle against school segregation. Bond prepared background information for the landmark 1954 Supreme Court case *Brown* v. *Board of Education,* in which the Court struck down racial segregation in public schools.

Bond also joined students in antisegregation demonstrations in the local communities. Because of these activities Lincoln's board of trustees, alumni, and faculty felt that Bond was neglecting some important duties of his administrative position. As a result, Bond's popularity sharply declined by 1956.

In 1957 Bond left Lincoln to become dean of the School of Education at Atlanta University. After ten years as dean, he became director of the university's Bureau of Educational Research. Bond retired in 1971 and died only a year later.

During their forty-two-year marriage the Bonds had three children. One of Bond's children, Julian Bond, became highly involved in the 1960s civil rights movement and served in the Georgia legislature for over twenty years, from 1965 to 1986. He also became president of the newly formed Southern Poverty Law Center in 1971, and in 1998 he became chairman of the NAACP. Julian was also on the staff of the American University in Washington, D.C., and a member of the history department at the University of Virginia in 2000.

For More Information

Bond, Horace M. *The Education of the Negro in the American Social Order.* 1934. Reprint, New York, NY: Octagon Books, 1966.

Bond, Horace M. *Negro Education in Alabama: A Study in Cotton and Steel.* 1936. Reprint, Tuscaloosa, AL: University of Alabama Press, 1994.

Neary, John. *Julian Bond: Black Rebel.* New York, NY: William Morrow, 1971.

Urban, Wayne J. *Black Scholar: Horace Mann Bond, 1904–1972.* Athens, GA: University of Georgia Press, 1992.

Williams, Roger M. *The Bonds: An American Family 1971.* New York, NY: Atheneum, 1971.

The Brain Trust:

Raymond Moley
Born September 27, 1886
Berea, Ohio

Died February 18, 1975
Phoenix, Arizona

Rexford Tugwell
Born July 10, 1891
Sinclairville, New York

Died July 21, 1979
Santa Barbara, California

Adolf Berle Jr.
Born January 29, 1895
Brighton, Massachusetts

Died February 17, 1971
New York, New York

Scholars, presidential advisers

Raymond Moley, Rexford Tugwell, and Adolf Berle were selected to advise Democratic candidate **Franklin D. Roosevelt** (1882–1945; served 1933–45; see entry) during his presidential campaign of 1932. These three experts were the core of Roosevelt's advisory group, which came to be known as the "Brain Trust." They offered major new ideas that shaped Roosevelt's campaign and the first years of his presidency as he struggled to restore economic health to the United States. All three were associated with Columbia University in New York City and believed in reforming America's economy through national planning. They represented a new kind of expert in American politics—the trained professional academic. Such expert advisers would become essential to future governmental leaders.

Raymond Moley, political adviser

Samuel Rosenman, general counsel (attorney) to Roosevelt while Roosevelt was governor of New York State (1929–33), convinced the future president to establish an ad-

"Tugwell wanted everyone to share in America's abundance.... As a result, he was often frustrated, and in those moments of frustration, his so-called radicalism appeared."

Michael V. Namorato in the 1988 book Rexford Tugwell: A Biography

Adolph Berle Jr. *AP/Wide World Photo. Reproduced by permission.*

27

visory group for the 1932 presidential campaign. Rosenman first asked Raymond Moley to provide political advice. Moley was a political science professor at Barnard College of Columbia University who had previously written speeches for Roosevelt. Moley would serve as leader of the Brain Trust and determine what topics the group needed to address.

The son of a clothing salesman, Moley was born in Berea, Ohio, and grew up in a financially secure home. Following graduation from a small Cleveland, Ohio, college in 1906, Moley became a teacher and superintendent of schools at Olmsted Falls, Ohio. However, in 1909 he was stricken with tuberculosis and had to leave his job. After recovering from the disease Moley chose a new path in life. In 1913 he entered graduate school in political science at Oberlin College in Oberlin, Ohio; he also taught high school in nearby Cleveland to earn a living. Moley went on to earn a Ph.D. from Columbia University in 1918 while teaching as an assistant professor at Case Western Reserve University from 1916 to 1919. Also during this time Moley married and had two sons. Upon graduation from Columbia, Moley was recruited to be director of the Cleveland Foundation, a fact-finding organization that promoted civic improvement projects. Through this foundation, Moley gained national prominence.

His success with the Cleveland Foundation led Moley back to New York City in 1923 to assume an associate professor position on Columbia University's Barnard College faculty. Moley quickly became involved in New York City legal affairs. He was also appointed research director for the New York City Crime Commission in 1926. In 1928 he was promoted to professor of public law (laws regulating government activities) at Columbia. From 1931 to 1933 he served on the New York Commission on the Administration of Justice. During this period Moley wrote reports on the criminal justice system and sharpened his administrative skills while working with volumes of complex data. Moley had excellent writing and speaking skills and the rare ability to explain complex ideas in simple language.

In 1932, as leader of the Brain Trust, Moley used his skills to examine large amounts of political material and ideas and shape them into manageable political policy for Roosevelt's presidential campaign. Moley is credited with coining

the term "New Deal," which Roosevelt first used in his speech accepting the presidential nomination of the Democratic Party. Moley was the chief author of that speech, which was delivered in August 1932. The term New Deal quickly became a label for the policies, programs, and legislation of the Roosevelt administration—all of which were designed to bring the United States out of the Great Depression, the most severe economic crisis in U.S. history.

Roosevelt easily defeated Republican incumbent **Herbert Hoover** (1874–1964; served 1929–33; see entry), who had been unable to find solutions for the Depression. Following the successful presidential campaign Moley continued as president-elect Roosevelt's chief adviser for the four months leading up to Roosevelt's inauguration. During that period Moley shaped general ideas into specific legislation. He advocated cooperation between business and government, development of unemployment and old-age insurance legislation, regulation of the stock market, reform of the U.S. banking system, regulation of private utility companies, and construction of public utilities.

Moley interviewed potential appointees for various high positions in the administration and was appointed by Roosevelt as assistant secretary of state. Moley was invaluable to Roosevelt in guiding numerous bills through Congress during the first few months of Roosevelt's term, a period frequently referred to as the "first hundred days" of the New Deal. Between 1932 and 1935 Moley assisted in drafting all of Roosevelt's speeches and "fireside chats," radio broadcasts the president made to inform the American public about the economic recovery efforts. He also founded *Today* magazine in 1934, which presented the New Deal perspective on issues. *Today* was absorbed by *Newsweek* magazine in 1937, and Moley wrote a political column for *Newsweek* for the next thirty years until his retirement from political life at age eighty-one.

Gradually Moley became disillusioned with the direction of the New Deal as it moved away from cooperation with business and towards placing restrictions on business. Moley wrote Roosevelt's 1936 acceptance speech for the Democratic nomination for reelection, but that was his last contribution to the New Deal administration. Moley progressively moved further away from Roosevelt and his New Deal policies. He would later become close friends with Herbert Hoover, and he supported Republican presidential candidate Wendell Willkie (1892–1944) in 1940 against Roosevelt. Moley, who remained associated with Columbia University until his academic retirement in 1954, continued as an adviser and speechwriter for Republican presidential nominees through the 1960s and wrote several books about his experiences. He was a great admirer of President Richard M. Nixon (1913–1994; served 1969–74) and advised him during his political career. In 1970 Nixon awarded Moley the prestigious Medal of Freedom at a White House ceremony. Moley died in February 1975 in Phoenix, Arizona.

Rexford Tugwell, agricultural adviser
For agricultural advice, Moley recruited Rexford Tugwell, another Columbia University professor. Tugwell was born in the small upstate village of Sinclairville, New York.

His mother was a teacher and loved to write. She taught in the nearby town of Chautauqua, a growing center of learning. She was quite individualistic and artistic, a good writer, an avid reader, a nature buff, and very outgoing. Tugwell gained his interest in writing and conservation of natural resources from her. His father was a successful businessman and banker. Often in poor health as a child, Tugwell spent a lot of his time reading. At the Chautauqua learning center he listened to lectures and debates presented by national figures in education, politics, and economics. He absorbed a variety of new ideas and approaches for dealing with issues of the day, such as the growing inequalities of the American economic system. Ironically, Tugwell was not a good student in school. He was bored with structured learning. Except in his favorite subjects of English and history, he worked just hard enough to pass his classes. However, he continued to be an eager reader. In 1904, when he was thirteen, his family moved to Wilson, New York, where Tugwell began writing local news columns for the *Niagara Falls Gazette*. By seventeen he was reporting on local court proceedings and financial news for the *Buffalo Courier*. During this period Tugwell became a follower of progressive politics as represented by President Theodore Roosevelt (1858–1919; served 1901–09). Progressive politics promoted using the powers of government to solve social and economic problems.

Rexford Tugwell. *UPI/Corbis Bettmann. Reproduced by permission.*

Tugwell was a man of wit and charm, very self-confident, often outspoken, and frequently considered arrogant. He wrote with intensity and was devoted to seeking social change in America through regulation of big business and finding economic security for the common citizen. While in college in 1914 Tugwell married and had two children. Moving on to graduate school, he earned a Ph.D. in 1922 from the University of Pennsylvania's Wharton School of Finance and

Commerce. Tugwell spent most of his academic teaching career at Columbia University, becoming a full professor in 1931 and specializing in farm economics.

Tugwell was certain America's simple times of small individual farms were in the past. He stressed national planning and government regulation to achieve agricultural modernization. He insisted that farmers and industry leaders should control their production, because overproduction was causing economic problems. He published two major books on the topic, *Industry's Coming of Age* (1927) and *The Industrial Discipline and the Governmental Arts* (1933).

As a member of Roosevelt's Brain Trust, Tugwell greatly influenced development of the Agricultural Adjustment Act, which set production limits for farmers. Tugwell served in the Department of Agriculture from 1933 to 1935 and then became director of the Resettlement Administration (RA) in 1935 and 1936. The RA was established to relocate farmers from poor farmland to areas of greater potential. The RA was also involved in the creation of several new communities made up of low-income housing. Known as "greenbelt towns," the new communities were located outside the decaying inner cities and were intended for the resettlement of industrial workers to get them out of the slums into a more productive environment. The RA programs introduced totally new approaches for solving the problems of the rural poor. As a champion for controversial programs, Tugwell was branded a political radical by his critics. He finally decided it best to resign from the Roosevelt administration in December 1936. He had become too much of a target for Republicans and anti-New Deal Democrats.

After a brief spell in private industry, Tugwell was appointed chairman of the New York City Planning Commission in 1938 and worked closely with the New York City mayor. Again hit with controversy over master plans and public housing programs, Tugwell resigned in 1941. President Roosevelt then appointed Tugwell governor of Puerto Rico, and Tugwell remained there until 1946. During that time Tugwell brought great economic and political change to Puerto Rico.

After his time in Puerto Rico, Tugwell returned to academic positions from 1946 to 1957 at the University of Chicago, the London School of Economics, Howard Universi-

Birth of the Brain Trust

During his early political life, when deciding how to address important policy issues, Franklin D. Roosevelt established a habit of seeking advice from academic scholars rather than other politicians or businessmen. He continued this approach through his term as governor of New York, from 1929 to 1933. By early 1932 it was clear that Roosevelt would be a serious contender for the Democratic Party's nomination for the presidential election that fall. The United States was in the depth of the Great Depression, the most severe economic downturn in the nation's history. Unemployment was rising toward 25 percent of the workforce; millions of workers had lost their jobs. Many more had their wages reduced. The economic and social issues were complex, and no one—including politicians and scholars—was sure what had caused the Depression or how it might be corrected.

In March Samuel Rosenman, Roosevelt's general counsel for the state of New York and a close friend, suggested that they bring together a group of advisers to sort out the issues. He recommended choosing advisers who were not businessmen, be-

cause businessmen would have substantial self-interests and concentrate only on problems affecting their businesses. Instead, Rosenman suggested, the advisers should be drawn from universities. The advisers who were chosen included Columbia University professors Raymond Moley, Rexford Tugwell, and Adolf Berle. They met often through 1932, arguing and debating policy issues. They were labeled the "brains trust," soon shortened to "brain trust," when James Kieran wrote an article about their activity in the *New York Times*. To control the abuses of economic power that were being carried out by a few dominant businessmen, the Brain Trust supported increased regulation of big business. After Roosevelt's election in November 1932 the group was formally dissolved. However, the members continued to play an active role in government; Moley and Tugwell became key members of Roosevelt's administration. Their work not only aided the campaign, but shaped legislation during the first hundred days of Roosevelt's presidency. The National Industrial Recovery Act and the Agricultural Adjustment Act were two key pieces of legislation influenced by the Brain Trust.

ty, Columbia University, Southern Illinois University, and other schools. Up to his death in Santa Barbara, California, in July 1979, Tugwell published numerous books and articles on topics such as Roosevelt and the New Deal, the atomic bomb, and national political and economic issues. Tugwell is remembered as the most colorful and perhaps the most radical of the Roosevelt insiders.

Adolf Berle Jr., business adviser

For economic and corporate matters, Moley and Tug-well recruited another Columbia University professor, Adolf Berle Jr. Berle was born in Brighton, Massachusetts. His father was a Congregational minister who strove to gain a reputation as an intellectual (a person with highly developed powers of thought). Berle's mother stressed strong work habits, spirituality, and an interest in science. Many intellectuals of the day visited the Berle home in Brighton, exposing young Adolf to varied ideas. He proved academically gifted and entered Harvard at age fourteen. Berle also earned money writing articles for the two Boston newspapers. Majoring in history and debate, he graduated from Harvard at age eighteen with both a bachelor's and a master's degree. He then entered Harvard Law School and graduated at twenty-one years of age, the youngest graduate in the school's history. However, having gained a reputation of being conceited, obnoxious, and difficult, Berle was not a very likable person to many. His first job in the legal profession was in the Boston law firm of Supreme Court justice Louis D. Brandeis (1856–1941).

During World War I (1914–18) Berle entered the army as an intelligence officer for the Army Signal Corps in the Dominican Republic. After the war, Berle began writing prolifically on economics, law, and foreign affairs. After providing legal services to a private charitable organization in Manhattan, he formed a small law firm, Berle and Berle, focusing on corporate (business) law. Berle remained academically oriented, writing articles for various progressive magazines such as the *New Republic* and the *Nation* and teaching at Harvard Business School. He married in 1927 and had three children. Berle teamed up with Harvard graduate student Gardiner C. Means to write a study of the rising influence of big business. In 1932 they published *The Modern Corporation and Private Property.* The highly influential book examined trends of American corporations during the early Great Depression years—approximately 1929 to 1932—and showed how U.S. wealth was concentrated in only two hundred corporations. The book was widely read during the Depression.

After Berle joined the Brain Trust, one of his most notable contributions was writing a September 1932 campaign speech delivered by presidential candidate Franklin Roosevelt in San Francisco, California. Historians look back on it as one of the most important speeches anticipating the New Deal national economic planning program. Unlike the other Brain Trust members, Berle wanted to remain in New York City, and he resisted a Washington appointment. In New York City he advised Mayor Fiorello La Guardia (1882–1947) and guided the city's dramatic financial recovery in 1934 and 1935. He also continued to advise Roosevelt on national economic issues. In 1938 Berle finally accepted a Washington position as assistant secretary of state specializing in Latin American politics. He was an architect of Roosevelt's "Good Neighbor" policy toward Latin America. During World War II (1939–45) Berle carried considerable authority as assistant secretary of state. He also returned to intelligence work and ran the State Department's international intelligence network. At the end of the war Berle was appointed U.S. ambassador to Brazil for a year. He returned to the United States to informally work with the Central Intelligence Agency (CIA) in its fight against communism in Europe and dictatorships in Latin America. Having joined an early think tank (an group organized to conduct research on a particular issue or problem), the Twentieth Century Fund, in 1934, Berle became chairman of its board of trustees in 1951. Under President John F. Kennedy (1917–1963; served 1961–63) Berle served as chairman of a Latin American task force to combat communist threats in the Western Hemisphere.

During his career Berle wrote many books and articles on corporations and foreign affairs. Remembered as a brilliant although somewhat arrogant public figure, Berle died in New York City in February 1971.

For More Information

Freidel, Frank, ed. *Realities and Illusions, 1886–1931: The Autobiography of Raymond Moley.* New York, NY: Garland Publishing, 1980.

Moley, Raymond. *After Seven Years.* New York, NY: Harper & Brothers, 1939.

Moley, Raymond, and Elliot A. Rosen. *The First New Deal.* New York, NY: Harcourt, Brace & World, 1966.

Namorato, Michael V. *Rexford Tugwell: A Biography.* New York, NY: Praeger, 1988.

Rosen, Elliot A. *Hoover, Roosevelt and the Brains Trust: From Depression to New Deal*. New York, NY: Columbia University Press, 1977.

Schwarz, Jordan. *Liberal: Adolf A. Berle and the Vision of an American Era*. New York, NY: Free Press, 1987.

Tugwell, R. G. *The Brain Trust*. New York, NY: Viking Press, 1968.

Tugwell, Rexford G. *The Economic Basis of Public Interest*. New York, NY: A. M. Kelley, 1968.

Charles Coughlin

Born October 25, 1891
Hamilton, Ontario

Died October 27, 1979
Detroit, Michigan

Catholic priest, radio personality

K nown as the "radio priest" during the 1930s, Father Charles Edward Coughlin broadcast to the nation from an office in his Catholic church. His first broadcasts were Sunday sermons primarily aimed at children. Then came more politically charged programs, in which he spoke on behalf of citizens disillusioned by the troubles of the Great Depression, the most serious economic crisis in U.S. history. By the 1930s the American radio audience was large. Despite economic hardships, most citizens found a way to purchase radios. Speaking out for the common people and against various targets—big business, communism, Jews, and eventually President Roosevelt and the New Deal—Coughlin reached nearly thirty million Americans during the peak of his popularity in the early 1930s.

Early on, Coughlin's personality and golden radio voice established him as a spokesman for the economic victims of the Great Depression. However, as his politics became steadily more radical, he preached hate and prejudice. Among an assortment of causes and demands, he called for nationalization (the U.S. government to assume ownership) of banks, utilities, and natural resources to ensure financial stability of

"Coughlin invented a new kind of preaching, one that depended on modern technology: the microphone and transmitter. He ushered in a revolution in American mass media...televangelism and political talk radio, stem back to him."

Donald Warren in Radio Priest: Charles Coughlin, the Father of Hate Radio

Charles Coughlin. *AP/Wide World Photo. Reproduced by permission.*

fairness in pay. He believed that everyone willing to work deserved a guaranteed living wage (an income whereby a family can afford all the basics in life, food, shelter, clothing, education, and transportation) and that farmers should be guaranteed payment of the cost of production plus a certain profit. As the years passed, Coughlin's once fiery and convincing radio delivery seemed more and more like the ravings of an unbalanced individual. Coughlin's public following steadily declined until he was forced off the air in 1942 by the government and his religious leaders.

A religious upbringing

Coughlin was born in Hamilton, Ontario, to a devoutly Catholic couple of Irish descent. He grew up as an only child (a younger sister died in infancy). His father was sexton (an official who maintains the church building) for a Catholic cathedral, and the family's house was on the church grounds. Coughlin's mother attended daily mass and dreamed of her son someday joining the priesthood. Coughlin attended St. Mary's parochial school in Hamilton and then St. Michael's College of the University of Toronto. He graduated in 1911 at the age of twenty with a Ph.D., specializing in philosophy and English. He spent the summer after graduation touring Europe. When he returned, he decided to begin studies for the priesthood. Coughlin entered St. Basil's Seminary at St. Michael's in Toronto for formal training and was ordained in June 1916 at the age of twenty-five. This branch of the Basilian Order, established in France in the early nineteenth century, generally opposed modern industrial economic growth and the resulting prominent role of money and banking systems in society. Coughlin taught at a Basilian boys' school, Assumption College, in Windsor, Ontario, from 1916 to 1923. Windsor is located just across the Detroit River from Detroit, Michigan. Though he taught many subjects, Coughlin put a great deal of time into drama classes, where he displayed a theatrical flair. During this period, Coughlin also began to exhibit a strong individualist mind-set and behavior that often did not conform with college rules.

In 1923 Coughlin left Windsor to become a parish priest in the Diocese of Detroit. He quickly gained a reputation for his speaking and fund-raising abilities. Overflowing

crowds often attended masses when Coughlin was scheduled to speak, causing resentment among fellow priests. After three years, in 1926, he was assigned to a newly established parish in the Detroit suburb of Royal Oak, which was populated by the rapidly growing number of automobile industry workers. Coughlin named the newly built, brown-shingled wooden church Shrine of the Little Flower. The Shrine of the Little Flower remained his home base for the rest of his life.

Charles Coughlin delivers a powerful sermon in Detroit, Michigan, circa 1936.
AP/Wide World Photo. Reproduced by permission.

The radio priest

The new parish was located where few Catholics lived; therefore, it struggled financially at first while trying to pay back the loans used for buying the property and building the church. In an effort to increase attendance and revenue, Coughlin asked a fellow Irish Catholic who owned a radio station, WJR in Detroit, if he would broadcast Coughlin's Sunday sermons in a radio program called "The Golden Hour of the Little Flower." With a strong signal, the station reached a large area of eastern Michigan. Beginning in October 1926, the broadcasts immediately became popular and secured a regular Sunday program spot. Coughlin's rich radio voice and Irish accent captured more and more listeners. By 1929 two more stations broadcast Coughlin's sermons, WMAQ in Chicago and WLW in Cincinnati. The following year the Columbia Broadcasting System (CBS) began broadcasting his program nationally. Over thirty million listeners of various religious affiliations were regularly tuning in every Sunday. To further expand his audience, Coughlin also began publishing a weekly newspaper, *Social Justice*.

Initially Coughlin's sermons were uncontroversial and nonpolitical. However, many of his parishioners were workers in the automobile industry and began to be affected by the Great Depression. Increasingly Coughlin addressed economics and politics in his sermons. He watched as many of his parishioners were laid off from their jobs as companies folded due to lack of funds. This experience moved him to focus on the greed and corruption in the banking and financial industry. Though he never fixed on a particular solution, Coughlin did begin to call for the government to take over the U.S. banking system. He preached that business leaders had a responsibility to the community. His sermons hit a popular chord with the public, who resented the modern industrial economy and the wealthy businessmen and bankers whom many blamed for causing the Depression. Coughlin delivered the sermons with a raised voice and clenched fist. Middle-class America was looking for someone to blame for its economic problems, and Coughlin provided his listeners with simple explanations in the form of conspiracy theories. For example, he argued big business and government conspired (worked together secretly) to concentrate the nation's wealth in the hands of a privileged few and leave the rest of society to struggle financially. His common targets for blame were political leaders and immigrants as well as both capitalism (an economic system in which property is privately owed and decisions on production and prices are largely privately determined) and communism (a theory that advocates elimination of private property).

Coughlin escalated the inflammatory political speech in his sermons, and in response CBS removed his program from the network in April 1931. Coughlin then established his own independent chain of radio stations, which by 1932 included twenty-seven stations from Maine to Kansas. With revenue and contributions flowing in, Coughlin built a lavish new church building in addition to comfortable homes for himself and his parents. He received so much mail, approximately eighty thousand letters a week, that 106 clerks and four personal secretaries were employed to keep up with it. Coughlin also established God's Poor Society, which distributed food and clothing to thousands of needy people in the Detroit area.

From supporter to critic

In 1932 Coughlin met presidential candidate **Franklin D. Roosevelt** (1882–1945; served 1933–45; see entry) and through his broadcasts became a major supporter of Roosevelt's campaign. Coughlin's slogans during 1932 and 1933 were "Roosevelt or Ruin" and "The New Deal Is Christ's Deal." However, by mid-1934, as Coughlin became more radical in his economic views, Roosevelt began to distance himself from the fiery broadcaster. Coughlin politically detached from the president and aligned himself with New Deal critics, including politician Huey Long (1893–1935) and Francis Townsend (1867–1960), an elderly medical doctor promoting a "retirement income" for senior citizens. Frustrated with the slow pace of reform and his inability to get closer to Roosevelt, Coughlin publicly denounced the New Deal in December 1935. He began calling the New Deal the "Jew Deal" and changed his earlier slogan to "Roosevelt and Ruin."

With his large following Coughlin was able to block some efforts by Roosevelt's administration by applying public pressure on Congress not to support the president's programs. For example, European governments were establishing an international World Court to help maintain peace and invited the United States to join. However, fears generated by Coughlin over greater foreign control over U.S. citizens swayed public opinion and Congress blocked Roosevelt from accepting the invitation. Concerned about the attacks coming from Coughlin and other critics, Roosevelt shifted New Deal support away from business and toward the common laborer, calling for legislation that would create social insurance, workers' compensation, and stronger labor unions.

Catholics and the Depression

By the 1920s the Catholic Church was actively promoting major social reform in the United States, urging minimum wage laws, social insurance programs, and labor rights in the workplace. The church's membership consisted largely of the lower working class and immigrants. As the Great Depression steadily worsened, Pope Pius XI (1857–1939) issued the *Quadragesimo Anno,* an official letter sent to church leaders in 1931. The letter stated church policy on social issues and called for governments to create laws and institutions that would benefit the general public and individual well-being. The letter also asserted that ownership of private property brought with it obligations to promote the common good of society. The *Quadragesimo Anno* condemned economic systems in which businesses operated without govern-ment regulation. The church argued that such systems had caused the Depression by concentrating wealth in the hands of a few and leaving many people in poverty.

By 1932, as the economic crisis deepened, American Catholic leaders were greatly dissatisfied with President Herbert Hoover's futile attempts at providing solutions. They strongly encouraged the government to adopt elements of the *Quadragesimo Anno* and quickly establish major direct relief programs. They also pushed for greater governmental control of industries to keep wages from dropping. Father Charles Coughlin was one of the church leaders supporting the Democratic candidate for the 1932 presidential election, Franklin D. Roosevelt. Roosevelt quoted from the *Quadragesimo Anno* in one cam-

A radical priest

In May 1936 Coughlin helped form the Union Party, with thoughts of nominating Huey Long as a presidential candidate. However, the assassination of Long left Coughlin with a lesser-known candidate. Coughlin had promised to re-tire from public life and his radio program if the Union can-didate received less than nine million votes in the November 1936 presidential election. When the candidate received less than nine hundred thousand votes, Coughlin briefly retired but returned to the radio program in early 1937.

Coughlin increased his hostile attacks on Roosevelt and the New Deal as his radio following steadily declined. He also promoted anti-Semitism (hostility toward Jews), and in 1939 he supported the formation of the militaristic Christian

paign speech, and many believed he had shown great courage by endorsing basic Christian social reform principles. Catholic leaders pushed for massive government spending on jobs and relief programs, increased taxes on the wealthy, and recognition of labor rights.

Following Roosevelt's election victory, Catholic leaders strongly supported Roosevelt's New Deal programs, which were designed to bring economic relief to the nation. Roosevelt appeared at the National Conference of Catholic Charities in 1933 to give a speech. His administration brought a sharp increase in the number of Catholics appointed to high-level government positions, including two cabinet positions: James A. Farley (1888–1976) as postmaster general and Thomas J. Welch as attorney general. Catholic support of Roosevelt continued through the 1930s, despite Father Coughlin's abrupt change in political views. Catholic leaders praised the Social Security Act of 1935 as a vital first step in a national social welfare system. It was estimated that 70 percent of Catholics voted for Roosevelt's reelection in 1936. Through his actions and policies Roosevelt had helped Catholics become part of mainstream American life. Previous to this, Catholics had been considered as largely representing Eastern European immigrant groups who came to the United States in the late nineteenth century, in contrast to the larger, more established Protestant majority that arrived from Western Europe in earlier centuries.

Front. The group, small and primarily located in a few Northeastern cities, accosted Jews and harassed Jewish-owned establishments. Coughlin began expressing sympathies with fascist leaders Adolf Hitler (1889–1945) of Germany and Benito Mussolini (1883–1945) of Italy. (Fascism is the belief in a central government led by a dictatorial leader, with the strictest social and economic restrictions and forcible suppression of any opposition to the government on the part of the people.)

Coughlin's radicalism was more than radio station owners could tolerate, and by early 1940 he was largely off the air. He continued to publish *Social Justice* for two more years until the U.S. government banned it from mail delivery. Under pressure from the government and the Catholic Church, by May 1942 Coughlin had withdrawn from political activities and resumed his pastoral duties at the Shrine of the Little Flower. He remained there until his retirement in 1966. He spent the next thirteen years out of the public eye and died in the Detroit area in 1979.

For More Information

Brinkley, Alan. *Voices of Protest: Huey Long, Father Coughlin, and the Great Depression.* New York, NY: Knopf, 1982.

Carpenter, Ronald H. *Father Charles E. Coughlin: Surrogate Spokesman for the Disaffected.* Westport, CT: Greenwood Press, 1998.

Fried, Albert. *FDR and His Enemies.* New York, NY: St. Martin's Press, 1999.

Tull, Charles J. *Father Coughlin and the New Deal.* Syracuse, NY: Syracuse University Press, 1965.

Warren, Donald I. *Radio Priest: Charles Coughlin, the Father of Hate Radio.* New York, NY: Free Press, 1996.

Dorothy Day

Born November 8, 1897
Brooklyn, New York

Died November 29, 1980
New York, New York

Journalist, advocate for the poor

The Great Depression, the worst economic crisis in the United States, had a stranglehold on Americans in May 1933. Newly elected President **Franklin D. Roosevelt** (1882–1945; served 1933–45; see entry) had launched his New Deal legislation to attempt to begin to pull America from the depths. On May 1, Dorothy Day, a tall, slender, thirty-five year old, walked among people at Union Square in New York City distributing for a penny a copy the first edition of her newspaper, the *Catholic Worker*. The edition boldly proclaimed: "To Our Readers: For those who are sitting on park benches in the warm spring sunlight. For those who are huddling in shelters trying to escape the rain. For those who are walking the streets in the all but futile search for work. For those who think that there is no hope for the future, no recognition of their plight—this little paper is addressed. It is printed to call their attention to the fact that the Catholic Church has a social program—to let them know that there are men of God who are working not only for their spiritual, but for their material welfare." Day, a convert to Catholicism, believed in applying Christian principles to help the poor. Beginning in the 1930s Depression era, Day and the *Catholic*

> "For those who think that there is no hope for the future, no recognition of their plight—this little paper is addressed."

From the first edition of the Catholic Worker

Dorothy Day.
©Bettmann/CORBIS.
Reproduced by permission.

Worker became a ray of hope for the poor and hungry, a voice for the powerless, challenging the wealthy, churches, government, and employers who had ignored the needy.

Early life

The third of five children, Dorothy May Day was born to John I. Day and Grace Satterlee Day in the shadow of the Brooklyn Bridge. John Day was a horse-racing enthusiast, and his career as a sportswriter centered on the horse-racing circuit. He was a respected but distant father who demanded an orderly, quiet family life, free of visitors. Dorothy rarely mentioned him except to say that when she was an adult, her radical ideas displeased him. On the other hand, Dorothy was close to her mother, who had an optimistic, cheery personality. Dorothy's sister Della was born two years after Dorothy. The two would be very close throughout their lives. Dorothy was the seeker and prober, always pushing boundaries, while Della's calm, good-natured personality would help moderate Dorothy's intensity.

In 1904 John moved his family to a bungalow in Oakland, California, near the Idora Park racetrack. Life was comfortable and uneventful for the family until April 18, 1906, when the earth shook mightily underneath them. While Oakland was not drastically affected, the earthquake left half of San Francisco in ruins. Within days John moved his family to Chicago. They lived in an apartment over a saloon, and for the first time the family experienced economic difficulties.

Religion was not a part of the Day household. John had been raised a Congregationalist and Grace an Episcopalian, but neither attended church in adulthood. Nevertheless, Dorothy always had an interest in "holy" things. An avid reader since the age of four, she came across a Bible in the house, spent several hours reading it, and experienced a "sense of holiness." She attended Methodist services with Chicago neighbors and visited with a Catholic girl in the neighborhood who told her about the Catholic religion. Dorothy attended an Episcopalian church with her brothers and sisters after a pastor visited John, who was slightly drunk at the time, and convinced him to let his children attend church.

By the time Dorothy reached her teen years, John had a good job as a sports editor for a Chicago newspaper, and the family was comfortable and happy in a large house near Lincoln Park. Dorothy's life consisted of going to school, helping with housework, and reading authors recommended by her father, such as Charles Dickens (1812–1870) and Robert Louis Stevenson (1850–1894). Dorothy also read books by Jack London (1876–1916), who described slum life and class struggles; Upton Sinclair (1878–1968), who was interested in socialism and wrote *The Jungle* (1906) about working conditions in the Chicago stockyards; and Carl Sandburg (1878–1967), a socialist and supporter of the common people. She followed with interest the labor movement struggles in Chicago and admired the activities of powerful labor leader Eugene Debs (1855–1926).

Late teens and college freedom

Day's interest in religion continued as she grew older. She was confirmed in the Episcopal Church in her teens and enjoyed reading about saints and religious teachings. She was deeply impressed by the formal prayer and psalms of the church. Day graduated from Waller High School in June 1914 and entered the University of Illinois at Urbana in the fall. She continued to be a very introspective young person who centered her life around reading and writing instead of college parties and empty chatter.

On her own for the first time and away from the watchful eye of her father, Day relished in attending or not attending classes as she saw fit. She always occupied a seat by the window during lectures. Day managed Bs and Cs but flunked biology, a subject that did not interest her. In her second semester at Illinois she met and became fast friends with Rayna Simons. Together they read and reread Russian writers such as Fyodor Dostoyevsky (1821–1881) and Leo Tolstoy (1828–1910). Rayna was destined to become a communist; Day, a Catholic.

Young journalist

In the spring of 1916 John Day accepted a sportswriter position on the *New York Morning Telegraph* and moved the family back to New York City. Day, at the same time, left the University of Illinois and took a reporter's job in New York for the Socialist journal *Call*. At the *Call* she reported on a variety of issues including housing conditions, evictions, labor troubles and strikes, and food riots. She also covered several groups opposed to the U.S. entry into World War I (1914–18).

In 1917 she left the *Call* and went to work for *Masses*, a radical Socialist journal. Day's writing dealt more with the individual experiences of poor and struggling people than with political issues. Government authorities soon suppressed *Masses*, and Day was unemployed. Around this time she joined a group of demonstrators at the White House who were protesting the treatment of a number of suffragettes (women who worked to attain voting rights for women). After the demonstration, Day ended up with a thirty-day jail sentence; in jail she experienced hunger and mistreatment.

Bohemian wanderings

After getting out of jail, Day began a Bohemian, or unconventional, wandering lifestyle that lasted almost a decade. She moved to Greenwich Village in New York City and became friends with many literary and artistic individuals who also lived in the vibrant Village. Day developed a particularly close friendship with playwright Eugene O'Neill (1888–1953). Continuing her journey through life, Day met and married literary promoter Barkeley Tobey, then followed him to Europe. Within a year she left Tobey and came back to the United States, first to Chicago, then to New Orleans, Louisiana.

In 1924 she published a semiautobiographical novel, *The Eleventh Virgin,* and was offered five thousand dollars for the movie rights. With the money Day bought a cottage on Staten Island in New York and began reestablishing her friendships within New York's literary circles. She counted author John Dos Passos (1896–1970) and Mike Gold as friends. Her circle of friends included socialists, communists, and anarchists (those who oppose government structure and believe people can govern themselves). At this point in her life she began a common-law marriage with Foster Batterham, an anarchist from an established Southern family.

A new Catholic

In June 1925 Day learned she was pregnant. She described her reaction as "blissful joy," and she later recalled that after hearing the news, she began to pray again rather spontaneously and make visits to a nearby Catholic chapel. In March 1926 Day and Batterham's baby, Tamar Teresa, was born. Day had her baptized into the Roman Catholic Church. Day began to explore joining the Catholic Church and was eventually baptized as a Roman Catholic on December 28, 1927.

Shortly after her baptism, Day left Batterham and traveled widely, taking various journalistic assignments. She even tried her hand at writing Hollywood scripts, but frustrated with the meaninglessness of the job, she quit and went to live in Mexico City, Mexico. There she wrote articles about the poverty and despair she found at every turn. She submitted these articles to *Commonweal,* a mainstream and respected Catholic journal, and they were accepted for publication. Articles by Day would appear in *Commonweal* for many years thereafter.

Day was constantly searching for a way to help the poor. She feared that the Catholic Church was not meaningfully addressing the problems of the poorest people in society. Day was actively trying to make sense of her own life and religious beliefs, but at the same time she was trying to figure out how she could improve the lives of others in a practical way.

By 1932 almost 25 percent of the U.S. workforce was unemployed. The Great Depression, the most severe economic crisis in America's history, was worsening. *Commonweal* sent Day to Washington, D.C., to cover hunger marchers in December 1932. To her dismay, Christians were not leading the marchers; instead it was communists who had organized the event. Although she was devoutly religious, which goes against the communist way of thinking, and was never a member of the Communist Party, Day sympathized with the communist doctrine calling for a government and an economic system that promote human dignity and social justice. In a book she published years later in 1952, *The Long Loneliness: The Autobiography of Dorothy Day,* Day remembered that while she was in Washington, D.C., she went to the national shrine at Catholic University, and "there I offered up a special prayer, a prayer which came with tears and with anguish, that some way would open up for me to use what talents I possessed for my fellow workers, for the poor."

Peter Maurin and the birth of the *Catholic Worker*

When Day returned to New York, Peter Maurin met her at her apartment. He had been sent by George Shuster, editor of *Commonweal,* because Shuster thought Day and Maurin had similar concerns. Born in 1877 in France, Maurin was educated by a Catholic order called the Christian Brothers. He became involved in Sillon, a radical democratic Christian farming movement that swept France in the early twentieth century. When the movement failed to take hold, he left France, moved to Canada, then arrived in New York in the late 1920s. Maurin talked intently about voluntary poverty, service to others, and Christian reform. He believed that if each Christian individually performed acts of kindness, Christians could collectively change the social order. Day realized that Maurin's ideas were a bridge to her own commitment to the poor. With his vision and her practicality, Maurin and Day established the Catholic Worker movement in 1933.

Together Day and Maurin created the newspaper *Catholic Worker* to present the official teachings of the Catholic Church on social justice and to address hunger, labor concerns, and race relations. In the newspaper Day and Maurin suggested ways for Christians to address the social realities of the day.

One of the suggestions, Houses of Hospitality, quickly caught on. Houses of Hospitality were started all over the country. By 1938 twenty-three houses fed and sheltered needy people—sometimes a few and sometimes hundreds each day. These Catholic Worker houses became the focus for a new Catholic social justice philosophy. The original Hospitality House, located in New York, moved to a larger house at 115 Mott Street and remained home to the movement for the next fifteen years. The *Catholic Worker* had a circulation of over one hundred thousand. From the start Day oversaw all aspects of the paper. For decades she wrote a monthly column for the *Worker* and traveled up to four months each year to

The Catholic Worker Movement

The Catholic Worker movement was founded in 1933 by two people. One was Dorothy Day, a journalist, a recent Catholic convert, and a friend of socialists, communists, and anarchists. The other, Peter Maurin, was an eccentric Frenchman and a Catholic intellectual without a penny to his name. Together they founded a movement whose philosophical cornerstones were Christian communal living (doing individual work to help others within a community specifically dedicated to following the teachings of Jesus); voluntary poverty (choosing to reject material possessions); and nonviolence and pacifism. They established a newspaper, the *Catholic Worker,* to explain and promote the philosophy and programs of the movement. From 1933 until her death in 1980, Day was the editor of the newspaper. Within only a few years Houses of Hospitality were set up in cities across the nation to provide food, clothing, shelter, and welcome to those in need. Rural self-sufficient Catholic Worker communities were also established. The Catholic Worker movement was never an official part of the Catholic Church but applied Catholic teaching by reaching out to the poor and the oppressed. The movement introduced a new form of Catholicism to America. Until the 1930s the U.S. Catholic population was made up entirely of immigrants intent on making a successful transition into American life and showing loyalty to their chosen country. The Catholic Worker movement, on the other hand, attracted more-liberal Catholics. They were involved in the labor union movement and social issues of the poor, both activities considered by the general public to be related to socialism and communism and disloyal to the United States. At first the movement was well received, but its unwavering pacifism—opposition to all military activities—lost it many followers during World War II (1939–45). Nevertheless, its message endured. At the start of the twenty-first century, 134 Catholic Worker communities still existed, and the *Catholic Worker* newspaper still cost one penny a copy. Besides clothing and feeding the poor, Catholic Workers support labor unions and civil rights and continue as pacifists during times of war.

speak out against the inhumane working conditions many laborers had to endure.

In the late 1930s tensions in Europe were building and would soon lead to the outbreak of World War II (1939–45). Both Day and Maurin found Christian teachings to be totally incompatible with war, and they said so through the *Worker.* Their pacifist (achieving goals through peaceful means) position angered many Catholics who chose to demonstrate their loyalty to the United States through service in the armed forces. By the mid-1940s *Catholic Worker* circulation had dropped to fifty-five thousand.

A role model in the fight for social justice

From the end of World War II until her death, Day advocated social, racial, and economic justice. She continued in her firm devotion to the Catholic Church. Day was considered a Catholic visionary, a role model in the fight for social justice, and an innovative advocate for the poor. From her baptism in 1927 to the end of her life, she attended mass and prayed daily.

Day remained active and outspoken until her death in 1980 at Maryhouse, a Catholic Worker hospitality house for destitute women in New York City. After a lifetime of voluntary poverty, Day left no money for a funeral. The Catholic Archdiocese of New York paid the expenses. A gifted and tireless writer, Day wrote thousands of essays, articles, and reviews, as well as several books in her eighty-three years of life. She put Christian principles into practice in the modern world. She chose a life of poverty, living at the Houses of Hospitality, eating the food, and wearing clothing from the secondhand clothing bins at the houses. Day was consistently several decades ahead of the Catholic Church on social issues and was a primary influence in the growth of the American Catholic community. In an article titled "The Pilgrimage of Dorothy Day" for the December 19, 1980, issue of *Commonweal,* Catholic historian David J. O'Brien calls her "the most significant, interesting, and influential person in the history of American Catholicism." In the September 11, 1982, issue of *Nation,* writer Linda Bamber describes Day as "the closest thing there is to a twentieth-century American saint." At the beginning of the twenty-first century a movement for her to be declared a saint was still in progress.

For More Information

Books

Day, Dorothy. *The Long Loneliness: The Autobiography of Dorothy Day.* New York, NY: Harper, 1952.

Miller, William D. *Dorothy Day: A Biography.* New York, NY: Harper & Row, 1982.

Roberts, Nancy L. *Dorothy Day and the Catholic Worker.* Albany, NY: State University of New York Press, 1984.

Thorn, William, Phillip Runkel, and Susan Mountin, eds. *Dorothy Day and the Catholic Worker Movement: Centenary Essays.* Milwaukee, WI: Marquette University, 2001.

Periodicals
Bamber, Linda. "A Saint's Life." *Nation,* September 11, 1982.

O'Brien, David J. "The Pilgrimage of Dorothy Day." *Commonweal,* December 19, 1980.

Web Sites
The Catholic Worker Movement. http://www.catholicworker.org (accessed on September 7, 2002).

Molly Dewson

Born February 18, 1874
Quincy, Massachusetts

Died October 21, 1962
Castine, Maine

Social reformer, Democratic Party leader,
promoter of women in government

"Molly Dewson arrived in Washington to take over as head of the country's Democratic women and to inaugurate a new deal of her own—a new deal for women in politics."

From Ladies of Courage

During the 1930s, Molly Dewson became America's first woman to take the lead role in a political organization. She was the driving force behind securing prominent positions for women in the Roosevelt administration. From 1932 until 1937 Dewson was director of the Women's Division of the Democratic National Committee. Director of the Women's Division was a full-time job on the staff of the national committee, and whoever held the position was the most powerful woman in the national party organization. During the 1936 presidential election campaign, Dewson directed the efforts of some eighty thousand women who served as a nationwide network recruiting the female vote for **Franklin D. Roosevelt's** (1882–1945; served 1933–45; see entry) reelection. Through her efforts, women voters became an important segment of the newly created Democratic Coalition. This coalition would influence U.S. political elections for decades to come.

Dewson held no desire for her own political gain but focused on promoting social reform and the participation of women in government. She preferred working quietly, but

Molly Dewson, sitting, played a key role in the 1932 election of Franklin Roosevelt to the presidency. *©Bettmann/CORBIS. Reproduced by permission.*

vigorously, behind the scenes rather than in the limelight. Instead of promoting women for political office, Dewson concentrated on getting women appointed to prominent government positions. She introduced the idea that women belonged at the highest governmental levels and moved the focus of women's issues from the state and local levels to the national level.

In the 1987 biography of Molly Dewson, *Partner and I: Molly Dewson, Feminism, and New Deal Politics,* author Susan Ware describes Dewson's ability to work effectively in the predominantly male world of politics: "She had a down-to-earth practical manner that male politicians liked. Unlike many political greenhorns [one who is inexperienced], she was not afraid to compromise; if a public fight seemed counterproductive, she found ways to achieve her goals behind the scenes." **Lorena Hickok** (1893–1968; see entry) and **Eleanor Roosevelt** (1884–1962; see entry) describe Dewson similarly in *Ladies of Courage*: "She has never been, to use a Dewson adjective, a 'buttery-uppery' person. Her forthright manner…reassured the men. They thought they understood her. Few of them ever realized how well she understood them."

Massachusetts years

Molly was born Mary Williams Dewson, the last of six children in a Massachusetts family that traced its American roots back to 1637. Her father, Edward Henry Dewson, was a Boston leather merchant. Her mother, Elizabeth Weld, focused on the home, family, and religion. The family was close, gathering daily to read aloud, often from the Bible. Her parents supported her desire to go to college even though higher education was an uncommon opportunity for women at that time. Molly attended Wellesley College, graduating in 1897. In college, she demonstrated leadership qualities and was elected senior class president.

Following graduation, Dewson worked with several organizations. She first found employment as a research assistant for the Women's Educational and Industrial Union in Boston. This organization was dedicated to helping women gain educational and vocational advancement. Dewson explored various topics concerning women workers in industry. The work introduced her to poverty and women's issues of the day. She had never seen women and children laboring long hours in unsafe, dirty factory conditions or people, who were either out of work or making poverty wages, living in crowded slums. In 1900 Dewson took a job as head of the parole department for delinquent girls at the Massachusetts State Industrial School for Girls at Lancaster. There she met her life partner of fifty-two years, Polly Porter. They moved to central Massachusetts in 1912 to operate an experimental dairy farm.

Also in 1912 Dewson became executive secretary for the Massachusetts Commission on the Minimum Wage. Politically Dewson considered herself a progressive. Progressives looked to the federal government to help solve the pressing social problems developing in modern industrial America. During this period of progressive politics, key issues for women were minimum wage guarantees and women's suffrage (right to vote). Dewson successfully fought for the nation's first minimum wage law for women workers, a major advance in social legislation. Eight other states passed similar laws in 1913, and by 1923 fourteen states had such laws. During the 1910s Dewson participated in the women's suffrage campaign. Women gained the right to vote in 1920 when the states ratified the Nineteenth Amendment.

An energetic and involved life

During World War I (1914–18), Dewson and Porter joined the American Red Cross in Europe and fearlessly traveled to France with other social workers. There Dewson became a zone chief working with immigrant refugees. Upon returning from the war, Dewson joined the National Consumers' League in New York City. She served as research secretary and worked on labor legislation from 1919 to 1924. The National Consumers' League attempted to use consumer pressure to change factory conditions by urging people not to buy products made in unsafe factories. In 1924, at the age of fifty, Dewson resigned from the league, with thoughts of settling into life in New York City's Greenwich Village. Dewson and Porter also spent time at Porter's large summer home in Castine, Maine. However, unable to contain her energy and curiosity within a retired lifestyle, Dewson soon took on the duties of civic secretary for the Women's City Club of New York, a social reform group. During 1924 and 1925 she helped develop a legislative program to address women's issues. Dewson next became president of the New York Consumers' League, a position she held until 1931.

Dewson and the New Deal

While serving on the city club and the New York Consumers' League, Dewson made many new friends including Eleanor Roosevelt. In 1928 Eleanor recruited Dewson to help with the women's campaign in the Midwest supporting the Democratic presidential candidate Alfred E. Smith (1873–1944). Dewson's success in resolving some complex situations led Eleanor to recruit Dewson once again in 1932 to assist with the presidential campaign of Eleanor's husband **Franklin D. Roosevelt** (1882–1945; served 1933–45; see entry). Dewson developed key campaign literature for Roosevelt: distinc-

Women of the New Deal

After Franklin Roosevelt's presidential election victory in November 1932, Molly Dewson met with Eleanor Roosevelt and others to compile a list of women who would make good appointees to public office in the Roosevelt administration. They considered, in particular, professionally trained social workers who would be familiar with formal organizational structures and key economic issues of the day. They compiled a list of one hundred women, with emphasis placed on fifteen, such as Francis Perkins, **Ellen Woodward** (1887–1971; see entry), and Nellie Tayloe Ross. Though success was slow in the number of appointments made through the years, some major gains were realized. In some cases Dewson had a direct role in the appointment and in other cases a more distant influence. Some of the resulting appointees included the following women:

Frances Perkins (1882–1965):
    Secretary of Labor
Jo Coffin:
    U.S. Government Printing Office administrator
Nellie Tayloe Ross (1876–1977):
    director of the U.S. Mint
Ruth Bryan Owen (1885–1954):
    minister to Denmark
Florence E. Allen (1884–1966):
    judge on the U.S. circuit court of appeals
Ellen Sullivan Woodward (1887–1971):
    Works Progress Administration administrator
Mary McLeod Bethune (1875–1955):
    director of the Negro Affairs Division of the National Youth Administration
Hallie Flanagan (1890–1969):
    head of the Federal Theatre Project

tive, brightly-colored, one-page fact sheets known as Rainbow Flyers. Six million flyers were distributed nationwide. When asked how she would like to be rewarded for her efforts in Roosevelt's successful campaign, Dewson requested that Roosevelt appoint **Frances Perkins** (1882–1965; see entry) as secretary of labor. (Perkins was appointed to this position in 1933 and became the first woman to hold a position in a U.S. presidential cabinet.) Dewson also established the Reporter Plan, a network of women who volunteered to study the impact of Roosevelt's New Deal programs and monitor the progress of government agencies in their communities. Five thousand women joined the network in 1934; by 1940 thirty thousand had joined. They shared their findings at community club meetings. Again organizing women's support for Roosevelt in the 1936 presidential election, Dewson was the head of the Women's Division of the Democratic National Committee from 1932 to 1937. In the 1940 campaign for

Roosevelt's reelection, she served in a much more limited capacity. Although she was primarily focused on increasing women's political participation, in 1937 Dewson did accept a position in the Roosevelt administration in Washington, D.C. She served briefly on the Social Security Board, but after nine months, she decided to return to a private life.

Dewson's close ties with Eleanor and Franklin Roosevelt and with Secretary of Labor Frances Perkins provided the foundation for Dewson's power. With President Roosevelt's sudden death in April 1945, Dewson's political influence suddenly ended. She retired to her personal life, serving in some limited duties such as on the board of the National Consumers' League. She would get together with Eleanor Roosevelt and Perkins on occasion. Sometimes referred to as the "Ladies Brain Trust" (in reference to President Roosevelt's advisors, dubbed the **Brain Trust**; see entry), the three carried the feminist cause and shaped Democratic politics for years to come. In 1952 Dewson and Porter retired to their home in Castine, Maine. In 1960, at age eighty-six, Dewson ran for a Maine state senate seat. Dewson died in October 1962, only two weeks before the death of Eleanor Roosevelt. Polly Porter died in 1972.

For More Information

Roosevelt, Eleanor, and Lorena A. Hickok. *Ladies of Courage*. New York, NY: Putnam, 1954.

Ware, Susan. *Beyond Suffrage: Women in the New Deal*. Cambridge, MA: Harvard University Press, 1981.

Ware, Susan. *Holding Their Own: American Women in the 1930s*. Boston, MA: Twayne Publishers, 1982.

Ware, Susan. *Partner and I: Molly Dewson, Feminism, and New Deal Politics*. New Haven, CT: Yale University Press, 1987.

The Du Pont Family

Industrialists

Lammot du Pont.
©*Bettmann/CORBIS.*
Reproduced by permission.

Du Pont is one of the most noted family names in U.S. industrial history. In 1802 Éleuthère Irénée du Pont (1771–1834), an immigrant from France, built a gunpowder mill on the Brandywine River in Delaware. Boosted by gunpowder sales to the government in the War of 1812 (1812–14), the company began to amass large profits during the American Civil War (1861–65) and World War I (1914–18). With its war profits, Du Pont greatly diversified; it was no longer just an explosives company but a world-leading chemical corporation. The du Pont family became one of the wealthiest families in the nation. In 1926 Lammot du Pont became the eighth consecutive family member to be named president of the family business. He continued to expand the Du Pont fortune during the 1930s Great Depression, the worst economic crisis in U.S. history. When President **Franklin D. Roosevelt** (1882–1945; served 1933–45; see entry) introduced new social and economic programs designed to help the country recover from its economic troubles, Lammot du Pont and other family members organized political opposition to these programs, which were collectively labeled the New Deal. The du Ponts feared the New

Deal programs would be too restrictive toward business and industry.

Building an industrial giant

In 1800 Éleuthère Irénée du Pont de Nemours fled to the United States from revolutionary France along with his father and other family members. Éleuthère, encouraged by President Thomas Jefferson (1743–1826; served 1801–09), founded E. I. Du Pont de Nemours & Company, which manufactured black powder in a factory on the Brandywine River just north of Wilmington, Delaware. Production of black powder, the prevailing form of gunpowder until later in the nineteenth century when it was replaced with a smokeless form of gunpowder, began in 1802 at the Du Pont factory. The War of 1812 gave the company's fortunes an early boost.

Éleuthère's sudden death in late 1834 placed his son, Alfred Victor du Pont (1798–1856) in charge of the business until 1850. Upon encountering health problems, Alfred turned the business over to his brother Henry (1812–1889) in 1850. Henry proved a shrewd manager and long-term president, greatly increasing the efficiency of gunpowder production. The Du Pont company made large profits during the American Civil War. The business expanded to a new factory built in New Jersey, and the new plant was producing a ton of dynamite a day in 1880. By 1881 the Du Pont company had cornered 85 percent of the explosives market, establishing itself as an industry giant during a period of rapid industrial growth in the United States. However, Henry left the company president position in 1889. Eugene du Pont took over but proved to be a less dynamic leader; under his leadership business began to slow.

Meanwhile, in October 1880 Lammot du Pont, the future Du Pont president, had been born in Wilmington, Delaware, home of the Du Pont dynasty. His father was also named Lammot, and his mother was Mary Belin du Pont. He had two older brothers, Pierre and Irénée. Young Lammot was largely raised by Pierre and Irénée after the death of their father in a nitroglycerin explosion in 1884. Like his older brothers, Lammot attended Massachusetts Institute of Technology. He graduated in 1901 with a degree in civil engineering and found work as a draftsman for a company in Philadelphia, Pennsylvania.

A new generation takes over

Upon Eugene's death in 1902, the elder members of the du Pont family decided to sell the family business. However, three of the younger du Ponts—Pierre and two of his cousins, Alfred and T. Coleman—were able to put an offer together to take control of the company and avoid the sale to nonfamily members. They invited Lammot to join the family business along with Pierre's personal secretary on financial matters, John Jakob Raskob. The more outgoing Coleman became president, Pierre ran the front office, Alfred oversaw research and production, and Raskob handled the complex financial arrangements. Lammot was named manager of the original Brandywine plant. Upon taking his new job, Lammot married Natalie Driver in 1903; she was the first of his four wives. Lammot would father ten children, eight by Natalie and two with his fourth wife.

Under the guidance of Pierre, Alfred, Coleman, Lammot, and Raskob, the company once again prospered. They greatly increased production efficiency and gained control of many other smaller powder firms. By 1905 Du Pont dominated the markets for blasting powder, dynamite, and gunpowder. It was producing 75 percent of the nation's explosives and had assets of $60 million. Because of its near monopoly of the explosives industry, Du Pont was among the industrial giants that attracted federal antitrust action in the first decade of the twentieth century. (Antitrust laws encourage business competition by breaking up monopolies.) In 1910 the government ordered Du Pont to break up its munitions monopoly. However, it left Du Pont in charge of the breakup, so the company suffered little.

With Coleman experiencing health problems, Pierre had become acting president in 1909. Pierre and Raskob restructured the Du Pont company into a modern management system with multiple management levels and separate departments responsible for the various products. Pierre also increased the active research and development program to regain government respect leading up to World War I in reaction to the earlier government antitrust lawsuits. Raskob was made treasurer of the giant company.

World War I profits

In 1915 the du Ponts along with other leading industrialists and bankers established the National Security League to lobby (attempt to persuade lawmakers) for U.S. entrance into World War I. The lobbying effort was supposedly based on patriotism and protection of the Allies, but many suspected the desire for profits was stronger. The United States did finally enter the war in 1917. The Du Pont company, with Pierre as president, brother Irénée now chief administrator, and Raskob directing finances, made profits of $59 million a year selling explosives to the U.S. government and Allied nations.

Rather shy in public but a highly competent businessman, Lammot moved up steadily, becoming vice president in charge of the black powder operation in 1916, when war production was rapidly increasing. He played a critical role in expanding the company's production capacity to meet the demand for military explosives. Du Pont supplied 40 percent of the explosives used by the Allies in World War I.

Diversification

The company needed to invest its large war profits, so Raskob encouraged the du Ponts to purchase stock in the newly formed General Motors Corporation (GM). By 1919 Du Pont held 27 percent of GM stock, and Raskob had left Du Pont to become chairman of GM's finance committee. When GM faced bankruptcy in 1920 during the postwar economic slump, Pierre du Pont took over as GM's president. Along with GM founder William Durant (1861–1947), Pierre and Raskob reorganized GM into a highly diversified company manufacturing many kinds of products. They named Lammot a director of GM. Du Pont's stock holdings in GM climbed up to 36 percent during this time. When Pierre retired from the GM board of directors in 1929, GM was the world's largest corporation. Lammot followed Pierre as chairman of the board from 1929 to 1937. He remained on the board until 1946.

When Pierre assumed leadership of GM, he turned the Du Pont corporation presidency over to Irénée. Lammot became vice president in the corporation, and then president in 1926. He was the eighth du Pont to head the family business. A critical issue was how to continue making use of the company's expanded production capacities following the war. Lammot and Irénée played leading roles in the acquisition of various companies that produced ammonia, plastics, varnishes, paints, insecticides, and other products that could be made from either the same materials as the explosives or from the by-products of explosives production. By expanding into these many new product lines, Du Pont profits continued to grow even after the war was over. Du Pont also purchased thousands of German patents and recruited German scientists. The company also acquired the rights to cellophane in 1923 from a French company, and sales grew quickly. Lammot and Irénée had transformed the company from primarily a munitions manufacturer to a highly diversified chemical company.

As company president, Lammot further expanded Du Pont by buying companies in new lines of business and promoting new research. Research brought new products, including Freon® (refrigerant) in 1929 and synthetic rubber in 1930. Rayon was developed, and methanol was formulated for use in antifreeze. By 1930 Du Pont was the largest chemical corporation in the United States. These new products kept company profits at a relatively healthy $26 million in 1932, the worst year of the Great Depression.

Political issues

The du Ponts were actively involved in political issues. In early 1928 the three du Pont brothers—Pierre, Lammot, and Irénée—and Raskob became active in the Association Against the Prohibition Amendment (AAPA). The organization was dedicated to repealing Prohibition, the nationwide ban on the manufacture and sale of alcoholic beverages enacted in 1920. AAPA's members argued that the ban on alcoholic beverage sales infringed on individual rights, created crime, and cost the government much revenue through loss of tax money while increasing costs of law enforcement. Also in 1928, Raskob, a lifelong Republican, resigned from GM and became the chairman of the Democratic

American Liberty League

The du Ponts, John Jakob Raskob, and many other leading industrialists and financiers in the United States disdained the New Deal social and economic programs introduced by President Franklin Roosevelt. By August 1934 they were becoming bolder despite the popular support of Roosevelt. Together they formed the American Liberty League (ALL) to combat business regulations and programs such as Social Security. A key goal was to defeat Roosevelt in the 1936 presidential elections and end his New Deal programs. The members of ALL were some of the same people who had formed the Association Against the Prohibition Amendment six years earlier to repeal Prohibition.

ALL argued that New Deal agencies such as the Agricultural Adjustment Administration and the National Recovery Administration violated personal property rights by attempting to regulate business. They claimed that relief programs represented the "end of democracy." They also opposed increased taxes, economic planning, and government deficit spending. Some members called the New Deal a communist concept. The league was not a large organization—membership peaked at almost 125,000 people in the summer of 1936—but it represented considerable wealth. In a massive campaign, ALL spent $600,000 to try to defeat President Roosevelt. The du Pont family contributed one quarter of the money. Membership dropped sharply after Roosevelt's reelection, and the league officially disbanded in 1940 as foreign issues began to take priority over domestic concerns.

Not all business leaders joined ALL, and some remained firmly behind President Roosevelt. Because of his past personal support for Roosevelt, Pierre du Pont refused to participate actively in ALL despite family pressure. Roosevelt found business opposition surprising because he thought the New Deal programs would save the capitalist economic system that had made business leaders so wealthy.

National Committee, which supported the candidacy of Alfred Smith (1873–1944) for president. Smith was more accommodating to the repeal of Prohibition than Republican candidate Herbert Hoover (1874–1964) was.

In the du Ponts' hometown of Wilmington, Pierre served on the Mayor's Emergency Unemployment Relief Committee in the early 1930s, during the depth of the Great Depression. Though a lifelong Republican, Pierre supported Democrat Franklin D. Roosevelt for president in the 1932 election, largely because of the Prohibition repeal issue. Herbert Hoover had won the previous election, and as a representative of the Republican Party he avoided taking a strong stand on the issue. The Democrats, on the other hand, favored repeal of Prohibition.

Except for Pierre, the du Ponts were greatly upset with Roosevelt's 1932 presidential election victory. To their dismay, Roosevelt's New Deal programs introduced in 1933 increased the role of government in the nation's business activities. However, Lammot and Pierre took an active role in the New Deal's National Recovery Administration (NRA) by drafting business codes for the chemical industry. Pierre was even appointed to the National Labor Board to oversee implementation of the NRA's industry codes. This experience in drafting codes and serving on the board hardened Lammot's disdain for the new government programs. He and Irénée charged that New Deal relief programs were unconstitutional because one segment of society was taxed in order to fund relief programs that would benefit only the unemployed, not the people who paid the tax. (At the time the du Pont brothers were among the wealthiest men in the world.)

In the summer of 1934 Lammot, Irénée, and Raskob along with other leading industrialists and financiers in the nation established the American Liberty League (ALL). The league, dedicated to defeating Roosevelt in his 1936 reelection bid and stopping his New Deal programs, met with little success.

Also in 1934 the U.S. Senate was investigating whether big business had pushed the United States into World War I for the purpose of making profits. Lammot, Pierre, and Irénée testified before a committee investigating munitions makers. Though no actual wrongdoing was uncovered, the public perception of the Du Pont corporation sharply declined when people learned of the vast profits Du Pont had made from the war. The press labeled the du Ponts "merchants of death." As a result, Du Pont took public relations steps to improve its image, sponsoring a popular radio program and creating catchy company slogans emphasizing the benefits of Du Pont products to society.

Forging on

Aside from politics and public relations in the 1930s, the company forged on, developing new products such as

nylon. Du Pont researchers had developed nylon by 1935, and it was unveiled to the public at the 1939 New York World's Fair. Nylon would become the hottest-selling product in Du Pont history and was used to make new consumer goods such as nylon hosiery.

Lammot retired from the Du Pont presidency and Pierre from the board of directors in 1940. Together they had built the top research and development programs in the industry. Under Lammot the budget for research rose from $2 million in 1926 to $11 million in 1940. Lammot was the last member of the du Pont family to be president of the family's business. He remained chairman of the board of Du Pont through World War II (1939–45) until 1948. During this time he contributed to many conservative political organizations that opposed the federal government's attempts to regulate big business.

For the public good

The du Pont family was known for more than its success in industry. The du Ponts developed elaborate gardens and donated millions of dollars to Delaware public schools and the state's highway system. The black American school system in Delaware was financed solely by the du Ponts, and the family gave substantial assistance to the state's college for blacks, the Delaware State College. Pierre du Pont was on the Delaware school board and became state school tax commissioner from 1925 to 1929 and state tax commissioner from 1929 to 1937 and from 1944 to 1949.

Lammot died on Fishers Island, New York, in July 1952. Though no member of the du Pont family was in the Du Pont company leadership by the end of the twentieth century, the family still owned 15 percent of the company's stock.

For More Information

Books

Burk, Robert F. *The Corporate State and the Broker State: The Du Ponts and American National Politics, 1925–1940.* Cambridge, MA: Harvard University Press, 1990.

Carr, William H. A. *The Du Ponts of Delaware.* New York, NY: Dodd, Mead, 1964.

Chandler, Alfred D., Jr., and Stephen Salsbury. *Pierre S. Du Pont and the Making of the Modern Corporation.* New York, NY: Harper & Row, 1971.

Duke, Marc. *The Du Ponts: Portrait of a Dynasty.* New York, NY: Saturday Review Press, 1976.

Zilg, Gerard Colby. *Du Pont: Behind the Nylon Curtain.* Englewood Cliffs, NJ: Prentice-Hall, 1974.

Zilg, Gerard Colby. *Du Pont Dynasty.* Secaucus, NJ: L. Stuart, 1984.

Web Sites

Du Pont Heritage. http://heritage.dupont.com (accessed on September 7, 2002).

Marriner Eccles

Born September 9, 1890
Logan, Utah

Died December 18, 1977
Salt Lake City, Utah

Businessman, banker, chairman of the Federal Reserve

Marriner Eccles played a major role in President **Franklin D. Roosevelt's** (1882–1945; served 1933–45; see entry) administration. Eccles guided economic policy, particularly the efforts to reform the U.S. banking system and strengthen the role of the Federal Reserve System. Historians recognize Eccles as a keenly perceptive observer of economic issues and a fierce battler in representing his views. Eccles was one of the most influential players in restructuring the ailing American economy during the 1930s.

> "He was more feared than loved; his economic titles made him a man whom people in the inter-mountain West addressed in tones of deference [respect]."
>
> *Sidney Hyman in* Marriner S. Eccles: Private Entrepreneur and Public Servant

A shrewd young businessman

Marriner Stoddard Eccles was the oldest of nine children born to Ellen Stoddard in Logan, Utah. His father, David Eccles, had grown up in poverty in the slums of Glasgow, Scotland. David never attended school and worked for only pennies a day by age eight. In 1863 the Eccles family had converted to Mormonism, or the religion of the Church of Jesus Christ of Latter-day Saints. The family immigrated to the United States and to the state of Utah, the center of the

Marriner Eccles. *AP/Wide World Photo. Reproduced by permission.*

Mormon Church. David Eccles was fourteen years of age and illiterate, but with a fresh beginning, he built a highly successful business career and amassed a fortune. The Mormon Church allowed polygamy (having more than one wife), and David Eccles had two wives, one of them Ellen Stoddard. The Eccles family became one of the wealthiest in Utah.

Marriner Eccles was raised in an atmosphere of thriftiness, honesty, self-reliance, hard work, and service to the Mormon Church. He attended a high school associated with Brigham Young College and then embarked on a required one-year Mormon mission. For his mission Eccles was sent to Scotland, and there he met his future wife, May Campbell "Maysie" Young. He and Maysie were married in 1913 and had four children.

David Eccles had died in 1912, leaving a fortune for Marriner to manage. At age twenty-two Marriner Eccles was a millionaire. After fierce legal battles with his half brothers, Marriner, the eldest son, assumed primary responsibility for his father's business enterprises, including various banks, a lumber company, and a sugar company. In 1916 he organized the Eccles Investment Company to help manage the various businesses, and he was the company's president. Eccles and a brother acquired more banks during the 1920s. By 1928 they had banks at seventeen locations in Utah, Wyoming, and Idaho. To manage the banks, they formed a holding company (a company that controls one or more other companies through stock ownership) called the First Security Corporation. Marriner Eccles was a shrewd and tough businessman. His banking and sugar interests grew until they were the largest such enterprises in the West. As director of the Utah Construction Company, he forged a partnership with other construction firms to form Six Companies, the lead construction firm for Hoover Dam on the Colorado River.

With the onset of the Great Depression in October 1929 and with bank failures occurring across the country, Eccles had to act decisively to save his banks. Eccles developed a strategy to maintain a public atmosphere of calm at his banks by having his employees interact with the depositors consistently in a calm manner. This strategy convinced depositors to retain their confidence in his banks. This was an

New Deal Banking Reform

The crash of the stock market in October 1929 brought tough times to the U.S. banking system. During the economic boom of the 1920s many banks flourished, with few regulations controlling the way they operated. But as the economy spiraled downward in late 1929 and early 1930, banks began to fail across the country. As bank failures mounted, public confidence in the banking system dramatically declined. If rumors indicated that a particular bank was weakening, depositors lined up to withdraw all their money. These mass withdrawals were called "bank runs." During the early 1930s bank decline, President **Herbert Hoover** (1874–1964; served 1929–33; see entry) called for Congress to investigate the U.S. banking system and consider revisions to U.S. banking laws. Congressional hearings on the matter of banking reform did not result in any helpful decisions, and Hoover resorted to other programs with little success. The number of bank failures increased steadily in 1931 and 1932. By March 2, 1933, twenty-one states had temporarily closed all their banks to prevent bank runs and additional bank failures. The U.S. banking system was paralyzed.

Resolving the banking crisis was the top priority facing newly inaugurated president Franklin Roosevelt on March 4. On that day Roosevelt declared a national banking holiday, temporarily closing all banks. The Emergency Banking Act was passed on March 9; it set standards for reopening the banks and providing loans to help banks. President Roosevelt delivered his first "fireside chat" over the radio waves on Sunday night, March 12, and restored the public's confidence in the banking system. He calmly and clearly explained what had been done to solve the problems. Most banks were reopened on March 13, and Americans responded by redepositing their money. The immediate crisis was resolved. Congress then passed the Banking Act of 1933, which included reform measures and created the Federal Deposit Insurance Corporation (FDIC), an agency that would insure depositors' accounts up to $2,500. The FDIC was further strengthened two years later in the Banking Act of 1935. By 1934 and 1935 the number of bank failures had significantly decreased. The three banking acts were monumental in restructuring the U.S. banking system.

amazing accomplishment at a time when the U.S. banking system seemed to be collapsing.

A New Deal banker

Eccles's Mormon background influenced his approach in tackling the difficulties of the Depression. Mormon children were taught to work together to solve problems. Accordingly, Eccles believed significant cooperation between government agencies was going to be necessary to stimulate consumption of goods and make the economy healthy again. He believed the Depression was caused by economic policies and social customs that could not be overcome simply by individual efforts.

An unexpected major turning point in Eccles's life came in February 1933. Although he was practically unknown to politicians on the East Coast, Eccles was invited to testify before the Senate Finance Committee in Washington, D.C. More and more banks were failing, hunger was increasing, breadlines were growing, and farmers were losing their farms at an alarming rate. The committee, headed by a senator from Utah, was eager to determine the causes and solutions of the Depression. Invited to testify were financial and industrial leaders as well as representatives of farm and labor organizations. Many of the selected speakers were unable to offer much sound advice on how to end the Depression, but Eccles surprised the committee with a well-thought-out program. Eccles was one of the first to call for government deficit spending—that is, spending more money than is taken in—with the goal of stimulating the economy. He urged establishment of minimum wage laws, additional federal regulation of the agricultural industry, and greater Federal Reserve control over the U.S. banking system. (The Federal Reserve System is a government agency that oversees the nation's banking system, manages the country's supply of money and credit, and provides a broad range of services to commercial banks.) Coming from a highly successful businessman, these were radical suggestions.

Eccles's proposals caught the attention of president-elect Roosevelt and his advisers. They recruited Eccles to assist in the drafting of the 1933 Emergency Banking Act and to help design the Federal Deposit Insurance Corporation (an agency designed to protect depositors against loss of savings in the case of bank failure). They also asked Eccles to assist in creating the 1934 National Housing Act. Then in 1934 President Roosevelt appointed Eccles as assistant secretary of the treasury under **Henry Morgenthau Jr.** (1891–1967; see entry). Eccles held that position for only a few months before being nominated governor of the Federal Reserve Board in

November 1934. He would remain a member of the board for seventeen years. In 1935 Eccles promoted the Banking Act of 1935, which gave the Federal Reserve greater control over banking and separated it from the Treasury Department. When the economy, after appearing to be on the mend, again slipped downward in 1937, Roosevelt continued to seek out Eccles for advice.

Marriner Eccles, center, and the rest of the members of the Federal Reserve Board after Eccles was sworn in as governor on November 15, 1934. *AP/Wide World Photo. Reproduced by permission.*

Later career

After World War II (1939–45) Eccles was deeply concerned about the postwar economy and the rapid rise in the prices of consumer goods. He disagreed with Secretary of the Treasury Henry Morgenthau Jr. and others on how to control the economy. As a result, President Harry Truman (1884–1972; served 1945–53) chose not to reappoint Eccles as chairman of the board of governors of the Federal Reserve in 1948, though Eccles did stay on as assistant chairman until 1951.

In 1951 Eccles left public life in Washington, D.C., and returned to Utah, where he again took charge of the family businesses. By this time First Security Corporation had become one of the largest bank corporations in the West, and Eccles's sugar company was making $25 million a year producing sugar beets. Also in 1951 Eccles very quickly published his memoirs from his years in Washington, titled *Beckoning Frontiers.* In addition to his successful business ventures, Eccles made significant contributions to academic institutions. He established the Marriner S. Eccles Library of Political Economy at the University of Utah in Salt Lake City and the Marriner S. Eccles Professorship of Public and Private Management at Stanford University in California. Eccles died in Salt Lake City in 1977.

For More Information

Eccles, Marriner S. *Beckoning Frontiers: Public and Personal Recollections.* New York, NY: Knopf, 1951.

Hyman, Sidney. *Challenge and Response: The First Security Corporation, First Fifty Years, 1928–1978.* Salt Lake City, UT: Graduate School of Business, University of Utah, 1978.

Hyman, Sidney. *Marriner S. Eccles: Private Entrepreneur and Public Servant.* Stanford, CA: Graduate School of Business, Stanford University, 1976.

Robert Fechner and Aubrey Williams

Robert Fechner:
Born 1876
Chattanooga, Tennessee

Died December 31, 1939
Washington, D.C.

Administrator, union leader

Aubrey Williams:
Born August 23, 1890
Springville, Alabama

Died March 5, 1965
Washington, D.C.

Social worker, reformer

By 1935 five million youths were unemployed. Deeply concerned, **Franklin D. Roosevelt** (1882–1945; served 1933–45; see entry) created both the Civilian Conservation Corps (CCC) and the National Youth Administration (NYA) to help youths in need during the Great Depression. Roosevelt appointed Robert Fechner as the CCC director. The CCC provided employment to young men between eighteen and twenty-five years of age and primarily accepted men from families on unemployment rolls. CCC enrollees were paid $30 a month, $25 of which had to be sent back home. At its peak in 1935 the CCC employed over five hundred thousand men in over twenty-five hundred camps across the nation. The CCC specialized in outdoor projects, such as controlling soil erosion, stocking fish, building public facilities, erecting markers and monuments, and planting trees. The public facilities that were built included bridges, fishponds, state parks, drinking fountains, lodges and museums, fire lookout towers, and water supply systems. The NYA was created in June 1935 to help students stay in school and to provide part-time jobs for youths no longer in school. The president appointed Aubrey Williams as executive director. The NYA assisted over 4.8 million youths from 1935 to

"Today, we hear again and again from CCC veterans about how the 3C's turned their lives around. Desperate young men in desperate times were given the chance to be gainfully employed...."

Craig Holstine, in the foreword to the 1990 book In the Shadow of the Mountain: The Spirit of the CCC *by Edwin G. Hill*

Robert Fechner. *AP/Wide World Photo. Reproduced by permission.*

1943. This program employed more youths than the CCC and included young women and more minorities.

Robert Fechner of the CCC

Robert Fechner was born in Chattanooga, Tennessee, in 1876, to a relatively poor family. He attended public schools but never graduated from high school. He left school to sell candy and newspapers on trains in Georgia for a year. He then became a machinist apprentice (person who is learning a trade) for the Georgia Central Railroad in Augusta. He joined the machinist union and, being an adventurous young man, traveled to Central and South America, where he worked as a machinist. Fechner returned to Savannah, Georgia, in the late 1890s and became active in labor union activities. By 1914 he was elected to the general executive board of the International Association of Machinists and then became a vice president of the American Federation of Labor (AFL), a position he held until 1933. Through these positions Fechner had become a skilled labor negotiator, a role that required much patience. During World War I (1914–18) Fechner served as a special adviser on labor policy and helped settle a railroad labor dispute in 1917. During the war he met Franklin Roosevelt, who was serving as assistant secretary of the navy. In 1932 Fechner worked hard for Roosevelt's presidential campaign, helping Roosevelt gain labor union votes.

When Roosevelt was first trying to push the CCC concept through Congress, organized labor opposed the idea. They thought CCC workers would compete for private jobs, increasing the pool of available labor and thus lowering wages. Therefore, Roosevelt decided to appoint a respected labor leader as head of the agency. He appointed Fechner on April 5, 1933, the same day the CCC was established. That day Fechner and the CCC received $10 million to fund CCC projects. Fechner selected another officer of the machinists union, James J. McEntee, as his assistant. The president wanted 250,000 men at work by early summer 1933. This required major efforts of organization, construction, and mobilization. By the end of June, 239,000 young males had been enlisted, divided into groups of 200, and assigned to freshly-built camps scattered across the nation.

Fechner's role was rather small since much of the CCC administration activity occurred in other parts of the government. Primarily his job was to coordinate the actions of the War Department, the Department of Labor, the Department of the Interior, and the Department of Agriculture, which together established and ran the CCC camps. One of Fechner's most important decisions came on August 17, 1933, when he approved use of CCC units to fight wildfires in Montana. The CCC would become well known for assisting local communities during emergencies such as floods, blizzards, tornadoes, hurricanes, and fires. As a result, the public held a highly favorable attitude toward the agency.

With his limited formal education, Fechner, a simple man, strongly contrasted with most New Deal administrators and advisers. However, Fechner was hardworking, honest, and friendly, and he became popular with his staff and CCC enrollees. He enjoyed traveling around the country visiting the CCC units. Through his travels he gained a thorough knowledge of the camps and supplied Roosevelt with detailed reports, much to the president's pleasure. Fechner's critics claimed that he lacked the vision to expand the CCC program to its fullest capabilities, including greater efforts to recruit black Americans to the CCC. Fechner brought to the administration the cautious and patient attitude he had acquired as a labor negotiator, causing much frustration among other, more dynamic New Deal leaders. Fechner kept the goals of the CCC simple throughout: Provide relief to the unemployed and perform useful work. Perhaps owing to Fechner's conservative ap-

CCC/NYA Facts

The two agencies created to employ youths during the Great Depression accomplished an astounding amount of work. The Civilian Conservation Corps (CCC) restored 3,980 historical structures, developed 800 state parks, treated over 20 million acres to prevent soil erosion, stocked rivers and lakes with over a billion fish, installed 5,000 miles of water irrigation ditches and canals, improved 3,462 beaches, transplanted 45 million trees and shrubs for landscaping, planted over three billion trees in reforested areas, and erected 405,037 signs, markers, and monuments. The CCC also built 8,045 wells and pump houses, 7,622 small dams, 28,087 miles of foot and horse trails, 8,304 footbridges and horse bridges, 32,149 wildlife shelters, 1,865 drinking fountains, 204 lodges and museums, 3,116 lookout towers, 27,191 miles of fences, and 38,550 vehicle bridges. The National Youth Administration (NYA) provided part-time jobs to 620,000 college students, 1,514,000 high school students, and 2,677,000 out-of-school youths. The NYA paved 1,500 miles of roads, built 6,000 public buildings (including 1,429 schools and libraries), and constructed 2,000 bridges.

proach, the CCC received much less criticism than more innovative programs, and it gained a reputation as a well administered agency for its size. However, the atmosphere of goodwill between Fechner and the four cooperating departments eroded through the years as communication declined.

In July 1939 the CCC was placed within the Federal Security Agency, losing its direct connection to the president. Later that year Fechner died of a heart attack at the age of sixty-three. The CCC shut down in 1942. During its nine years of operation the CCC enrolled 2.5 million youths including two hundred thousand black Americans.

Aubrey Williams of the NYA

Born in Springville, Alabama, Aubrey Williams was the third child in a family of five sons and two daughters. His father was a poor provider, and the family moved frequently, finally ending up in Birmingham, a booming industrial town. Williams had to leave school after the first grade to get a job. Only seven years old, he worked as a delivery boy for a laundry wagon, earning a dollar a week. He later got a job in a department store as a change boy, running change from one station to another in the store. By age twelve, Williams had worked his way up in responsibility and was put in charge of the wrappings department. Later he sold suits in the clothing department.

Williams's mother was deeply religious, and church was the center of the family's social life. Having to leave school at a very early age to find work, Williams even learned to read and write through the church. Tagging along with local church leaders, Williams learned a great deal about poverty. He would accompany the church pastor when he made Sunday rounds visiting convicts and mine workers. As a young teen, Williams was committed to serving the underprivileged and pursuing social activism through Christianity. At age sixteen Williams began touring on his own, preaching to the poor and outcast. He taught literary skills to mill workers on Sunday afternoons. At eighteen years of age, Williams organized a boys' club at the Birmingham YMCA and was in charge of thirty ten-year-olds.

By age twenty-one, Williams had become such a successful department store salesman, known for his reliability and hard work, that he was able to save some money to complete school. He entered Maryville College near Knoxville, Tennessee, to complete his high school education. After four years Williams had completed his high school education and one year of college, and he had become an avid reader. While at Maryville, he continued his habit of traveling to remote villages to preach on Sundays.

Running short of money, Williams left Maryville and got a job with the Redpath Chautauqua, a group that traveled to rural areas, giving lectures and concerts. Williams would travel ahead of the speakers and performers, making final arrangements and collecting fees. In the fall of 1916 Williams entered the University of Cincinnati but could only stay for one year because of money concerns. Disheartened, he joined the French foreign legion during World War I and survived bloody battles in Europe. When the United States entered the war in late 1917, Williams joined the American First Division and again took part in heavy fighting.

Aubrey Williams. *AP/Wide World Photo. Reproduced by permission.*

After the war, Williams returned to Cincinnati to attend school and serve as pastor for a small Lutheran church in nearby Dayton, Kentucky. Completing his degree in 1920, he accepted a position as assistant director of the Cincinnati Community Service Association, an organization providing public recreation opportunities. In December 1920 Williams married and had one child.

In 1922 Williams was hired as executive secretary for the Wisconsin Conference of Social Work. The conference was dedicated to preventing delinquency and crime, fighting poverty, and caring for neglected children. Williams worked hard for ten years on behalf of underprivileged children in

Wisconsin. He was involved in the revision of the juvenile court system there, making it much more sensitive to the needs of juveniles; he considered this work his key accomplishment. The Great Depression led to a substantial decline in private donations to the organization at a time when they were needed most. Williams took up an active fight for a public relief bill in the state.

Under President **Herbert Hoover** (1874–1964; served 1929–33; see entry), Congress passed the Emergency Relief and Construction Act in July 1932 to provide funds to states for public relief projects. Williams was hired by the American Public Welfare Association to travel in the Midwest and the South persuading governors to apply for the available federal funds.

With the inauguration of Franklin Roosevelt as president in March 1933 and passage of the Federal Emergency Relief Act, Williams was offered a position by **Harry Hopkins** (1890–1946; see entry), director of the Federal Emergency Relief Administration (FERA) created by the act. By this time the forty-three-year-old Williams had accumulated many years of experience finding ways to aid the less fortunate. As FERA's Southeast field representative he was responsible for determining whether state relief organizations were appropriately set up and free of racial discrimination. As a result of his work, Williams established a close working relationship with **Eleanor Roosevelt** (1884–1962; see entry), who shared his concern for needy youths. The president created the National Youth Administration (NYA) on June 26, 1935, and appointed Williams as its director. Williams remained in that position until the program ended in 1943. Unlike Robert Fechner of the CCC, Williams became a leading figure in promoting social change during the 1930s. For example, Williams established the Negro Affairs Division in the NYA and hired educator **Mary McLeod Bethune** (1875–1955; see entry) to be its head.

In 1960 Williams was named chairman of the National Committee to Abolish the House Un-American Activities Committee. He served in that position until 1963. After a long battle with cancer, he died in March 1965 in Washington, D.C.

For More Information

Hill, Edwin G. *In the Shadow of the Mountain: The Spirit of the CCC.* Pullman, WA: Washington State University, 1990.

Lacy, Leslie A. *The Soil Soldiers: The Civilian Conservation Corps in the Great Depression.* Radnor, PA: Chilton Book Company, 1976.

Salmond, John. *The Civilian Conservation Corps, 1933–1942: A New Deal Case Study.* Durham, NC: Duke University Press, 1967.

Salmond, John. *A Southern Rebel: The Life and Times of Aubrey Willis Williams, 1890–1965.* Chapel Hill, NC: University of North Carolina Press, 1983.

Hallie Flanagan

Born August 27, 1890
Redfield, South Dakota

Died July 23, 1969
Old Tappan, New Jersey

Theater educator, administrator

"Fred [Hallie's father] began organizing home talent shows in the family living room on weekends.... Once Hallie had discovered the pleasure of thrilling an audience...there was no stopping her."

From Hallie Flanagan: A Life in the American Theatre

Hallie Flanagan. *AP/Wide World Photo. Reproduced by permission.*

Hallie Flanagan, multitalented in the theater arts, exhibited her abilities in acting, playwriting, and directing while teaching at Grinnell College in Grinnell, Iowa, and then at Vassar College in Poughkeepsie, New York. In 1935 Flanagan was appointed director of the Federal Theatre Project (FTP), a program established under President **Franklin D. Roosevelt's** (1882–1945; served 1933–45; see entry) administration. The FTP was one of the many New Deal programs designed to put people back to work and bring the nation out of the 1930s Great Depression. The FTP put unemployed theater personnel to work and allowed Flanagan to present high-quality theatrical productions to the general public. In carrying out this task, Flanagan introduced major changes in American theater: Theater became more relevant to everyday life and was a source of entertainment and inspiration for a wider audience than ever before.

Growing up in the Midwest

Flanagan was born Hallie Mae Ferguson in Redfield, South Dakota. Her father, Frederic Miller Ferguson, was a traveling salesman who urged his daughter to express and use her unique talents to their full potential. Her mother, Louisa Fischer, stressed the importance of helping others. Hallie's father had a difficult time maintaining a steady job, so the family kept moving from one place to another—from South Dakota to Nebraska to Illinois and then to Sonora, Iowa, where her grandparents had a farm. By late 1900 Frederic was selling telephone switchboards in nearby Grinnell, Iowa, and the family finally enjoyed a permanent residence.

Hallie graduated from Grinnell College in 1911 and began working as a high school teacher. In 1912 she married her college boyfriend, Murray Flanagan, and they had two children before his death in 1919. As a young widow and single parent, Hallie Flanagan returned to high school teaching and also assisted in classes at Grinnell College. Tragedy struck again in 1922 when Hallie's oldest son died suddenly of spinal meningitis.

Building a career in theater

To ease the grief she felt after losing both her husband and her son, Flanagan poured herself into theater, her first love. She accepted a position teaching theater at Grinnell College and began directing plays for the college theater, the Colonial Theatre. She also began writing plays and acting. While at Grinnell she wrote *The Curtain,* which won an award for playwriting and was subsequently produced in Des Moines, Iowa. She was accepted into 47 Workshop, a training ground for playwriting, headed by noted Harvard University professor George Pierce Baker (1866–1935). Flanagan also entered nearby Radcliffe College for women and earned a master's degree in the arts in 1924. After briefly returning to teach again at Grinnell, Flanagan accepted a teaching position at the elite Vassar College for women in New York. In addition she received a Guggenheim Fellowship to study theater in Europe for one year.

While traveling in Europe, Flanagan observed and studied many new forms of theater and innovative techniques, including the use of theater in Russia to influence political and social change. Inspired by her journey, she returned to Vassar and established the Vassar Experimental

Theatre. Productions at the Experimental Theatre caught the attention of both critics and scholars. One production was in Greek, which led Flanagan to her second husband, Philip Davis, a professor of Greek studies at Vassar. They married in 1934 but had no children.

Federal Theatre Project

In March 1933 Franklin D. Roosevelt was inaugurated as the thirty-second president of the United States. The Great Depression, the most severe economic crisis in U.S. history, was at its worst: Up to 25 percent of America's workforce was unemployed. President Roosevelt immediately began introducing programs to bring relief and recovery to the nation, programs that were collectively called the New Deal. In 1935 the Works Progress Administration (WPA), a New Deal agency, was established to put people to work on public works projects that would benefit the country. Although 75 percent of the jobs were construction related, the WPA also set up programs for unemployed artists, including painters, writers, musicians, and actors. **Harry Hopkins** (1890–1946; see entry), the head of the WPA, had been Flanagan's classmate at Grinnell College, where he had the lead in the senior play. Knowing Flanagan's sterling credentials, he called upon her to be the director of the WPA's Federal Theatre Project (FTP).

Flanagan seized the opportunity to provide relief work to unemployed actors and theater workers; she also hoped the project might lead to the development of a national theater for the United States. Flanagan sought to establish theater groups in many local communities so they would become part of the fabric of those communities and last well beyond the FTP.

Flanagan had some definite ideas about what a national theater should be. Early American theater reflected the interests of the social elite, but Flanagan believed theater must relate more to the common people of the communities. By reflecting everyday life in theater productions, she sought to reach a diverse public. Flanagan also believed that for theater to remain vibrant, it would have to continually push the boundaries of what people found acceptable or comfortable. Accordingly, the FTP tackled all the major topics of the

day, including many controversial issues, through its "Living Newspapers" productions. Flanagan dramatized the struggles of Americans caught in the Depression, in hopes of enlightening her audiences and moving some people to action.

The conservative U.S. Congress soon became alarmed with the kinds of topics being addressed in FTP productions. The House Un-American Activities Committee began investigating many New Deal programs and made the FTP one of its

Federal Theatre Project

Part of the Works Progress Administration, the Federal Theatre Project (FTP) was designed to bring work relief to unemployed actors, directors, playwrights, stagehands, technicians, and others associated with theater production. Established in June 1935, the FTP employed over 3,350 people by December. The FTP was composed of four major divisions: the Popular Price Theater, the Living Newspapers, the Negro Theater, and the experimental theater. There was also a Yiddish theater unit, a children's theater unit, a dance unit, and a puppet unit. The units performed not only in theaters, but also at parks and hospitals in an effort to bring theater to the people. Some of the most successful productions were T. S. Eliot's *Murder in the Cathedral* and Sinclair Lewis's *It Can't Happen Here,* which the FTP staged simultaneously in eighteen cities. The Negro unit employed almost nine hundred blacks and produced seventy plays, including a highly acclaimed "voodoo" version of Shakespeare's *Macbeth* in New York. The Living Newspapers unit was the most innovative and controversial part of the FTP, tackling foreign affairs and domestic politics. The Popular Price Theater presented original plays by new authors. Free or fairly inexpensive, FTP productions reached a large audience. It was estimated that 65 percent of attendees were seeing theater for the first time. An average of five hundred thousand people attended FTP performances each week. Over thirty million people attended FTP performances before the program was shut down in 1939. In its four years of existence, the FTP employed over twelve thousand people in 158 theaters located in twenty-eight states. Though she was not able to establish a national theater, the dynamic leader of the FTP, Hallie Flanagan, greatly influenced American theater by making it relevant and accessible to the common citizen.

primary targets. Flanagan was invited to testify before the committee to plead her program's case. Despite her testimony in defense of the FTP, Congress ended the program's funding in June 1939. The committee considered the FTP potentially too heavily influenced by communists. Flanagan's dream of a national theater had been shot down.

Life after the FTP

With the demise of the FTP, Flanagan returned to Vassar College and the Experimental Theatre. She soon wrote the story of the FTP in *Arena,* published in 1940. She also suffered another personal tragedy, in February 1940, when her second husband died suddenly. Flanagan continued her teaching career. From 1942 to 1955 she served as dean, director of the college theater, and full professor in drama at Smith College in Northampton, Massachusetts. In 1955 Flanagan retired at age sixty-five.

Flanagan received a number of awards during her retirement, including a 1957 Creative Arts Award from Brandeis University and a citation from the National Theatre Conference in 1968. Following her death from Parkinson's disease in Old Tappan, New Jersey, in July 1969, a memorial was held at the Lincoln Center in New York City.

For More Information

Books

Bentley, Joanne. *Hallie Flanagan: A Life in the American Theatre.* New York, NY: Alfred A. Knopf, 1988.

Flanagan, Hallie. *Arena: The Story of the Federal Theatre.* New York, NY: Duell, Sloan and Pearce, 1940.

O'Connor, John, and Lorrain Brown. *Free, Adult, Uncensored: A Living History of the Federal Theatre Project.* Washington, D.C.: New Republic Books, 1978.

Web Sites

Federal Theatre Project Collection. http://www.gmu.edu/library/special collections/theater.html (accessed on September 8, 2002).

Woody Guthrie

Born July 14, 1912
Okemah, Oklahoma

Died October 3, 1967
Queens, New York

Songwriter, folksinger, social activist

"He'd stand with his guitar slung on his back, spinning out stories like Will Rogers [popular 1930s entertainer], with a faint, wry grin."

Pete Seeger, in the foreword of Bound for Glory, *by Woody Guthrie*

Woody Guthrie. *Archive Photos. Reproduced by permission.*

Woodrow Wilson "Woody" Guthrie's musical career lasted just seventeen years. At the age of thirty-nine Guthrie was struck with Huntington's chorea, an inherited disease that had killed his mother. He nevertheless wrote over a thousand songs before his career came to a premature end. Guthrie's songs reflected his experiences of the 1930s Great Depression, severe drought on the Great Plains, President **Franklin D. Roosevelt's** (1882–1945; served 1933–45; see entry) New Deal programs, and World War II (1939–45). The New Deal was a collection of federal legislation and programs aimed at relieving the effects of the Great Depression, the worst economic downturn ever experienced in America. In the mid-1930s the New Deal increasingly focused on the common people—the Americans with whom Guthrie most identified. Through his music Guthrie became a spokesman for the oppressed and the victims of the Depression. His music focused on farmers, workers, unions, and the common people and the injustices these groups experienced. His seemingly simple songs are about complex social and environmental issues that were affecting the nation at that time. Some of his songs became American standards, including "This Land Is Your Land" and "Pastures of Plenty."

Early life

Woody Guthrie was born in 1912 in the small frontier farming community of Okemah, Oklahoma. His grandfather had been a Kansas farmer before moving the family to Oklahoma. Woody's father, Charles Guthrie, was a cattle rancher and sold real estate. His mother, Nora Belle Sherman, was a schoolteacher. Okemah, in existence for only ten years, was settled by people from diverse backgrounds who brought various music traditions with them. At gatherings the sounds of ballads, hillbilly music, church songs, and fiddle music all mingled together.

At age seven, Woody endured a series of family tragedies that would shape his life. His sister was killed in a fire possibly set by his mother, his father's business failed, and his mother was institutionalized when she began showing early signs of a hereditary disease called Huntington's chorea. Huntington's chorea affects the muscular system, leads to mental deterioration, and is eventually fatal.

In 1927 the family moved to Pampa, Texas, where Woody began learning how to play a guitar. Full of musical talent, the fifteen-year-old quickly mastered the guitar. He performed locally with his aunt playing accordion and his uncle playing fiddle under the name Corncob Trio and the Pampa Chamber of Commerce Band. He also learned to play the fiddle and mandolin and his stock of tunes grew. In the ninth and tenth grades, Woody performed in school plays, dancing, singing, playing guitar, and doing anything to get laughs. All the while the family struggled financially as Woody's father was in and out of work.

During his later teens, Woody left home at times and took up the hobo life. Wandering about the South, Guthrie studied and learned to play various forms of music, including country music, blues, gospel, and hoedown. He also developed a style of writing songs that involved forever rewriting them and playing them differently each time. Few of Guthrie's songs would ever make it to a finished state. He would often change them from performance to performance depending on the nature of the audience.

Identifying with the downtrodden

Guthrie returned to Pampa and began dating his good friend's sister, sixteen-year-old Mary Jennings, in 1933. He and Mary soon married and quickly had three children. Even though he was only twenty-one years old when he married, Guthrie had fascinating stories to tell of his days on the road. Everyone wanted to get to know and talk to him.

It was in Pampa, which is located in the Texas Panhandle, that Guthrie experienced his first dust storm. Mary described it as seeming like the end of the world, with everything going dark and dust getting into even the lightbulbs. The Texas Panhandle was in the southern part of the Dust Bowl. The term "Dust Bowl" refers to the Great Plains region of the United States where years of severe drought in the 1930s led to a great loss of crops. Strong winds blew across the region, stirring up huge clouds of dust, causing serious erosion, and creating a barren landscape—a dust bowl.

As the Dust Bowl conditions grew worse, Guthrie observed the desperation of the farmers. He began to see farmers who were "dusted out"—defeated by the drought—heading down the road, their cars packed with family and household goods. They had to move on in search of new land or a new occupation. Guthrie often referred to the Dust Bowl refugees as "my people." Soon Guthrie began to write his "Dust Bowl Ballads." One of the earliest ballads was "Dust Storm Disaster." Between 1936 and 1941 Guthrie would write approximately twenty ballads about the dust storms, the farmers, and the farmers turned migrants.

Crisscrossing the United States

By 1937 Guthrie had again become restless. He wanted to go to California, so with guitar and bag he hitchhiked west. His talent was soon recognized, and he landed a spot on a radio show on KFVD in Los Angeles. The station paid Guthrie one dollar a day to sing his songs; with that security, Mary and the kids headed to Los Angeles to be with him. Guthrie spent a great deal of time getting to know people, "getting their story." He had a special fondness for people who worked the land, for the migrants who followed the harvest of the West, for the unemployed, and for anyone who was struggling. These are the people he wrote about in his songs.

One of Guthrie's acquaintances in Los Angeles was actor Will Geer (1902–1978), who promoted radical politics.

He talked Guthrie into playing his music at a rally supporting socialism and communism as potential solutions to America's economic problems. Because he associated with such groups and because he wrote songs about workers and common people, Guthrie developed the reputation of being a political radical. However, those who best knew Guthrie scoffed at the idea. They maintained that his songs were not political but social protest music calling attention to the plight of the poor. Democrats, Republicans, Socialists, or Communists—Guthrie often said it made no difference to him; he played for them all. He played for whomever would listen.

In 1940 Geer was in New York and persuaded Guthrie to again leave Mary and the kids and hitchhike across the country to New York City. There, thanks to the efforts of folk music historian Alan Lomax, Guthrie was featured on a nationwide CBS radio network program and began to make good money. His family soon joined him. But before long Guthrie became disgruntled when he was told that all the songs he wrote and sang would have to be approved by the CBS staff. Besides, Woody Guthrie never liked to make too much money because it seemed like a violation of his relationship with the poor. So the whole Guthrie family piled into the new Plymouth car they had purchased and headed back to California.

Twenty-six songs in thirty days

Unable to find work in Los Angeles, Guthrie jumped at the chance to go to Portland, Oregon, in the summer of 1941 to work for a New Deal agency, the Bonneville Power Administration (BPA). His family accompanied him once again. The job was for one month and paid $266. Guthrie was to do what he did best: talk to people and write songs. The Bonneville Dam had just been finished, and the Grand Coulee Dam was under construction on the Columbia River in Washington State. Guthrie was asked to write one song a day for thirty days about the people and the river and how beneficial the power generated by the dams would be. The hydroelectric power was to be transmitted to businesses and homes by the BPA. Guthrie ended up writing twenty-six songs in thirty days. In those songs he caught the spirit of the people and of a beautiful, powerful river. Four of the most fa-mous songs are "Roll On, Columbia," "Grand Coulee Dam," "Jackhammer Blues," and "Pastures of Plenty."

When the job with the BPA ended in mid-1941, Guthrie headed back to New York City, where he recorded the songs he had written for the BPA. He received thirty dollars for the recordings. Mary and the children did not follow Guthrie this time. Instead, they went to El Paso, Texas. Mary felt she must give the children a permanent home and put them in school. The separation was the end of Guthrie's first marriage.

Life after the Depression

After the bombing of Pearl Harbor in December 1941, the United States entered World War II (1939–45). As the country mobilized for war, factories needed workers to help manufacture weapons and other war supplies. The armed ser-vices also offered instant employment. By creating new jobs, the war effectively put an end to the Great Depression.

During World War II Guthrie first served in the mer-chant marine, where he wrote songs in support of the war ef-fort. Also during the war Guthrie published an autobiogra-phy, *Bound for Glory,* about his early life. In 1943 he joined the Almanac Singers along with folksinger Pete Seeger (1919–). Their music supported the work of political activists promoting the rights of the common worker. With the Al-manac Singers, Guthrie developed a "talking blues" style, telling a story through his music. Later folksingers such as Bob Dylan (1941–) adopted this style. Late in the war Guthrie was drafted, and he served a year in the U.S. Army.

After the war, Guthrie traveled the country again, writing about what he saw. He focused on labor struggles and the rights of workers. He married two more times and had five more children. However, Guthrie's career was cut short when he was struck with Huntington's chorea, the hereditary disease that earlier caused his mother's death. With the onset of symptoms he returned to New York and spent much of the rest of his life hospitalized at Creedmore State Hospital in Queens, New York. He managed to complete two books, *American Folksong* (1947) and *Born to Win* (1965), both of which included autobiographical writings, poems, and lyrics

"He wrote most every minute of everyday"

In 2000 Michael Majdie and Denise Matthews of the University of Oregon produced and directed the short film *Roll On, Columbia: Woody Guthrie and the Bonneville Power Administration*. While working for the Bonneville Power Administration (BPA) for one month in the summer of 1941, Guthrie wrote twenty-six songs in thirty days about the Columbia River valley and the people in the region. Guthrie's family and friends and the BPA employees who worked with him were interviewed for the film.

Woody Guthrie's daughter Nora and son Arlo, a singer and songwriter in his own right, provide insight into the writing habits of their father. In the film Nora explains, "His writing was drippings from a faucet that no one could turn off and he couldn't either—he wasn't that much in control of the situation that he could turn off his faucet—he kept writing till there was nothing more left in him to write." Arlo agrees, "He was a guy who wrote everyday of his life. He wrote most every minute of everyday.... If you left him alone at night after everybody was tired out—

and this was not a man who was afraid to party either, he would be up there with the best of them drinking and a'singing—after everybody went to sleep he would be there writing.... Rolls of toilet paper, single spaced on both sides, went through the typewriter. Nothing was safe from the man. All the paper bags, all, everything that was paper that could be wrote on, he wrote on. There was no scrap, no napkin from the table, no piece of paper...nothing was safe from him.

"I think only somebody who had that kind of training [Woody Guthrie's years of experience] could sit down and take a project of this size [the BPA project] and nature in those times and be able to *[snaps his fingers]* just nail it. That's all—just write it down like it was everyday 'cause that's what he was doing everyday. Couldn't be a part-time writer, part-time thinker, or part-time anything and in one month write songs that have lines like the ones that are in these songs. Just can't do it. You got to have discipline or you've got to be crazy and he was both."

to many of his songs. However, he eventually lost all ability to write, because he could no longer hold a pencil.

Guthrie's music inspired a generation of folksingers in the 1950s and 1960s, when his ballads were again popular. In 1966 he received a Conservation Service Award from Secretary of the Interior Stewart Udall for raising public awareness of the need to care for the land. Guthrie died in 1967 at the age of fifty-five. In 1999 the Smithsonian Institution created an exhibit about Woody Guthrie, which, like Guthrie himself, traveled around the country for all to enjoy.

For More Information

Books

Gold, John R. "From 'Dust Storm Disaster' to 'Pastures of Plenty': Woody Guthrie and Landscapes of the American Depression." In *The Place of Music,* edited by Andrew Leyshon, David Matless, and George Revill. New York, NY: Guildon Press, 1998, pp. 249–268.

Guthrie, Woody. *Bound for Glory.* New York, NY: E. P. Dutton, 1970.

Guthrie, Woody. *Woody Guthrie Songs.* Fort Lauderdale, FL: TRO Songways Service, 1992.

Klein, Joe. *Woody Guthrie: A Life.* New York, NY: Ballantine Books, 1986.

Santelli, Robert, and Emily Davidson, eds. *Hard Travelin': The Life and Legacy of Woody Guthrie.* Hanover, NH: University Press of New England, 1999.

Web Sites

Bound for Glory: A Tribute to Woody Guthrie. http://www.themomi.org/museum/Guthrie/index.html (accessed on September 8, 2002).

Other Sources

Majdie, Michael, and Denise Matthews (producers). *Roll On, Columbia: Woody Guthrie and the Bonneville Power Administration.* University of Oregon, 2000. Short film.

Lorena Hickok

Born March 7, 1893
East Troy, Wisconsin

Died May 1, 1968
Rhinebeck, New York

News journalist, investigator

A lthough her adult life was closely associated with **Eleanor Roosevelt** (1884–1962; see entry), wife of President Franklin D. Roosevelt (1882–1945; served 1933–45; see entry), Lorena Alice Hickok independently overcame ingrained sexual discrimination in the male-dominated field of newspaper journalism. She became an outstanding reporter and investigative writer.

Hickok's talent was first recognized and rewarded in the early 1920s at the *Minneapolis Tribune,* where she rose to the position of general news reporter. In 1928 Hickok was one of the first women reporters hired by the Associated Press (AP). Working in the AP New York City office, she covered politics and sensational stories. She achieved a status with AP that no other woman had reached. During the 1932 U.S. presidential election Hickok developed a lasting friendship with Eleanor Roosevelt. Hickok was the first reporter to recognize Eleanor's ability to make news and pursue issues in her own right. Hickok would serve as a supportive friend and adviser to Eleanor. During the mid-1930s Hickok worked for **Harry Hopkins** (1890–1946; see entry), Roosevelt's chief administra-

"What I want you to do is to go out around the country and look this thing [New Deal programs] over. I don't want statistics from you. I just want your own reaction, as an ordinary citizen."

Harry Hopkins speaking to Lorena Hickok from One Third of a Nation

Lorena Hickok. *AP/Wide World Photo. Reproduced by permission.*

tor of federal relief programs. She traveled through approximately thirty-two states, meeting with people from all walks of life and reporting back to Hopkins on how the New Deal relief programs were being carried out. The New Deal was a series of programs instituted by the Roosevelt administration to bring relief, recovery, and reform to the United States, which was suffering through the worst economic crisis in its history, the Great Depression.

The confidential, insightful reports Hickok sent to Hopkins and the letters she wrote to Eleanor Roosevelt provide one of the best historical accounts of how the Depression affected the lives of Americans. From her fact-finding travels, Hickok ultimately sent back 120 reports to Hopkins, and she kept up a daily correspondence with Eleanor.

Early life

Born in East Troy, Wisconsin, to a traveling butter maker, Addison J. Hickok, and a dressmaker, Anna Waite Hickok, Lorena was the oldest of three girls. Lorena's childhood was marked by physical abuse at the hands of her father, who had been abused when he was a child. He repeatedly whipped Lorena, most likely because of her defiant attitude toward him. Lorena would never give in to him. Later she recalled that her mother had tried—generally ineffectively—to protect her from his abuse. Lorena's father also whipped her puppy and threw a kitten against a barn door, causing its death.

The Hickok family moved from Wisconsin to Illinois to Minnesota to South Dakota because of Addison's temper and inability to hold a job. Lorena never had time to make any friends. When Lorena was a thirteen-year-old eighth-grader, her mother died. At that time the family was living in Bowdle, South Dakota. Soon after Anna Hickok's death, Lorena's father told her to find another place to live. As a result, from age fourteen to sixteen Lorena worked as a live-in "hired girl," doing domestic work, cleaning, and child care for various families. She changed families frequently, working for at least nine families in that two-year period. At age fifteen and a half Lorena managed to return to school as a ninth-grader at Bowdle High School. Living with one of Bowdle's more prosperous families, she often scrubbed clothes until late at night, but she still found time to complete homework. Her talent for writing emerged, and she won every essay contest at the school.

During this time, Lorena was hired by Mrs. O'Malley, the colorful seventy-year-old wife of Bowdle's first saloon owner. For the first time, someone took an interest in Lorena's future. Mrs. O'Malley contacted Lorena's Aunt Ella in Chicago, Illinois, and explained the plight of the teenager. Aunt Ella was Lorena's mother's sister. Before long Lorena was on the train bound for Chicago and Aunt Ella. Shortly thereafter, Aunt Ella arranged for Lorena to move in with another relative in Battle Creek, Michigan, where she lived until she finished high school. She was a big, lumpish girl who wore unbecoming clothes and showed no interest in social events. Nevertheless, her intellectual talent was clear: She made almost all As on her report card. Following graduation, Lorena entered Lawrence University in Appleton, Wisconsin, in the fall of 1912. Self-conscious about her size—5 feet 8 inches tall and 200 pounds—she felt like a misfit and stayed only one year.

Begins career as a journalist

Returning to Battle Creek, Hickok took her first paid job as a reporter for the *Battle Creek Journal*. As a cub reporter she wrote about train arrivals and ice cream socials for seven dollars a week. In 1915 she took another job as a society editor of a large city paper, the *Milwaukee Sentinel*. She loathed society reporting and longed to impress the city editor with her writing skills, but at that time, society editor was the only reporting job open for a woman. Hickok made fifteen dollars a week, lived at the YWCA, and ate beans to stretch money between paychecks. She nevertheless found her way almost daily to a European-style coffeehouse where she enjoyed creamy hot chocolate and pastries and listened to other reporters talk about their work. There she began to learn how journalists lived and worked in the real world.

Hickok's most striking physical characteristic was her blue eyes, which revealed much of her thoughts and personality. Acquaintances always remembered her eyes, full of humor, pain, pleasure, or piercing understanding. Hickok was coming into adulthood, and she was developing not only a "nose for news" but personality traits that endeared her to many.

It was at the *Sentinel* that Hickok first broke into general news coverage. Her break came when she wrote a humorous story about her attempts on a rainy day in Milwaukee to interview Geraldine Farrar (1882–1967), the most famous opera singer of the day. The story so amused the city editor that he placed it on the front page. However, restless for big-time reporting, Hickok headed for New York City, only to be overwhelmed by its enormity. At this time Hickok decided she must have a college education, so at the age of twenty-five she went back to the Midwest to the University of Minnesota in 1918.

To support herself Hickok worked as a night rewriter for the *Minneapolis Tribune.* Her hours were 7:00 P.M. to 8:00 A.M. She took down the stories reporters called in from their assignments in the evening. If a big story such as a fire or a trolley accident broke, she had to know the right person to call to get the best information. Soon Hickok became known simply as "Hick" and fit well into the newsroom full of men. Hick's stories caught the spirit of events whether they were happy or tragic. Hickok's news-gathering career took off, and she quit school for good. She continued to work for the *Tribune* and lived in Minneapolis with Ellie Morse, a wealthy young woman with a sunny disposition. Hickok and Morse lived as companions for the next eight years.

In 1923, Hickok wrote a story for the *Tribune* about the funeral train bearing the body of President Warren G. Harding (1865–1923; served 1921–23) through Iowa. The story won an Associated Press award. Hickok's stories soon regularly appeared on the front page. Hickok was also assigned to cover the football games of the University of Minnesota Gophers and had great fun doing it.

Hickok gave credit to the *Tribune*'s managing editor, Thomas J. Dillon, for teaching her the newspaper business and assigning her varied stories. On her way to becoming the *Tribune*'s top reporter, she had taken to drinking straight whiskeys and constantly smoking cigarettes. She was a perfectionist in her work. If she made a mistake or realized she had violated the journalistic code of conduct, she could fall into

an emotional slump for days. In 1926 Hickok was diagnosed with diabetes and told to take a rest.

After a disastrous attempt at writing fiction in San Francisco, California, Hickok headed back to New York City and in 1927 worked for the *Daily Mirror,* a newspaper published by ultraconservative William Randolph Hearst (1863–1951). Then in 1928 Hickok was one of the first female reporters to be hired by the Associated Press (AP). Hickok was assigned to cover the Democratic National Committee headquarters located in New York City. From 1928 to 1932 she covered the activities of Franklin Roosevelt, who was governor of New York at that time. Although she had met Roosevelt's wife, Eleanor, Hickok avoided doing any stories on her. She was afraid that such writing would only end up on the women's pages.

Hickok's social life was nonexistent in New York. In the evening, she wrote, and she focused all her emotional expression on her new German shepherd puppy named Prinz. Prinz remained Hickok's faithful companion for fifteen years.

Friendship with the Roosevelts

In 1932, when the United States was deeply mired in the Great Depression, Hickok, like many Americans, tried to tell herself that economists would somehow figure out what was wrong and fix it. Hickok had already taken one 10 percent pay cut and was expecting another. However, she had also been given a prestigious assignment: covering Democrat Franklin Roosevelt's campaign for the president of the United States. Hickok was the only woman in the country assigned this coverage, and thanks to the assignment, she and Eleanor Roosevelt struck up a friendship. Eleanor increasingly chose Hickok to accompany her on the campaign trail. In October 1932, AP asked Hickok to specifically cover Eleanor's activities. Hickok had already come to understand Eleanor's potential to do great things. She persuaded Eleanor to hold weekly press conferences for women reporters only. Her stories about Eleanor were flattering, and she always cleared them first with Eleanor or Louis Howe, an adviser to the newly elected President Roosevelt. Realizing that this practice violated journalism's rule of reporting without bias—positive or negative—Hickok left her groundbreaking post at AP in mid-1933. By this time Hickok and Eleanor had become close friends. Eleanor confided all to Hickok, and Hickok carefully advised her. In July 1933 the two women took off on a holiday together through New England and the Canadian peninsula of Gaspé. Upon returning from the month-long road trip, Hickok began a job that Eleanor had secured for her. Hickok would work under Harry Hopkins, administrator of the newly created Federal Emergency Relief Administration (FERA).

Investigator of the New Deal

On May 22, 1933, Hopkins had been given the title of Federal Emergency Relief Administrator and $500 million to provide immediate relief to struggling Americans living in the financially strapped states. He had set up a nationwide organization to run the program but needed a chief investigator to find out how the relief programs were being administered by state and local officials and how the programs were being received by the people. That investigator would be Lorena Hickok. Hopkins did not want statistics; he wanted firsthand reports of the conditions Hickok found. Hickok

Hickok Paints A Picture With Words

Hickok's first report to Harry Hopkins was written August 6, 1933, and reprinted in *One Third of a Nation: Lorena Hickok Reports on the Great Depression,* published in 1981. In the report Hickok apologizes for its great length and detail. Hickok then ends the report with "Don't tell me to leave it all out, please, because I like this job. Believe me, it's absorbing."

The reports were exactly what Hopkins wanted. They were focused, highly readable, and riveting, and they told Hopkins how the American people were faring. He always wanted to hear more, not less. President Roosevelt often asked Hopkins or Eleanor if Hickok had sent anything back lately that he could read. Hickok's captivating reports no doubt helped shape New Deal policy. Her writing style is well illustrated in the following description, reprinted from the 1981 book, of the ordinary people she met in her travels, people from walks of life she had never before experienced.

One by one, sometimes bold, sometimes hesitant, sometimes demanding, sometimes faltering, they emerged— individuals. People, with voices, faces, eyes. People with hope. People without hope. People still fighting. People with all courage squeezed out of them. People with stories.

There was the Negro woman in Philadelphia who used to walk eight miles every day over the scorching pavements just on the chance of getting, perhaps, a little cleaning to do, at 10 cents an hour.

There was the chauffeur in New York who, on the day before he reported for the first time to work as a laborer on a park project, stood about for hours watching how the other men handled their picks and shovels, so he would "get the hang of it and not feel so awkward."

There was the little Mexican girl, aged 6, in Colorado, who said, sure, she'd worked "in the beets." Two summers already and, yes, sometimes she did get pretty tired."

began her investigative travels across the United States immediately. Her reports could be angry or amusing in tone but were always insightful and to the point. Hickok had no patience for government inefficiency and sharply criticized it when she found it. In a matter of minutes, she could correctly interpret the needs and mood of a community. Her reports were secret, read only by Hopkins, Eleanor, and President Roosevelt. While on this assignment, Hickok corresponded daily with Eleanor. She also frequently traveled with Eleanor on similar fact-finding trips. When Hopkins became administrator of two more relief programs, the Civil Works Administration (CWA) in the winter of 1933–34 and the Works

The Lorena Hickok Papers

As early as 1958 Lorena Hickok began to donate boxes of her letters to the Franklin Delano Roosevelt Library in Hyde Park, New York. Hickok stipulated that the boxes could not be opened until ten years after her death but then placed virtually no limits on their examination. By the time the staff of the FDR Library opened the papers in 1978, Eleanor Roosevelt had been dead sixteen years and Hickok ten years. The thirty-five hundred letters written between Eleanor and Lorena and spanning their thirty years of friendship revealed a surprisingly close relationship. The letters spawned an ongoing debate about whether Eleanor and Lorena had a lesbian love affair or whether the relationship simply involved an exchange of affection between two women who had grown up without the love of their natural parents. Earlier while living at the White House, Hickok never publicized the fact that she was living there, and she kept a low profile going to and from work. The Roosevelt family consistently denied that a same-sex relationship existed. The Lorena Hickok Papers as well as the Harry Hopkins Papers, which contain many of Hickok's investigative reports for New Deal agencies, are both located at the FDR Library.

Progress Administration (WPA) starting in 1935, Hickok served in the same investigative capacity. When she was not traveling, she lived at the White House in a room adjacent to Eleanor's. The two women, besides discussing all their activities, were fond of reading out loud to each other from poetry books.

In April 1936 Hickok had more health problems related to her diabetes. Her blood sugar had gone so far off normal that the doctor said she must take insulin daily for the rest of her life. Attempting to live a slower paced life, in January 1937 Hickok took a job as a publicity person for the upcoming 1939 New York World's Fair at a hundred dollars a week. In 1937 Hickok and her beloved Prinz moved into Aunt Ella's "Little House," located on 2 beautiful acres at Mastic, Long Island, New York. Little House would be Hickok's refuge from 1937 to 1955.

Return to the White House

In 1941 Hickok joined the staff of the Democratic National Committee. She would head the Women's Division and again live as a guest of the Roosevelt's at 1600 Pennsylvania Avenue, the White House. Hickok's room was part of the Lincoln Suite in the northwest corner of the White House living quarters. The only meal she ate there was breakfast with Eleanor, if Eleanor was not traveling. Hickok continued to keep Little House in Mastic. In 1943 Prinz died at the age of fifteen, and her neighbors buried him, as instructed, wrapped in Hickok's old raincoat at the entrance to a favorite trail on the grounds of Little House.

Hickok remained at the White House for four years but decided to resign her Women's Division post in early 1945. After farewell parties Hickok returned to Little House on March 21, 1945. President Roosevelt died the following month on April 12, 1945.

Later years

For the next ten years Hickok led a quiet life. However, she did serve part-time on the New York State Democratic Committee from 1947 to 1952. In 1954 Hickok and Eleanor Roosevelt published *Ladies of Courage,* a book about women in politics. By 1955 Hickok had a falling-out with Aunt Ella at Little House, and Eleanor sent her chauffeur to bring Hickok and her belongings to Eleanor's residence in Hyde Park, New York. Hickok remained there a year, then moved to other quarters close by. Eleanor persuaded her to write more, and Hickok produced six biographies for young readers, including *The Story of Helen Keller.*

In 1962 Hickok wrote and published *Reluctant First Lady* about Eleanor, who was by then seventy-eight and in failing health. Eleanor died that year. Hickok's health was also poor and her eyesight all but gone. She died on May 1, 1968.

For More Information

Faber, Doris. *The Life of Lorena Hickok: E. R.'s Friend.* New York, NY: William Morrow, 1980.

Lowitt, Richard, and Maurine Beasley, eds. *One Third of a Nation: Lorena Hickok Reports on the Great Depression.* Urbana, IL: University of Illinois Press, 1981.

Roosevelt, Eleanor, and Lorena A. Hickok. *Ladies of Courage.* New York, NY: Putnam, 1954.

Herbert Hoover

Born August 10, 1874
West Branch, Iowa

Died October 20, 1964
New York, New York

Thirty-first president of the United States

"Hoover pursued his private and public careers…based on this cooperative work ethic, whereby all members of the community did their best in their particular 'callings' in life for the good of everyone."

Joan Hoff Wilson in Herbert Hoover: Forgotten Progressive

Herbert Hoover. *AP/Wide World Photo. Reproduced by permission.*

Herbert Hoover was the thirty-first president of the United States. Elected in November 1928 and inaugurated in March 1929, Hoover had the misfortune of being president as the U.S. economy began a dramatic downward spiral into the Great Depression. Attempts by his administration to address the severe economic crisis were not enough to slow the decline. As a result, Hoover faced much of the blame for the financial troubles of many Americans.

Engineer turns humanitarian

Hoover was born to a farming family in West Branch, Iowa, and had a strict Quaker upbringing. The Quakers are a religious group known for their humanitarian activities, strong belief in education, and rejection of war; a humanitarian is a person who promotes the general welfare of others. Hoover was orphaned at age nine: His father died of heart trouble in 1880 and his mother of typhoid fever in 1884. After living with various Iowan relatives, Hoover left for Oregon, where he spent his teen years with an uncle in Newberg and Salem. In Salem at age fifteen Hoover worked in the sales office for the Oregon Land Company, selling orchard plots, and quickly showed his business skills. A good student, Hoover went to Stanford University, where he earned a geology degree. In 1895 he was part of Stanford's first graduating class. While at Stanford he met his future wife, Lou Henry, who was also a Stanford graduate in geology. They married in 1899 and had two sons.

Hoover became a mining engineer just as the United States began a period of exploration for foreign minerals. Developing mines in South America, Hoover became a millionaire by the age of forty. From his Quaker roots, he had also adopted a progressive political outlook, maintaining that social good could be attained by cooperation, volunteerism, and business self-regulation. Progressives believe in using the organizational powers of the government to stimulate voluntary efforts toward solving social and economic problems. Beginning public service during World War I (1914–18), Hoover created and was head of the Commission for Relief in Belgium. At the time, the United States was still neutral and not participating in the war. Belgium had been defeated by German troops and was running short on food. Hoover's agency saved thousands of lives. Catching the attention of President Woodrow Wilson (1856–1924; served 1913–21), Hoover was appointed U.S. food administrator when the United States entered the war. He served in that position from 1917 through 1919. As administrator, he led a program of voluntary food rationing in America so food could be shipped to Europe. (Rationing means fairly distributing food or goods that are in short supply.) After the war, Hoover returned to Europe as director general of the American Relief Administration in 1919 and 1920, directing food supplies to millions of needy people. Hoover had become an internationally famous humanitarian.

Secretary of commerce

Having established a reputation as a humanitarian and an excellent administrator, Hoover was sought by both the Democrats and the Republicans to be their candidate in the 1920 presidential election. However, he was not ready to take on such an ambitious position, so he declined the offers. The victor in the election, Republican Warren G. Harding (1865–1923; served 1921–23), appointed Hoover secretary of commerce, a position he would continue to hold through President Calvin Coolidge's administration (1923–29). Hoover brought major change to the Commerce Department, building it into a major governmental department. By the late 1920s Hoover became very concerned with the widespread speculation in the stock market. Speculation at that time involved buying stocks using borrowed money, with the assumption that stock prices would continue to rise. Bankers would speculate using depositors' money. They then loaned money to stockbrokers, who, in turn, would allow their customers to invest with the borrowed money. Hoover tried to convince the bankers to stop these risky practices. However, he found few people, in government or in the banking and financial communities, who shared his concerns. With stock prices zooming upward, easy fortunes could be made, and Hoover's warnings were ignored.

Troubled presidency

When Coolidge decided not to run for reelection in the 1928 presidential election, the highly popular Hoover was chosen as the Republican candidate. Amazingly, this was the first time Hoover had ever run for public office. Riding the wave of economic prosperity through the 1920s under two previous Republican presidents, Hoover defeated Democratic candidate Alfred E. Smith (1873–1944). With his engineering and business background, Hoover represented technical efficiency in a time of booming industrial production. However, Hoover also brought progressivism to the White House. Hoover wanted to make the U.S. capitalist system more humane. For example, in early 1929 Hoover called a special session of Congress to solve the lingering economic problems of farmers. Farmers had been suffering from overproduction and low crop prices since the end of World War I. Under Hoover's leadership, Congress passed the Agricultural Marketing Act in June 1929. The act attempted to help farmers stabilize and improve their economic situation. Specifically, it established the Federal Farm Board to loan federal funds to farmers' cooperatives (organizations of farmers formed to economically cooperate by coordinating the production and marketing of their produce).

In October 1929 the stock market crashed, beginning a long period of economic difficulties, first for the United States and later for the world. Hoover did not think the economic situation would become severe, because he believed that the problem was largely due to overspeculation in stocks and that it was limited to the United States. To try to solve the problem, Hoover applied his personal beliefs in cooperation and voluntary actions and exercised his powerful role in government: He organized various groups to help quickly turn the economy around. He urged citizens to make private contributions to relief organizations to aid the poor and requested voluntary cooperation among business leaders to stabilize economic conditions. He used fact-finding commissions, business associations, and educational conferences to bring industrial and labor leaders together to work toward solutions.

On November 21, 1929, Hoover hosted conferences at the White House. Attending were leaders from business, labor, and farming, who were being asked to help the government solve the nation's economic difficulties. Hoover sought promises from industry and labor to maintain existing wages, employment, and production levels, and to refrain from strikes. Hoover also urged state and local governments and the federal departments to speed up already scheduled public works projects and other construction activities. (Public works projects, which would provide jobs for the unemployed, involved government-funded construction of public buildings, roads, and bridges.) In December the National

Hoover and the Depression

Despite his worldwide reputation as a humanitarian and successful businessman, Hoover was uncomfortable in front of crowds. To the public he seemed cold and insensitive; his shyness came off as uncaring aloofness. Few were aware that President Hoover donated his presidential income to charity. At the onset of the Depression, Hoover called for voluntary cooperation of business, industrial, and labor leaders. He believed direct federal aid would lead to political corruption and low public morale. As the economy struggled and Hoover's efforts to promote volunteerism fell short, the public came to believe Hoover was responsible for their plight. Hoover's name became associated with the widespread suffering caused by the Depression. As unemployment grew, tens of thousands became homeless. In vacant lots and parks, on riversides, and even in dumps, shantytowns of makeshift shelters appeared; they were called "Hoovervilles." Shelters in the Hoovervilles were made of scrap metal, cardboard, and any other available materials. St. Louis was home to the largest Hooverville, which contained more than one thousand people. There were also "Hoover blankets" (newspapers), "Hoover heaters" (campfires), and "Hoover tourists" (hoboes on trains).

Business Survey Conference, consisting of four hundred business leaders, was established to enforce the voluntary agreements. On February 18, 1930, Hoover optimistically announced that the worst was over.

With the economy still struggling in April, Hoover guided through Congress a bill for $150 million to put people to work constructing public buildings. He also approved the start of construction of the Hoover Dam on the Colorado River, a project that would employ thousands of engineers and construction workers. In early 1930 Hoover called for another special session of Congress to follow through on his promise to increase tariffs on foreign farm products. Tariffs are fees imposed on goods imported to the United States from foreign countries. Because tariffs made foreign goods more expensive, Americans tended to buy only products made and grown in the United States, thereby helping American farmers. However, it would take fourteen months for Congress to pass the Hawley-Smoot Tariff Act in June 1931. The controversial measure to raise tariffs on imported farm produce led to a major decline in world trade and spread the Depression to the rest of the world.

Despite funding increases coming from all levels of government, private construction decreased substantially, and nationwide unemployment grew from four million in 1930 to over eight million in 1931. Americans who managed to hold on to their jobs saw their salaries cut. The loss of jobs and income led to many bank failures because borrowers could not pay back bank loans and depositors had to take money out of their savings to meet daily expenses. To assist failing banks, Hoover pressured bankers and insurance executives to voluntarily organize the National Credit Corporation (NCC) in October 1931. The NCC was given $500 million in federal funds to loan to banks in need. However, members of the NCC were not enthusiastic about the program, and it proved ineffective. Likewise, having lost almost $350 million by 1932, the Federal Farm Board program proved a costly and ineffective way to halt overproduction of farm products. Overproduction kept prices for the products very low. Hoover asked farmers to voluntarily cut back crop production, but few did.

Hoover's plan of relying on volunteerism was clearly failing. He had to turn to a more direct involvement of the federal government. Hoover created the Reconstruction Finance Corporation (RFC), a federal agency, in January 1932 to provide loans to banks. In addition $750 million was made available to industry and business by the Glass-Steagall Act of February 1932. Seeing that local government efforts and private organizations were not meeting the needs of the unemployed and the hungry, Hoover signed the Emergency Relief and Construction Act in July 1932, providing $2 billion for public works and $300 million in loans to states for cash payments to the poor and the unemployed. Some believed these actions by Hoover in 1932 prevented a complete collapse of the U.S. economy. Even though unemployment rose to twelve million workers, some saw signs of economic improvement by the summer of 1932.

The Bonus Army and election defeat

A major event unfolded during the summer months of 1932 that would dash Hoover's hopes for reelection. Thousands of unemployed World War I veterans, called the Bonus Army, had marched on Washington, D.C., in the spring and set up camps. They demanded early payment of cash bonuses promised to them by Congress but not scheduled to begin until years later. Despite the marchers, Hoover and Congress defeated a bill that would have approved early payments. Following the legislative defeat, most of the Bonus Army left, but some two thousand stayed in their makeshift camps to continue the protest. Finally, Hoover sent the U.S. Army in late July to clear out the remaining protesters. Against his orders the army used considerable force, leading to bad publicity about Hoover's handling of the situation.

Blamed for the Depression and the Bonus Army incident, Hoover lost the 1932 presidential election by a landslide to Democratic candidate **Franklin D. Roosevelt** (1882–1945; served 1933–45; see entry). Despite the ineffectiveness of Hoover's efforts to respond to the difficulties brought on by the Depression, his programs marked a major new trend in the federal government's involvement in domestic economic affairs. For the first time in U.S. history the federal government established public works projects to address unemployment and set up federal loan programs to aid Americans confronting debts they could not repay. Hoover also adopted

Herbert Hoover and president-elect Franklin Roosevelt ride to Roosevelt's inauguration ceremony on March 4, 1935. *Hulton Archive/Getty Images. Reproduced by permission.*

foreign policies quite different from his predecessors. For example, rather than focusing only on U.S. military domination over the region's political and economic developments, Hoover sought a more equal relationship with Latin American nations through international trade and economic assistance. Roosevelt would take many of these ideas and expand them to a much grander scale to combat the domestic effects of the Depression and to forge his "Good Neighbor" policy with Latin America.

After leaving office, Hoover did not comment publicly on the Roosevelt administration for two years. But in 1935 he became a major critic of the New Deal. The New Deal was a collection of legislation and programs designed by the Roosevelt administration to relieve the economic problems of the Depression. The New Deal programs were wide-ranging and affected the daily lives of Americans. Hoover remained a firm believer in limited federal government and thought that capitalism should regulate itself. He maintained that industry should have essentially unrestricted control over their production goals and means of distributing their goods as opposed to the New Deal efforts at regulating production and dictating work conditions. Hoover reentered politics in 1936 but failed to gain the Republican nomination for president. He failed again in 1940 even though he had played a role in Republican victories in the 1938 congressional elections.

Later life

With his vast experience in food relief in Europe during World War I, Hoover was consulted in the development of food relief policy during and immediately after World War II (1939–45). He was named chairman of the Famine Emergency Commission and stayed in the public spotlight traveling, giving speeches, and writing. In keeping with his Quaker roots, Hoover opposed the U.S. decision to drop two atomic bombs on Japan to end World War II, the U.S. involvement in the Korean War (1950–53), and the establishment of the North Atlantic Treaty Organization (NATO) in Europe. Membership in NATO placed the United States in a defense alliance with European nations against the threat of the Union of Soviet Socialist Republics (USSR). Hoover was critical of early cold war (an intense political and economic rivalry from 1945 to 1991 between the United States and the USSR falling just short of military conflict) policies regarding the USSR and did not support the anticommunist fervor that ran through Congress in the late 1940s and early 1950s. He headed two commissions under President Harry Truman (1884–1972; served 1945–53) and President Dwight Eisenhower (1890–1969; served 1953–61), guiding reorganization of the federal government during the postwar period. His popularity, severely damaged by the Great Depression, was well restored with his long service to society and government following his presidency. Hoover died at age ninety in New York City in October 1964 and was buried in West Branch, Iowa.

For More Information

Books

Burner, David. *Herbert Hoover: A Public Life*. New York, NY: Alfred A. Knopf, 1979.

Hoff-Wilson, Joan. *Herbert Hoover: Forgotten Progressive*. Boston, MA: Little, Brown, 1975.

Holford, David M. *Herbert Hoover*. Berkeley Heights, NJ: Enslow, 1999.

Nash, George H. *The Life of Herbert Hoover*. 3 vols. New York, NY: W. W. Norton, 1966–88.

Smith, Richard N. *An Uncommon Man: The Triumph of Herbert Hoover*. New York, NY: Simon & Schuster, 1984.

Web Sites

Herbert Hoover Presidential Library and Museum. http://hoover.nara.gov (accessed on September 8, 2002).

J. Edgar Hoover

Born January 1, 1895
Washington, D.C.

Died May 2, 1972
Washington, D.C.

Director of the Federal Bureau of Investigation

J. Edgar Hoover first joined the U.S. Department of Justice as a law clerk in 1917, rising to director of the Department's Bureau of Investigation (later the Federal Bureau of Investigation, or FBI) by 1924. He would remain in that position for the next forty-eight years until his death in 1972, serving under both Democratic and Republican presidents. Hoover transformed the bureau from an agency ridden with scandal to an elite corps of highly regimented Special Agents. The American public wanted protection from the outlaws of the early 1930s, and Hoover's agency was able to end the crime wave and restore public confidence in law enforcement. During the later 1930s President **Franklin D. Roosevelt** (1882–1945; served 1933–45; see entry) along with many other Americans feared that the fascism in Europe and the Communism of the Soviet Union could gain a foothold in the United States. (Fascism is a political system characterized by dictatorship, militarism, and racism. Soviet Communism was a political doctrine that aimed to eliminate private property so that goods would be equally available to all people. Such an economic system cannot co-exist with capitalism, which is primarily based on the private ownership of proper-

"Hoover directed the Bureau [Federal Bureau of Investigation] so long that he seemed fixed in the political landscape of Washington. The grim scowl was that of a man who had seen all evil, heard all evil, and could be counted on to warn of any evil that would put the nation in danger."

Richard Gid Powers in Secrecy and Power: The Life of J. Edgar Hoover

J. Edgar Hoover.
©Bettmann/CORBIS.
Reproduced by permission.

ty and business.) Roosevelt relied on Hoover to oversee the national security of the United States. Following World War II (1939–45) the United States and the Soviet Union fought each other for several decades with words and threats. During this period of nonviolent hostility, referred to as the cold war (1945–91), Hoover and his agency staunchly guarded against the spread of communism to American soil. The FBI made a regular practice of undercover surveillance (spying) and maintaining secret files on citizens who seemed suspicious in any way. The legality of these and other activities was often questioned. Yet even amid these concerns, Hoover managed to single-handedly establish an internationally respected law enforcement agency.

Early life

John Edgar Hoover was the last of four children born to Dickerson Naylor Hoover and Annie Marie Scheitlin Hoover. He arrived on New Year's Day in 1895 in Washington, D.C. His family's home was located on Capitol Hill just behind the Library of Congress in a white, middle-class, Protestant neighborhood known as Seward Square.

Hoover's father was a printer with the U.S. Coast and Geodetic Survey. Hoover's mother paid careful attention to her youngest child because he was frail. He also had a stuttering problem that he overcame by speaking very fast. As an adult Hoover would remain close to his mother, living with her in the house where he was born for forty-three years until her death in 1938.

Rising through the ranks

Hoover was very bright and graduated at the top of his class from the prestigious Central High School in 1913. After high school, Hoover got a job as a file clerk with the Library of Congress and attended night classes at National University Law School. He received his law degree in 1916 and a graduate degree in law the following year in 1917 just when the United States entered World War I (1914–18). That same year the Alien Enemy Bureau in the Department of Justice hired twenty-two-year-old Hoover to process newly arriving

German citizens to determine if any of them might pose a threat to America. Also in 1917, a revolution brought the Communists to power in Russia. Federal government leaders feared that the Communist influence might spread to the United States. The General Intelligence Division (GID) was established within the Justice Department to track down, arrest, and deport alien radicals. U.S. Attorney General A. Mitchell Palmer chose Hoover to head the agency. Hoover also became assistant to the attorney general in November 1918. In that position Hoover planned and directed raids on foreign anarchists and communists in three U.S. cities in November 1919 and January 1920. The raids resulted in mass arrests, and some well-known anarchists (those who oppose government rule over individuals) were deported (officially forced to leave the country). The investigations Hoover conducted during this period made him the nation's expert in communist activities taking place in the United States. He held this role for the rest of his life. His campaign against radicals ended amid charges that he and other law enforcement officials were disregarding the civil liberties of the accused. Nevertheless, Hoover, despite his youth, had gained a reputation of being extremely efficient and effective in each assignment he undertook.

In 1921 the attorney general placed the GID within the Bureau of Investigation (BOI) and appointed Hoover assistant director of the BOI. The BOI would be renamed the Federal Bureau of Investigation (FBI) in 1935. Congress gave the agency the task of investigating federal crimes such as bank robberies, kidnappings, and car thefts. At twenty-nine years of age Hoover rose to the director's position on May 10, 1924. The BOI was filled with scandal and corruption. As director, Hoover worked diligently to improve the image and effectiveness of the organization. He raised the standards for agents by firing those he considered unqualified and replacing them with an elite group of men who were mostly young, white, and college-educated. Hoover also brought scientific law enforcement techniques to the agency, establishing a fingerprint identification department, modern investigation laboratories, and maintenance of comprehensive crime statistics. As a result, the BOI was able to take on greater responsibilities. Under Hoover's leadership it had become an important and prestigious agency.

The Federal Bureau of Investigation

The catastrophic attacks on the World Trade Center in New York City and on the Pentagon in Washington, D.C., on September 11, 2001, brought the Federal Bureau of Investigation's (FBI's) chief concern—national security—into clear focus. It is the FBI's responsibility to investigate over two hundred categories of federal crime, and domestic terrorism has top priority. It is the FBI's job to defend the United States against any similar attack in the future and against the threat of nuclear, biological, or chemical attack.

For almost a century, the FBI saw its mission grow and shift as new threats to the United States arose. The agency had its beginnings in 1908, when the U.S. attorney general hired thirty-four special law enforcement agents to work within the U.S. Justice Department. In March 1909 they were given the name Bureau of Investigation (BOI), and in 1935 the name was changed to Federal Bureau of Investigation. The FBI headquarters, located in Washington, D.C., provides direction and support to fifty-six field offices, several hundred related agencies, four specialized

field facilities, and over forty foreign offices. The foreign offices work with American and local authorities on federal crimes. At the start of the twenty-first century, the FBI had 11,400 Special Agents and over 16,400 other employees including professional, administrative, technical, and maintenance positions. About 9,800 of these employees worked at the Washington headquarters, and the other 18,000 worked in the numerous field offices.

Training for agents is provided at the FBI National Academy located in Quantico, Virginia. The academy was founded on July 29, 1935, by J. Edgar Hoover, and twenty-three students were enrolled that year. By 1999 the program had graduated over 32,000 students. The academy has a strong reputation among international law enforcement; 128 foreign countries send trainees through the program. The curriculum includes eleven weeks of training for higher-level law enforcement officers. To qualify for FBI Special Agent training, a candidate must be between twenty-three and thirty-seven years of age, meet certain physical requirements, and hold a college degree.

Restoring confidence in law enforcement

The economic hard times of the Great Depression spawned the rise of notorious outlaws in the Midwest in 1933 and 1934. Driving fast cars and carrying machine guns, they robbed isolated banks and service stations, leaving a bloody trail behind. Among the outlaws were Bonnie and Clyde, "Ma" Barker, George "Machine Gun" Kelly (1895–1954), Charles "Pretty Boy" Floyd (1901–1934), John Dillinger

(1903–1934), and George "Baby Face" Nelson (1908–1934). Hoover, seeking to raise the public's awareness of the BOI, targeted these well-known criminals to gain the maximum publicity benefit for his agency. With the help of the Texas Rangers, BOI agents, only recently authorized to carry weapons and make arrests, shot and killed Bonnie and Clyde in May 1934. BOI agents then gunned down Dillinger in July 1934, Floyd in October 1934, Nelson in November 1934, and Barker in 1935.

The agents, including Hoover, became national heroes and the subjects of considerable media attention. The movie *G-Men,* released in 1935, features a main character (played by James Cagney, 1904–1986) who is patterned after Hoover. "G-men" reportedly was short for government men. The movie was a big box-office hit. That same year the BOI was renamed the Federal Bureau of Investigation, and its G-men became known as FBI agents. The FBI's successes and related publicity helped restore public confidence in law enforcement that had been badly shaken by the lawlessness of the Prohibition era (1920–33) when organized crime supplied much of the population with banned liquor. To maintain his heroic image, Hoover would at times personally lead raids with reporters on hand. For example, a classic case of heroics for Hoover occurred in 1937, when a top New York City criminal surrendered personally to Hoover just as one of his primary critics, New York State attorney general Thomas Dewey (1902–1971), was closing in. Newspaper reporters and photographers were on hand to record the event.

Despite his success against the Midwest outlaws and individual criminals, Hoover chose not to attack organized crime. By supplying banned alcohol to Americans during the years of Prohibition, between 1920 and 1933, organized crime had become incredibly wealthy and powerful. By taking on such a powerful adversary, Hoover might have jeopardized the new winning image of the FBI. Instead he focused on the easier targets of lawless individuals. Hoover denied the existence of organized crime in the United States, and he continued to deny it throughout his career. This denial contributed to the growth of organized crime, which continued to prosper through the mid-twentieth century. The FBI did not earnestly enter the battle against organized crime until after Hoover's death.

J. Edgar Hoover, right, congratulates Melvin Purvis, chief of the Chicago FBI office, who was in Washington, D.C., to give his report on the slaying of outlaw John Dillinger in July 1934. *©Bettmann/CORBIS Reproduced by permission.*

Threats from abroad

Tensions in Europe rose during the 1930s as Adolf Hitler (1889–1945), leader of the Nazi Party, became the dictator of a fascist Germany. President Franklin D. Roosevelt assigned the FBI to secretly monitor the activities of fascists in the United States. Hoover rose in prominence as the head of domestic counterintelligence (preventing enemies from gathering information), counterespionage (detecting and preventing enemy spying), and countersabotage (preventing enemy destruction of U.S. facilities) in the United States. He compiled information on the daily habits and organizational memberships of numerous people, searching for those who might turn into enemies of democracy. In 1942 FBI agents captured German saboteurs who had landed in a submarine near Long Island, New York. This incident received great attention in the media and gave the public confidence that the FBI was on top of threats to the U.S. homeland.

Protecting America from communism

World War II was followed by the cold war (1945–91), a prolonged struggle for world dominance between the capitalist United States and the communist Soviet Union. The weapons of conflict were words of propaganda and threats. The campaign against communism dominated Hoover's life. In the late 1940s the FBI investigated the backgrounds of numerous government employees, checking for communist infiltration of the U.S. federal government. The Republican Party in particular supported these investigations and established the House Un-American Activities Committee (HUAC) in Congress. Hoover eagerly supplied HUAC with information, intent on exposing communists in labor unions and other organizations. In another high-visibility case, Hoover uncovered an atomic spy ring seeking to sell nuclear bomb secrets to foreign nations. The arrests led to convictions and executions in 1953 of Julius and Ethel Rosenberg. To educate the public about the domestic threat of Communism, Hoover authored a widely read book, *Masters of Deceit,* in 1958. In twelve years and twenty-nine printings the book sold 250,000 copies in hardback and two million in paperback. Still seeking positive publicity to maintain his public prestige, Hoover worked with the national media on the production of radio and television programs and Hollywood movies. These productions included *The FBI Story* (1959), starring James Stewart (1908–1997), and a popular television series, *The FBI,* that ran from 1965 to 1974.

Noting Hoover's success in weeding out hidden threats, President John F. Kennedy (1917–1963; served 1961–63) directed Hoover to target the Ku Klux Klan, an antiblack terrorist hate group. Hoover identified more and more groups that he believed threatened traditional American values. He targeted black American organizations such as the militant Black Panthers and protesters opposing the Vietnam War (1954–75). Hoover also waged a smear campaign against civil rights leader Dr. Martin Luther King Jr. (1929–1968). Claiming King had communist ties, he tried to destroy King's credibility and career.

Methods questioned

Hoover was in his forty-eighth year as director of the FBI when he died in his sleep in Washington, D.C., in May 1972. His body lay in state in the Capitol's rotunda, an honor given to only twenty-one Americans in the history of the United States. Hoover had worked hard to maintain a clean public reputation through the many decades he served as the head of the FBI. However, casting a shadow of suspicion over his past activities as head of the agency, Hoover ordered his personal secretary to destroy all of his personal files upon his death. His tactics of surveillance, wiretaps (secretly listening to telephone conversations), and keeping detailed files on numerous citizens never charged with crimes had posed a major threat to civil liberties. After his death, in 1975 and 1976, Hoover became the subject of a Senate investigative committee, the Select Committee to Study Governmental Operations with Respect to Intelligence Activities. The committee determined that Hoover greatly abused his governmental authority, violating the civil liberties of free speech and association (freedom to meet with others) by harassing those he considered a threat.

For More Information

Books

Nash, Jay R. *A Critical Study of the Life and Times of J. Edgar Hoover and His FBI*. Chicago, IL: Nelson-Hall, 1972.

Powers, Richard Gid. *Secrecy and Power: The Life of J. Edgar Hoover*. New York, NY: Free Press, 1987.

Sullivan, William C. *The Bureau: My Thirty Years in Hoover's FBI*. New York, NY: Norton, 1979.

Summers, Anthony. *Official and Confidential: The Secret Life of J. Edgar Hoover*. New York, NY: G. P. Putnam's Sons, 1993.

Theoharis, Athan G., and John S. Cox. *The Boss: J. Edgar Hoover and the Great American Inquisition*. Philadelphia, PA: Temple University Press, 1988.

Web Sites

Federal Bureau of Investigation. http://www.fbi.gov (accessed on September 8, 2002).

Harry Hopkins

**Born August 17, 1890
Sioux City, Iowa**

**Died January 29, 1946
New York, New York**

**Social worker, relief
administrator, diplomat**

"Roosevelt trusted Hopkins implicitly [totally]—trusted his instincts and trusted his loyalty. No president had ever placed such confidence in another man; no president had given another man such power and influence."

June Hopkins, granddaughter of Harry Hopkins, in Harry Hopkins: Sudden Hero, Brash Reformer

Harry Hopkins. *Courtesy of the Library of Congress.*

From humble beginnings Harry Hopkins rose high in the U.S. government during the 1930s and 1940s. Hopkins's loyal service to his country helped President **Franklin D. Roosevelt** (1882–1945; served 1933–45; see entry) guide the United States through the Great Depression (1929–41) and World War II (1939–45), two of the worst crises of the twentieth century. Hopkins was uniquely qualified to administer the New Deal relief programs of the Roosevelt administration. Tutored by Roosevelt throughout the 1930s in the art of politics and diplomacy, Hopkins became the president's representative and messenger during World War II.

Young Harry

Hopkins gathered the philosophies he would live his life by from his family, his college years, and his experiences as a young social worker in New York City. Born in Sioux City, Iowa, to David Aldona Hopkins and Anna Picket Hopkins, Harry was the fourth of five children.

His father, known as Al, was highly outgoing, made friends easily, participated in community organizations, and was a fierce competitor in the sport of bowling. Anna was a self-disciplined woman and a devout Methodist. She was generous, sympathetic, and devoted to home mission work. Al paid considerably less attention to business matters than to bowling and friends, which often left the family struggling financially. As a result, they moved frequently from town to town in Iowa, Nebraska, and Illinois. In 1901 Anna chose Grinnell, Iowa, a town where she believed her children could be well educated, to permanently settle her family. Anna looked on education as a means to a greater spiritual awareness for her children. Al opened a harness and leather shop there.

Harry excelled in school. His personality seemed to be a blend of characteristics from his parents. Like his dad, he was friendly, optimistic, and competitive. He had little concern for social standing; on the contrary, he delighted in outsmarting snobbish people or those he considered too self-centered. Although Harry rejected his mother's strict religious practices, the missionary zeal Harry demonstrated later in life for social work and New Deal relief programs likely came from his mother. Harry took all of these characteristics with him to Grinnell College.

College days

Hopkins often recalled his years at Grinnell College as the happiest time of his life. Grinnell, a small liberal arts college, had long been a school at the center of social reform and taught the application of Christian principles as a method of lessening the troubles brought on by rapid modernization.

At Grinnell Hopkins learned that a person must accept others of different races or nationalities, and that working to improve the living conditions of the less fortunate would improve the condition of all society. Grinnell students often looked toward a life of serving others. Economic and social status were considered unimportant compared to the quality of one's character.

Hopkins was well known on campus and involved in an array of activities, including newspaper productions, tennis, baseball, basketball, and drama. He was elected senior class permanent president, meaning he would serve as leader of the class after graduation.

Hopkins's favorite professor was Jesse Macy. Macy taught political science, a brand new subject on college campuses, and embraced Progressivism, a political and economic doctrine that advocated bringing an end to the power of corrupt city politicians, returning the government to the people, and supporting labor rights. Progressivism also included the belief that government should aid in improving the lives of the poor. As a freshman and sophomore Hopkins had concentrated on fun and ranked near the bottom of his class, but during his last two years he made As and Bs. In Hopkins's senior year, Macy considered Hopkins his top student.

Birth of a social crusader

Upon graduation in 1912 Hopkins took a summer job at a boys' summer camp in Bound Brook, New Jersey. The camp was run by the Christadora Settlement House in New York City's Lower East Side, a poverty-stricken slum area. The camp was just across the Hudson River from New York City. Taking the summer job mainly to get to New York City, Hopkins never anticipated the impact it would have on his life. What happened to Hopkins is described by Robert E. Sherwood in his 1948 book, *Roosevelt and Hopkins: An Intimate History*:

> On arrival at the Christadora Summer Camp at Bound Brook, he [Hopkins] confessed that he was bewildered by his first contacts with the products of the East Coast slums. He had certainly known poverty in his own family and friendly neighborhood in the Middle West, but that kind of poverty involved the maintenance of a kind of dignity and self-respect and independence; it did not involve hunger, or squalor [filth], or degradation [poor conditions]. The poverty of the city slums was, to him, something alien, shocking and enraging.... This was his real birth as a crusader for reform. The missionary impulse that he had inherited from his mother became the most powerful force within him. As with other changes in the circumstances of his life, he adjusted himself to his new environment with remarkable rapidity. After two months in the camp at Bound Brook he was the zealous champion of the underprivileged which he would always remain.

From that summer on, Hopkins held only jobs as a social worker or relief giver. His first full-time job was at Christodora House; his title was Director of Boys Work. He married fellow social worker Ethel Gross in 1913, and they had three sons. Hopkins worked for a large Manhattan private charity, the Association for Improving the Condition of the Poor; the reform administration of Mayor John Mitchel; the Board of Child Welfare; the Red Cross during World War I (1914–18); and the New York Tuberculosis and Health Association through the 1920s. At the Tuberculosis and Health Association, Hopkins met and fell in love with a secretary, Barbara Duncan. He divorced Ethel and married Barbara in June 1931. They had one daughter, Diana.

Hopkins's efficient and effective work caught the attention of Franklin Roosevelt (1882–1945), who was governor of New York at the time. Governor Roosevelt appointed Hopkins New York relief administrator in 1931. By that time the economic crisis of the Great Depression was severely affecting New York City, and Hopkins set out to relieve the suffering. It was in New York that Hopkins developed his firmly held belief that people wanted work, not handouts, and that work was far superior for morale and the economic health of the community.

Chief relief administrator

Franklin Roosevelt, a Democrat, ran for president and easily won the November 1932 election over the incumbent Republican, **Herbert Hoover** (1874–1964; served 1929–33; see entry), whose policies had been ineffective against the Depression. Roosevelt was inaugurated on March 4, 1933, and immediately set in motion his New Deal programs to bring relief, recovery, and reform to an ailing nation. He appointed Harry Hopkins his chief relief administrator. On May 22 Hopkins was handed the reins of the newly formed Federal Emergency Relief Administration (FERA) and $500 million to bring immediate relief to people devastated by the Depression. FERA gave cash grants to cities and states to provide direct relief assistance for groceries and rent. Hopkins also quickly initiated the Works Division within FERA to hire those on relief to work and earn pay for their labor on federal, state, and local projects such as road improvement.

According to the *Time* magazine issue of February 19, 1934, which pictured Hopkins on the cover, Hopkins worked in a tiny office in the Hurley-Wright Building overlooking the Washington Monument in Washington, D.C. The writer of the article notes, "It [the office] has no clock because Harry Hopkins does not want to know how late he works. Frequently he skips lunch altogether.... [Hopkins immediately] made a reputation for himself ... as the greatest disburser of ready cash in the country's history ... a professional giver of relief ... [who] had done a thoroughly professional job."

In June 1933 Congress passed the National Industrial Recovery Act. Title II of the act allowed creation of the Public Works Administration (PWA) to relieve unemployment by funding public works projects that would provide jobs. Secretary of the Interior **Harold Ickes** (1874–1952; see entry) was put in charge of developing the work relief projects, but Ickes worked slowly and methodically, debating every aspect of each project. In October 1933, as winter came on, an impatient Roosevelt took $400 million out of PWA funds, created a temporary agency called the Civil Works Administration (CWA) by executive order, and put Hopkins in charge. Hopkins was fond of saying, "Hunger is not debatable." He immediately cut through the red tape—unnecessary, time-wasting procedures that were delaying action and progress—and by February over four million Americans had been put to work on short-term projects suggested by local authorities, such as repaving streets, repairing schools, improving parks, and assisting with sanitation projects.

Congress was so impressed by the boldly determined yet totally honest and sincere Hopkins that they would have allocated however much money he asked for. But as planned back in the fall of 1933, Hopkins ended the CWA program in the spring of 1934. Nevertheless, he continued to urge the president to create expanded work relief programs, even as the PWA was finally getting into gear.

New Deal Agencies Administered By Harry Hopkins

The Federal Emergency Relief Administration (FERA): FERA was created by Congress on May 12, 1933, under the Federal Emergency Relief Act. Congress allocated $500 million to be immediately spent in direct relief of the hungry and the unemployed. Each state received money according to need, to pay for rent and food for its residents. The Works Division of the FERA was the forerunner of the CWA.

The Civil Works Administration (CWA): CWA was created by Executive Order 6420-B on November 9, 1933. The CWA offered jobs for people in need of work through the winter of 1933–34. Unlike the FERA, the CWA was operated entirely by the federal government, with Hopkins and his staff delivering the paychecks. The program ended in the spring of 1934 but was a forerunner of the WPA.

The Works Progress Administration (WPA): WPA was established by Executive Order No. 7034 on May 6, 1935, under authority of the Emergency Relief Appropriation Act. The WPA was an innovative work relief program that employed an average of 2.3 million workers each year between 1935 and 1940. Seventy-five percent of the WPA workforce worked on engineering and construction projects. But the WPA also established work relief programs for artists, musicians, writers, and actors, and youth programs such as the National Youth Administration (NYA). The WPA shut down in 1943.

On May 6, 1935, President Roosevelt created the Works Progress Administration (WPA) and placed Hopkins in charge. The WPA operated between 1935 and 1943. Over $11 billion was spent on work relief projects, from huge construction projects to local arts and music programs. Millions of Americans were put to work. Hopkins appointed two of his former classmates from Grinnell College, Deborah Herr and **Hallie Flanagan** (1890–1969; see entry) to administer two of the WPA's divisions, the Women's Division and the Federal Theatre Project. The president's wife, **Eleanor Roosevelt** (1884–1962; see entry), eagerly supported Hopkins's work, as did Roosevelt's close friend and personal secretary, Louis Howe. Hopkins was firmly entrenched in the innermost circle of the White House.

Personal tragedy struck Hopkins in 1937, when his wife, Barbara, died of cancer. Shortly thereafter Hopkins had much of his stomach removed; he, too, had cancer. Hopkins

Harry Hopkins was a persuasive, often arrogant, speaker whose directness offended some and gained support from others.
AP/Wide World Photo.
Reproduced by permission.

would remain in fragile health for the next nine years. Nevertheless, he managed to carry out the policies of President Roosevelt in a tough, courageous, but sometimes sarcastic manner. Critics abounded, saying Hopkins spent too much money or was "too big for his breeches," but Hopkins persisted in realistically assessing the needs of those devastated by the Depression and delivering appropriate relief. By 1941 as the United States prepared to enter World War II, WPA projects focused on defense, and by 1943, with jobs in the private sector plentiful, the WPA ceased operations.

World War II mobilization

By early 1941 the United States had begun full mobilization for World War II. Factories were rapidly manufacturing war materials, and suddenly there were more jobs than there were people to fill them. Many young Americans entered the armed forces. The Great Depression had ended.

The war effort completely consumed President Roosevelt's attention. Hopkins, now a seasoned governmental figure, became the president's trusted representative in meetings with European leaders. Despite his fragile health Hopkins became Roosevelt's emissary to Britain's prime minister, Winston Churchill (1874–1965). Hopkins organized the Lend-Lease program to supply England with defense equipment. Hopkins met with the Soviet Union's leader, Joseph Stalin (1879–1953), to help him prepare for defense against German invaders.

The United States formally entered the war after Japan's December 7, 1941, attack on Pearl Harbor. Hopkins played key roles in munitions allocation, continued overseeing the Lend-Lease program, and served as a major adviser to Roosevelt in foreign policy. Hopkins and his daughter, Diana, lived at the White House from 1940 to 1943. During this time, he married Louise Macy, but tragedy would again enter his life: In February 1944 Hopkins lost his youngest son in fighting in the Marshall Islands of the Pacific. Then in the spring of 1944 he again underwent surgery and returned to work in a greatly weakened state. But once more Hopkins persevered and was credited with superbly preparing the Americans for the Yalta Conference in February 1945. The Yalta Conference was one of the most important meetings between the victorious Allied nations of the United States, Great Britain, and the Soviet Union. Their goals were to determine the character of postwar Europe, including the division of Germany into East and West Germany, and the need for a world peacekeeping organization, later known as the United Nations.

President Roosevelt died suddenly in April 1945. Hopkins, at President Harry Truman's request, returned to the Soviet Union for talks with Stalin. Truman awarded Hopkins the nation's highest civilian honor, the Distinguished Service Award. Hopkins, in rapidly failing health, hoped to write his memoirs but died in January 1946.

Hopkins's legacy

Although Hopkins served as a powerful diplomat during World War II, historians more often speak of the legacy of his Depression-era work. Largely through the tireless actions of Hopkins and his staff, the federal government extended a helping hand to the poor and the unemployed during the 1930s Great Depression. The government offered not only food and jobs but reassurance, hope, and renewed confidence in the American political and economic system. As decades passed, millions of American families remembered that during those desperate years of unemployment, government efforts halted further loss of their mental and physical health. The thousands of CWA and WPA projects Hopkins directed brought work and respectability for the unemployed as well as new and improved roads, schools, hospitals, parks, power and irrigation systems, and airports throughout the nation.

For More Information

Books

Adams, Henry H. *Harry Hopkins: A Biography*. New York, NY: G. P. Putnam's Sons, 1977.

Charles, Searle F. *Minister of Relief: Harry Hopkins and the Depression*. Syracuse, NY: Syracuse University Press, 1963.

Hopkins, Harry L. *Principal Speeches of Harry L. Hopkins: Works Progress Administrator*. Milwaukee, WI: Milwaukee State Teachers College, 1938.

Hopkins, June. *Harry Hopkins: Sudden Hero, Brash Reformer*. New York, NY: St. Martin's Press, 1999.

McJimsey, George. *Harry Hopkins: Ally of the Poor and Defender of Democracy*. Cambridge, MA: Harvard University Press, 1987.

Sherwood, Robert E. *Roosevelt and Hopkins: An Intimate History*. New York, NY: Harper, 1948.

Periodicals

"National Affairs: Professional Giver." *Time* (February 19, 1934): pp. 11–13.

Harold Ickes

Born March 15, 1874
Hollidaysburg, Pennsylvania

Died February 3, 1952
Olney, Maryland

Public administrator,
reformer, spokesman

Harold Ickes had a reputation of being crusty and combative, but he was also noted for honesty and thoroughness. He fought for the rights of America's minorities and for the orderly development of the nation's rich natural resources. Ickes served as secretary of the interior for thirteen years, from 1933 to 1946, longer than anyone else in U.S. history. Never hesitant to speak his mind, he also served as the Roosevelt administration's spokesman for publicly opposing or supporting a variety of controversial issues. With an incredible record of achievement and well-run programs, Ickes is known as one of the greatest public administrators in U.S. history.

A hard childhood

Harold LeClair Ickes was born in March 1874 in Hollidaysburg, Pennsylvania, the second of seven children. Soon after his birth the family moved to nearby Altoona, where Harold spent the first sixteen years of his life amid rolling forested farmland. The area's population was predominantly Scots-Irish and had a reputation for industriousness. Harold's

"It is clear from Ickes' account of his childhood that to earn his mother's love and respect required a great deal of hard work, conformity, and good behavior. It is also plain that from a very early age these demands found a ready acquiescence [acceptance] in Harold."

Graham J. White in Harold Ickes of the New Deal: His Private Life and Public Career

Harold Ickes. *AP/Wide World Photo. Reproduced by permission.*

father, Jesse Boone Williams Ickes, was a salesman and accountant who operated a tobacco store for a time but who drank heavily. Harold's mother, Matilda "Mattie" McClune Ickes, was a homemaker and devout Presbyterian. The Ickes family traced their ancestral roots in the region back to pre–American Revolution times. They had at one time been large landowners, and Harold's grandfather served several terms in the state legislature. However, family fortunes had slipped away through time, and Harold's family struggled to make ends meet.

Mattie held strong religious convictions, raised her children under strict behavior codes, and constantly endeavored to keep a clean, tidy home. On Sunday the only songs or books family members could sing or read were hymns and religious books. The children could not play or whistle or even walk in the sunshine on Sundays. Sensing in Harold a special dedication to work and a drive to succeed, Mattie enjoyed a special relationship with him. Harold both admired his mother and resented her for the strict religious codes she enforced.

Harold's mother died of pneumonia in 1890, a devastating loss to the sixteen-year-old Ickes. Ickes and his sister were sent to live with an aunt and uncle in Englewood, Illinois, a suburb of Chicago. His father provided little support, and his uncle was very demanding. Ickes worked long hours in the family drugstore while in high school. He would open the store every day at 6:30 A.M., then go to school, and return in the afternoon to work until 10:00 P.M. Still, Ickes not only got his homework done but excelled to such a degree that the school let him combine his junior and senior years. It was in high school that his relentless dedication to work and achievement became apparent. Ickes graduated with honors in 1892 and was president of his senior class.

Progressive politics

Ickes worked his way through the University of Chicago while teaching English to immigrants at night. The Democrats held their national convention in Chicago in 1896, and William Jennings Bryan (1860–1925), a populist, won the party's nomination for president. Young Ickes eagerly followed the convention proceedings and was strongly impressed by the populists within the party, who stressed the needs of the common people. After graduating in 1897, Ickes became a newspaper reporter for the *Chicago Tribune* and the *Chicago Record,* where he was educated on the often corrupt world of Chicago politics. Through his news gathering Ickes also familiarized himself with the ideas of the progressive reform movement, which demanded good government free from big-business domination and political corruption. Progressives believe in using governmental power to stimulate private efforts toward solving social and economic problems. In 1903 John Harlan ran for mayor in Chicago and hired Ickes to manage the campaign. Although the campaign was unsuccessful, Ickes impressed others with his hard work, and the campaign brought him into contact with many people involved in the progressive social reform movement in Chicago. As elsewhere, the movement sought a greater role for government in guaranteeing public welfare. One of the city's progressives was businessman and city planner Frederic Delano, uncle of future president **Franklin D. Roosevelt** (1882–1945; served 1933–45; see entry).

Ickes entered the University of Chicago's law school. Graduating in 1907, he established a law practice in the city. He also joined the Progressive wing of the Republican Party, a wing led by President Theodore Roosevelt (1858–1919; served 1901–09). The Progressives' focus on the common people appealed to Ickes. He was also greatly influenced by Teddy Roosevelt's commitment to conserving natural resources and creating a system of national forests and wildlife reserves. In 1912 Theodore Roosevelt decided to run again as a presidential candidate, this

Whistling on Sundays

An early episode between Harold Ickes and his mother, Mattie, would tell a lot about Harold's character in later life. One of Mattie's many rules for Sundays was that whistling was irreverent. It was considered disrespectful to God. One weekend Harold was staying with some cousins, and a visiting minister was also staying at the house. Later on Sunday after listening to the minister's sermon, Harold overheard him whistling. After seriously weighing the situation, young Ickes figured that if a pastor could whistle and get away with it with God, then so could he. The following Sunday while his mother was nearby, he began whistling. When she corrected him, he told her that he had heard a minister whistling the previous week. Having no adequate response, Mattie relented, and Harold could whistle on Sundays from then on. This episode reflected his respect for her and her authority—he did not challenge her directly—but also his drive for justice and equality, in this case the desire to have the same, or equal, right to whistle as the minister had. Such pursuit of equality was later reflected in his efforts to correct laws that discriminated against women and minorities.

time for the newly formed Progressive Party, which had split away from the Republican Party. Ickes became campaign manager in the critical Cook County area encompassing the city of Chicago. However, Democrat Woodrow Wilson (1856–1924) won the presidential election. Ickes remained a leader in the Progressive Party in Illinois for several years until the party's collapse in 1916. He then returned to the Republican Party.

During this period of involvement in Chicago politics, Ickes married Anna Wilmarth Thompson, a woman from a wealthy background. The marriage was stormy but freed Ickes from the day-to-day struggles of making a living. The couple had one child. Continuing in politics, Ickes guided his wife's successful political campaigns for the Illinois General Assembly in 1928, 1930, and 1932. During the 1920s Ickes continued his private law practice in Chicago, fighting the power of big business. Showing deep concern for equal opportunity among all people, he represented the legal interests of women industrial workers without charging fees. He also served as director of the Chicago branch of the National Association for the Advancement of Colored People (NAACP) in 1923, promoting greater economic opportunity for black Americans.

Ickes and the New Deal

Through the 1920s the Republican Party held the White House. However, Ickes became disillusioned with his party as big business steadily gained greater power, greater wealth, and greater influence within the party—and within the government. Aware of his dissatisfaction with the Republican Party, the Democrats recruited Ickes in 1932 to lead the Western Independent Republican Committee for Democratic presidential candidate Franklin D. Roosevelt, a distant relative of Teddy Roosevelt. Democratic Party leaders wanted to win the support of progressive Republicans for the Democratic candidate. Ickes worked hard for the Franklin Roosevelt campaign, and when Roosevelt won the election, Ickes was rewarded with an appointment as secretary of the interior. The appointment was a surprise to many because at the time Ickes was fifty-eight years old and relatively obscure on the national level.

Over the next decade, Ickes promoted the orderly development of natural resources through careful planning. In addition to serving as secretary of the interior during the New Deal era, Ickes played other key roles in the administration. He identified projects for the Civilian Conservation Corps (CCC) and directed the Public Works Administration (PWA), both New Deal agencies. President Roosevelt's New Deal programs were designed to bring relief and recovery to the United States, which was suffering the worst economic crisis in its history, the Great Depression of the 1930s. Through the PWA, Ickes guided the spending of $6 billion of federal funds on public works projects, including construction of large dams, tunnels, hospitals, schools, highways, post offices, and other public structures. The projects provided desperately needed jobs for Americans during the Depression. With his strong commitment to service and honesty, Ickes personally reviewed all projects to make sure they were economically sound and useful. Nineteen thousand projects were completed, including 622 sewerage systems, 522 schools, 263 hospi-

Harold Ickes, seated, signs the paperwork for a slum-clearance and low-rent housing project in New York City sponsored by the Public Works Administration, August 1937. New York mayor Fiorello LaGuardia looks on. *AP/Wide World Photo. Reproduced by permission.*

tals, and many miles of streets and highways. The projects also included Hoover Dam on the Colorado River, Grand Coulee Dam on the Columbia River, and many other large water and power projects. Despite the thousands of projects and billions of dollars, there was never a hint of corruption. Ickes also aggressively led the nation's natural resources conservation programs, promoting major soil conservation efforts and establishing new national parks.

Ickes's aggressiveness in getting the job done led to friction with other New Deal leaders, including Secretary of Agriculture **Henry Wallace** (1888–1965; see entry) and Works Progress Administration (WPA) director **Harry Hopkins** (1890–1946; see entry). They competed over control of the many new conservation and public works programs being created at this time. They wanted the new agencies assigned to their own departments. Ickes trusted few people, and because of the harsh personality traits he acquired during his strictly disciplined childhood, he did not generate a strong public following.

Besides directing resource development and conservation programs, Ickes also continued his earlier push for equality and social justice for all. Ickes was quick to speak out on controversial social issues and became very close to **Eleanor Roosevelt** (1884–1962; see entry), who shared his desire to promote civil rights causes. Ickes was the first to end racial segregation in a major federal department. He also made sure that blacks received a fair share of jobs on construction projects funded by the Interior Department. He promoted the appointment of the first black American federal judge, William Hastie (1904–1976). When internationally famous black singer Marian Anderson (1897–1993) was denied use of a private concert hall in Washington, D.C., Ickes, with the support of Eleanor Roosevelt, arranged for her to perform at the Lincoln Memorial. Thousands attended the open-air concert. He would also later oppose the U.S. government's imprisonment of Japanese Americans during World War II (1939–45).

Spirited and always ready to take on new challenges, Ickes was a key campaigner for Roosevelt in the 1936, 1940, and 1944 presidential campaigns. He was the first to publicly support Roosevelt's decision to run for a third term in 1940. Ickes also served as a spokesman for the administration on other controversial issues: During the 1930s he was the first in Roosevelt's administration to publicly speak out against the isolationist stance of popular aviator Charles Lindbergh (1902–1974). (Isolationists oppose involvement in war and formal international relations.) Ickes was also the most aggressive speaker against the dictatorships growing in Europe during the 1930s.

After the New Deal

As the United States prepared to enter World War II in 1941, Ickes assumed an additional responsibility. He became head of the Petroleum Administration, which was created to ensure the supply and distribution of oil and gasoline in the United States. When Ickes resigned on February 13, 1946, he was one of the last key members of the New Deal administration to leave office.

As a reprieve from the fast-paced Washington life, Ickes retired to a farm in Olney, Maryland, that he had owned for some time. He commuted to an office he established in Georgetown, a section of Washington, D.C., and worked on various writing projects. Recognizing his own crustiness, Ickes titled his 1943 memoirs *The Autobiography of a Curmudgeon.* (A curmudgeon is one who is difficult to get along with, a rude or surly person.) His personal diary detailing his career as secretary of the interior was published in three volumes in the early 1950s after his death. Titled *The Secret Diary of Harold L. Ickes,* it provides a unique behind-the-scenes view of the New Deal. Persisting as a watchdog over the Department of the Interior and U.S. affairs in general, Ickes also wrote columns for the *New York Post* and *New Republic* magazine, and a series of articles for the *Saturday Evening Post.* His articles tackled controversial issues such as the anticommunist crusade of Senator Joseph McCarthy (1908–1957) in the early 1950s. Ickes also maintained an active speaking schedule. He died at age seventy-seven near his home in Olney, Maryland, in February 1952.

For More Information

Clarke, Jeanne N. *Roosevelt's Warriors: Harold L. Ickes and the New Deal.* Baltimore, MD: Johns Hopkins University Press, 1996.

Ickes, Harold L. *The Secret Diary of Harold L. Ickes: The First Thousand Days, 1933–1936; The Inside Struggle, 1936–1939; The Lowering Clouds, 1939–1941.* 3 vols. New York, NY: Simon & Schuster, 1952–54.

Watkins, T. H. *Righteous Pilgrim: The Life and Times of Harold L. Ickes, 1874–1952.* New York, NY: Henry Holt, 1990.

White, Graham J. *Harold Ickes of the New Deal: His Private Life and Public Career.* Cambridge, MA: Harvard University Press, 1985.

Dorothea Lange

Born May 25, 1895
Hoboken, New Jersey

Died October 11, 1965
Berkeley, California

Photographer

Dorothea Lange, considered one of America's most important twentieth-century photographers, began her career as a traditional portrait photographer. However, by 1933, observing the desperate conditions of people who had lost their jobs and homes in the Depression, Lange felt compelled to leave her studio and go onto the streets in San Francisco and then into the farm country to photograph the situation. Never seeing her photographs as art, she instead wanted to use the photos to get action on aid for the poor. Eventually she would be one of the most famous Farm Security Administration (FSA) photographers. She was a perceptive observer of the human condition and used her camera to document the faces of Americans struggling through the Depression.

"I saw and approached the hungry and desperate mother, as if drawn by a magnet. I do not remember how I explained my presence or my camera to her, but I do remember she asked me no questions."

Dorothea Lange in "The Assignment I'll Never Forget: Migrant Mother"

Dorothea Lange. *Courtesy of the Library of Congress.*

Early life

Dorothea Lange was born in Hoboken, New Jersey, across the Hudson River from New York City. Her parents, Heinrich (Henry) Martin Nutzhorn and Joanna Caroline Lange, were of German heritage. Dorothea's birth name was

Dorothea Margaretta Nutzhorn, but she later dropped her middle name and took her mother's maiden name for her last name. Dorothea's grandmother, Sophie Vottler, lived in the household throughout Dorothea's youth and was perhaps the first to recognize the acute intelligence, perception, and sensitivity of her granddaughter.

When Dorothea was seven years old, she contracted polio, which left her with a damaged right leg and a limp. Being called "Limpy" by other children caused her much pain as a child. When Dorothea was twelve years old, her father abandoned the family, which by then included Dorothea's six-year-old brother, Henry Martin. Luckily her mother, Joanna, found work in a branch-library on the Lower East Side in Manhattan, the most densely populated square mile in the world. Each morning Dorothea rode the ferry with her mother across the Hudson, then walked through the crowded streets to Public School (P.S.) 62, where her mother dropped her off before going to the library to work. The streets were full of Chinese people, Irish people, black Americans, Italians, and most of all, Jews. Later in life Dorothea would recall that she had noticed the clamor and lifestyles in the neighborhood "like a photographic observer." The Lower East Side helped develop her intense awareness of all about her. Two evenings a week her mother worked late, and Dorothea would have to walk to the ferry alone. She had to walk by the poverty-stricken area of the Bowery, which was littered with drunken men. Intimidated, the young teen developed a technique she would use throughout her photographic career. She learned to keep an expression on her face that did not draw any attention. No one took notice of her. She called it her "face of invisibility."

Dorothea did not do well academically at P.S. 62 and made no friends. In February 1909 she entered Manhattan's Wadleigh High School, a school for girls only. Her favorite subjects were English, drawing, and music. However, the strict school concentrated on developing teachers and paid no particular attention to the arts. Dorothea remained a loner, but she did meet one girl who became a lifelong friend, Florence Ahlstrom. At graduation in June 1913, Dorothea announced what she intended to do with the rest of her life—she would be a photographer.

Lange had never snapped a picture or even owned a camera. Yet, as related in Milton Meltzer's book *Dorothea Lange: A Photographer's Life*, Lange once commented, "I've never not been sure that I was a photographer any more than you would not be sure that you were yourself." Because her mother insisted she have something to fall back on, Lange enrolled in New York Training School for Teachers and found work in photographers' studios at night and on weekends. Soon she landed a job in the studio of Arnold Genthe (1869–1942), a top portrait photographer whose clients were all members of the privileged classes. Why Genthe hired the young Lange is a mystery, but perhaps like her grandmother, he sensed the young woman's intense perception and eye for the inner essence of humans. Genthe paid her fifteen dollars a week, a good wage, and in his studio Lange quickly learned photographic techniques. Her first camera was a gift from Genthe. The only photography class Lange ever took was from well-known photographer Clarence H. White (1871–1925), who taught Art Photography I and II in the extension department of Columbia University in New York City.

A portrait photographer

After apprenticing at several other New York studios, Lange, along with her apartment mate Florence Ahlstrom, decided to travel around the world. They got no farther than San Francisco, where they fell victim to a pickpocket. With only four dollars to their name, the young women had no choice but to seek employment in San Francisco. Lange immediately found a job doing photofinishing at Marsh and Company on Market Street. Lange often referred to Marsh's counter as the beginning of her life. There the interest she showed in what people left for photofinishing soon made her friends in the art and photography world. Two of her first friends were Roi Partridge, an etcher, and his wife, photographer Imogen Cummingham. Lange also joined the San Francisco Camera Club. Before long, with the help of wealthy San Franciscans, she was able to open a studio of her own at 540 Sutter Street. Her studio prospered as word spread about her talent for portrait photography. Soon Lange was photographing the wealthiest families in San Francisco. She thought of her work as a skilled trade; she was making a living in portrait photography. She did not see herself as an artist, and she rarely did any personal photography. In the fall of 1919, her friend Roi Partridge introduced Lange to Maynard Dixon, an already well-known painter of Western scenes, landscapes, people, and animals. Although Dixon was twenty years older than Lange, they married on March 21, 1920.

Lange's first child, Daniel Rhodes Dixon, was born on May 15, 1925, and a second son, John Eaglefeather Dixon, arrived on June 12, 1928. Lange and Dixon maintained separate studios for their work, and Dixon frequently traveled to the Southwest on "sketching trips."

Onto the street

In October 1929 the stock market crashed, sending stock values plummeting. In the weeks and months that followed, Lange's and Dixon's wealthy customers stopped ordering portraits and paintings. By 1934, in a money-saving move, Lange and Dixon gave up their house, boarded their young sons at school, and began living separately in their respective studios.

As more and more unemployed people began wandering the streets, Lange, with time on her hands, peered out the windows of her studio, observing the neighborhood much as she had done as a child in New York's Lower East Side. Her instincts then led her out onto the streets to photograph the humanity below. She had recently been thinking that she needed something more satisfying than studio portrait photography. Near Lange's studio a wealthy woman known as the "White Angel" had set up a breadline to feed the hungry. Lange donned the "face of invisibility" that she had used as a child walking through the Bowery in New York City and began to shoot photos of people along the breadline. One exposure was of a man in torn clothing leaning against a barricade holding a tin cup. She pinned the picture on her wall and called it "White Angel Breadline."

Lange left her studio more and more often to photograph people whose lives had been destroyed by the Depression, those on the breadlines and those living on the streets. She also photographed common laborers, including those involved in strikes for better working conditions.

In the summer of 1934 gallery owner Willard Van Dyke exhibited Lange's work at his gallery in Oakland, California. It was there Lange first met Paul Schuster Taylor, an associate professor of economics at the University of California, Berkeley. In 1935 Taylor began serving as the field director for the Division of Rural Rehabilitation of the California Emergency Relief Administration known as SERA. SERA was the California state division of the Federal Emergency Relief Administration (FERA),

Dorothea Lange snapped this 1935 photo of a homeless Oklahoma family. *Liaison Agency. Reproduced by permission.*

an agency established in 1933 by President **Franklin D. Roosevelt's** (1882–1945; served 1933–45; see entry) administration to bring relief to Americans devastated by the Depression. In February 1935 Taylor hired Lange to photograph the migrant workers who were flooding into California in search of work in the fields. Lange closed her portrait studio and followed Taylor into the field. Although she left behind commercial portrait photography, she took with her the skills of portraiture. She also frequently put on her face of invisibility as she moved among the migrant farmworkers. At other times she sat down and talked to those she photographed, collecting their stories. She looked upon her work as photography with a purpose—the goal was to make the conditions under which migrants lived visible to others and to thereby bring about change. Working as a team for SERA, Taylor wrote notes and Lange provided photos for illustration. The Taylor-Lange reports were sent back to FERA in Washington, D.C.

RA/FSA photographer

In May 1935 the Resettlement Administration (RA) was established as part of the federal government's effort to aid the rural poor. The RA brought together the various government agencies that were attempting to deal with agricultural problems, including the Land Programs and the Rural Rehabilitation Division of FERA. Taylor and Lange became employees of the RA. (In 1937 the RA would be absorbed by the Farm Security Administration, or FSA.) **Rexford Tugwell** (1891–1979; see Brain Trust entry) was appointed head of the RA, and he hired **Roy Stryker** (1893–1975; see entry) to head the Historical Section in the RA. Under Stryker's guidance, the Historical Section mounted an extensive documentary photography project to capture on film the conditions of the rural poor and publish those photos for the general public. Stryker and his staff hoped the photographs would help the public understand rural poverty and therefore support the RA projects. By the end of 1935 Stryker had hired a group of amazingly talented photographers: Arthur Rothstein (1915–1985), Ben Shahn (1898–1969), Walker Evans (1903–1975), Carl Mydans (1907–), and Dorothea Lange. Even though they had never met, Stryker hired Lange on the strength of her photos in the Taylor-Lange reports. Lange merely had to

Who Were the Rural Poor?

By the late 1800s tenant farmers (farmers who rented the land they worked) operated approximately one-third of Southern farms. By 1920 one-half of Southern farms were cultivated by tenant farmers. And by 1930 at least three-fourths of the farmers in Mississippi, Georgia, and Louisiana were tenant farmers. Translated, these figures meant that approximately eight and one half million persons—over one million white families and seven hundred thousand black families in the South—worked as tenants on someone else's land in 1930. Up to one-half of the tenant farmers were sharecroppers, who were required to share a portion of their crop with the landowner. Few tenants or sharecroppers ever earned more than two hundred or three hundred dollars a year, and often they had large families to support. Cotton was the principal crop grown, and landowners generally demanded that crops be grown right up to the doorstep of the farmer's shack, which left no room for vegetable gardens to supply the tenant family's needs.

Great Plains farmers had different problems than their Southern counterparts. In the United States the Great Plains extend from North Dakota down to Oklahoma and Texas. During the early 1930s great black clouds of dust began to roll over the land in this region as strong winds blew down from Canada. A severe drought had caused wheat and other grain crops to fail, and because the land had been plowed up for wheat for many years, there were few native grasses left to anchor the topsoil when the winds came. The temperature stayed about a hundred degrees week after week in the mid-1930s. In 1936 a seven-county survey in southeastern Colorado revealed that half of the farmhouses were abandoned. Oklahoma reported the loss of approximately eighteen farms a day. The stricken farm families generally headed west to greener pastures in California, Oregon, and Washington. From 1935 to 1939 an estimated 70,857 Oklahomans, or Okies, went to California in search of farmwork. Soon, regardless of what state they were from, all poor farm families migrating into California were called Okies. Some went into cities in search of work, but almost half stayed in the central valleys of California, following crop harvests and living in squalid camps. Unable to find the better life they had hoped for, they lived with starvation and filth through the last half of the 1930s.

transfer to the Historical Section. Stryker and Lange finally met in May 1936.

Another major change took place in the forty-year-old Lange's life in 1935. Realizing she and Taylor were an extraordinary match, she divorced Maynard Dixon in October

1935 and married Taylor on December 6, 1935. Taylor had transferred to the research division of the newly formed Social Security Board in late 1935, but they continued to travel together as Taylor researched farm labor difficulties in various regions. On an RA/FSA assignment between 1935 and 1939, Lange traveled extensively, visiting hundreds of agricultural communities, many not on any map. She moved through the West, Southwest, and South. In March 1936 she photographed a migrant woman and her children in a pea pickers' camp in Nipomo, California. Known as the "Migrant Mother," the photograph has been reproduced many thousands of times, becoming a lasting symbol of hard times during the 1930s Depression era. Lange produced a large number of other superior-quality photos. Her photos express her intimate sense of the people and a compassionate awareness of their living and working conditions. Lange's photographs were never staged; that is, she never arranged or posed her subjects. She usually photographed from a low angle, which automatically gave her subjects a look of dignity.

Lange and Stryker communicated extensively by letter. The main problem they encountered was a difference of opinion about where her negatives should be kept. Lange wanted to keep them in her Berkeley studio, where she could control the quality of prints made from them. Stryker wanted and needed them in the central file in Washington, D.C. They debated endlessly over the negatives. Also, Stryker was forced to constantly juggle the Historical Section's budget by letting photographers go and then rehiring them, so Lange was not actually on the RA/FSA payroll continuously between 1935 and 1939.

Career as a photographer continues

As work wound down for the FSA, Lange and Taylor worked together on a book that would combine her photographs and his field notes. They worked on the project intensively from late 1938 through the spring of 1939. Published as *An American Exodus* in 1939, the book met with little success as Americans turned their attention to events in Europe and the looming war.

During World War II (1939–45) Lange worked for the War Relocation Authority, photographing the Japanese Americans who were relocated to internment camps. After the war she covered the birth of the United Nations. During this time Lange developed digestive tract problems including ulcers, and her poor health prevented her from doing much field work for several years. In 1958 Taylor traveled to Asia as a consulting economist for both the government and private companies, and he took Lange with him. They visited Vietnam, Korea, Indonesia, Bali, India, and Pakistan. Lange had no particular plans for photographing but shot pictures as opportunities presented themselves. In Saigon, Vietnam, she photographed three generations of a family planting onions. In Bali she photographed the hands of a dancer. Soon after this trip Lange and Taylor traveled to South America, to Egypt, and to Europe. Rather than attempting pictures with social implications, Lange focused more on beauty.

By the 1960s, still in poor health, Lange concentrated on photographing subjects close at hand, such as the oak trees in her yard and her family. In early 1964 Lange learned that the Museum of Modern Art in New York City had committed to a retrospective show of her work for February 1966. Retrospective exhibits present a comprehensive selection of an artist's work. Two years seemed like short notice to plan an exhibition of a lifetime of work. Themes had to be selected, prints produced and mounted, captions written, and catalog material gathered and printed. Lange set about the task. In August 1965 she was diagnosed with inoperable cancer of the esophagus. Lange's last year had been consumed in preparing for the special exhibition, which opened three months after her death in October 1965.

For More Information

Books

Cox, Christopher. *Dorothea Lange*. New York, NY: Aperture, 1981.

Elliott, George P. *Dorothea Lange*. Garden City, NY: Doubleday, 1966.

Hurley, F. Jack. *Portrait of a Decade: Roy Stryker and the Development of Documentary Photography in the Thirties*. Baton Rouge, LA: Louisiana State University Press, 1972.

Lange, Dorothea, and Paul Schuster Taylor. *An American Exodus: A Record of Human Erosion*. Reprint. New York, NY: Arno Press, 1975.

Lange, Dorothea, and Paul Schuster Taylor. *Lange Looks at the American Country Woman*. Los Angeles, CA: Ward Ritchie Press, 1967.

Levin, Howard M., and Katherine Northrup, eds. *Dorothea Lange: Farm Security Administration Photographs, 1935–1939,* Volume 1. Glencoe, IL: Text-Fiche Press, 1980.

Meltzer, Milton. *Dorothea Lange: A Photographer's Life.* New York, NY: Farrat, Straus, & Giroux, 1978.

Ohrn, Karin B. *Dorothea Lange and the Documentary Tradition.* Baton Rouge, LA: Louisiana State University Press, 1980.

O'Neal, Hank. *A Vision Shared: A Classic Portrait of America and Its People, 1935–1943.* New York, NY: St. Martin's, 1976.

Periodicals

Lange, Dorothea. "The Assignment I'll Never Forget: Migrant Mother." *Popular Photography* (February 1960): pp. 42, 126.

Henry Morgenthau

Born May 11, 1891
New York, New York

Died February 6, 1967
Poughkeepsie, New York

Secretary of the treasury

DOES IT
CONTRIBUTE
TO
RECOVERY?

Though a poor student throughout his school career and very awkward during public appearances later in life, Henry Morgenthau Jr. served as secretary of the treasury for eleven years during some of the most challenging economic times in U.S. history. From 1934 to 1940 he tried to maintain a stable monetary system in the face of the Great Depression, the worst economic crisis the United States had ever experienced. In the early 1940s Morgenthau was in charge of financing the massive U.S. war effort during World War II (1939–45). Throughout this time he remained sensitive to the hardships of poor Americans and was dedicated to easing the suffering of those in need.

Challenging early years

Henry Morgenthau Jr. was born in May 1891 to Henry Morgenthau Sr. and Josephine "Josie" Sykes. The third of four children, he was the only son. The family resided in a New York apartment at Central Park West and Eighty-first Street. Henry Sr.'s father, Lazarus Morgenthau, had immigrated from

"[A]lthough obviously bright, the boy [Morgenthau] suffered from what today would be called a learning disability.... Despite hard work, the boy developed an aversion to conventional schooling."

Henry Morgenthau III, in the 1991 book Mostly Morgenthaus: A Family History

Henry Morgenthau. *AP/Wide World Photo. Reproduced by permission.*

Germany to the United States when Henry Sr. was ten years of age. Henry Sr. became a lawyer who made a fortune in real estate transactions in Harlem and the Bronx. He and Josie were active in the Democratic Party and supported a variety of social welfare causes.

Henry Sr. took great interest in his only son and established a very close relationship with him. Young Henry Jr. was outgoing and fun-loving. When he reached school age, it soon became apparent that he had a significant learning disability. Henry did poorly in every level of school and was miserable in the academic environment. Learning language skills and math proved quite difficult for him. On the other hand, apart from his school subjects, he was very bright and had a strong imagination. Following kindergarten Henry went into the Sachs Collegiate Institute, then to New Hampshire's Phillips Exeter Academy, and back to Sachs by 1906. At that time he received tutoring from Prussian instructor Otto Koenig. Through the tutor's assistance, Henry graduated from high school and entered Cornell University to major in architecture. Henry Sr. wanted his son to join his real estate business as an architect. However, despite the availability of a personal tutor, Henry Jr. was unsuccessful in the college classroom and left Cornell in the spring of 1911.

Henry got a job as a timekeeper for a construction company, but his father had other ideas. Henry Sr. and Josie had been involved in an organization providing social services for the needy in Manhattan's Lower East Side. It was called the Henry Street Settlement House. They encouraged Henry Jr. to serve as a volunteer there. The Henry Street House in particular aided impoverished Jewish immigrants from Poland and Russia. Settlement houses in the late nineteenth and early twentieth century frequently served as a training ground for individuals who would later become social workers or pursue public careers. Henry spent the summer of 1911 at the Henry Street House. The dire poverty of the people there made a lasting impression on him.

A New York farmer

In the fall of 1911, after only a few days of working as a laborer at the Underwood Typewriter Company in Hartford,

Connecticut, Morgenthau became seriously ill with typhoid fever. When he was well enough, his father sent him to a Texas ranch to complete his recovery. The experience changed Henry's life: He decided to become a farmer. Morgenthau returned to Cornell to major in agriculture. He completed his studies in 1913 at age twenty-two (though he did not receive a degree) and purchased a 1,700-acre farm in Dutchess County near the town of Poughkeepsie, New York. Morgenthau grew apples and maintained a dairy. Although comfortably at home on his farm, he retained a circle of personal friends who had connections to wealth and influence. One acquaintance was young **Franklin D. Roosevelt** (1882–1945; served 1933–45; see entry), the future president. Henry Jr. married Elinor Fatman, known as Ellie, in April 1916. He and Ellie had known each other for years. She, too, had volunteered at the Henry Street House before finishing her college education in 1913. Ellie gave birth to a son in January 1917, and the couple would have two more children.

When Roosevelt was struck with polio in 1921, Morgenthau spent many hours with him during his initial recovery, endlessly discussing issues of the day and playing board games. Also during this time Morgenthau purchased the farm journal *American Agriculturist,* to pursue his interest in agricultural science. Through the magazine he promoted soil conservation and application of new scientific advances in agriculture.

As Roosevelt began to resume his political activity, Morgenthau served as his driver and personal assistant. Upon winning the New York governor's election in 1928, Roosevelt appointed Morgenthau chairman of the state's Agricultural Advisory Commission. In 1930 after his reelection as governor, Roosevelt appointed Morgenthau the state commissioner of conservation, placing him in charge of New York's $2 billion reforestation program. The program provided jobs for thousands of the state's workers during the early Depression years, and they planted nearly ninety million trees.

Head of finance

Morgenthau followed Roosevelt to Washington, D.C., after Roosevelt's successful presidential campaign in 1932. Morgenthau had privately hoped to become secretary of agriculture, but in March 1933 Roosevelt appointed him head of the Farm Credit Administration (FCA). Morgenthau was responsible for consolidating the programs of nine existing farm loan agencies into one agency. Eventually the FCA was loaning a million dollars a day to farmers to help them meet their mortgage payments and avoid bankruptcy.

Before long an opportunity for a cabinet appointment did arise for Morgenthau. In November 1933 Secretary of the Treasury William Woodin was in failing health, and he submitted his resignation to Roosevelt. The president appointed Morgenthau as Woodin's replacement on January 1, 1934. He would remain secretary of the treasury for the next eleven years. Many thought Morgenthau an odd choice for the position. He had little background in finance and often came across very poorly in public appearances, such as at press conferences. He always appeared shy and ill at ease. Nonetheless, Morgenthau maintained a close relationship with Roosevelt, lunching with the president every Monday, much to the envy of others.

As secretary of the treasury during the Depression years, Morgenthau spent most of his energy ensuring a stable U.S. dollar. By the end of the 1930s U.S. currency was the strongest in the world. Morgenthau's job became increasingly complex as the federal budget dramatically increased. From 1934 to 1945 the annual federal expenditures rose from $5 billion to $98 billion. Some problems did occur along the way: Morgenthau had long sought a balanced federal budget (in which the government spends no more money each year than it receives in revenue). In early 1937, with the nation's economy seemingly on better footing, Morgenthau finally convinced Roosevelt to cut back federal expenditures on relief programs. However, the economy soon went into a steep decline, and many thought the decreased federal funding was a key contributing factor. Morgenthau fought to maintain the balanced budget, but others convinced Roosevelt to increase federal spending once again.

As war spread across Europe from 1939 to 1941, Morgenthau called for U.S. support of Britain's war effort against Germany. He drafted the Lend-Lease Act, creating a major program for supplying Britain with war materials. He also helped create the War Refugee Board to assist Jews and other refugees arriving from Europe. With the U.S. entry into the

Farm Credit Administration

Henry Morgenthau's keen interest in agriculture prior to 1933 was clear; he operated a farm and published an agricultural magazine. Accordingly, newly elected president Franklin D. Roosevelt appointed his good friend head of the Farm Credit Administration (FCA). The nation's farm economy had struggled throughout the 1920s. The international demand for U.S. produce dropped significantly following World War I (1914–18) and stayed down. Economic conditions grew even worse with the beginning of the Great Depression in late 1929. During the 1920s and early 1930s Congress passed several pieces of legislation making loans more readily available to farmers so they could stay in business. However, by early 1933 farm prices remained low, and farmers continued to struggle. In addition, the large number of federal agencies making farm loans caused much confusion and inefficiency. These agencies included the Federal Farm Board, the Federal Farm Loan Board, the Reconstruction Finance Corporation, the Department of Agriculture, and various federal banks.

To pump more money into the nation's farm economy and better organize services to farmers, Roosevelt signed an executive order on March 27, 1933, creating the Farm Credit Administration, an independent federal agency. It was Morgenthau's responsibility to consolidate all the various farm loan programs into one. Congress passed the Farm Credit Act on June 16, making the FCA permanent. Congress next passed the Farm Mortgage Refinancing Act in January 1934, establishing the Federal Farm Mortgage Corporation, known as Farmer Mac, under the FCA with $2 billion in funds. The number of loans the FCA processed was staggering—three hundred loans a day at its peak. Over 20 percent of U.S. farms had been refinanced through FCA loans by late 1934. By 1941 the FCA had loaned almost $7 billion and saved thousands of farmers from bankruptcy. In the twenty-first century the FCA remains responsible for regulating the various banks and associations that make up the U.S. farm loan system.

war in December 1941, Morgenthau became responsible for financing the massive U.S. war effort. Morgenthau was also a leading figure in planning the postwar international monetary system. At an international conference attended by forty-four nations in July 1944 at Bretton Woods, New Hampshire, Morgenthau led in creating the International Monetary Fund and the World Bank. The two international financial organizations were established to help stabilize national currencies and provide funds to underdeveloped nations.

In regard to postwar Germany, Morgenthau promoted a controversial plan to dismantle German industries and divide the nation into two agricultural countries. However, in early 1945 Roosevelt decided on a different plan, which called for Germany to be rebuilt and maintained as a key part of the European economy. Three months after President Roosevelt's sudden death in April 1945, Morgenthau turned in his resignation because he did not have a good working relationship with the new president, Harry Truman (1884–1972; served 1945–53).

An advocate for Jews

After leaving public office, Morgenthau became heavily involved in Jewish causes. He served as general chairman of the United Jewish Appeal (UJA) from 1947 to 1955. The UJA is an international organization created to support Jewish communities throughout the world and to care for those in need. From 1951 to 1954 Morgenthau was also chairman of the board of governors for the American Financial and Development Corporation for Israel. The corporation assisted Israel, the newly established Middle Eastern state, in its efforts to become economically stable.

In 1949 Morgenthau's wife, Elinor, died. In November 1951 he married Marcelle Puthon Hirsch. Morgenthau lived for over a decade in retirement before dying of a heart and kidney condition in February 1967. He was seventy-five. An incredible volume of materials from Morgenthau's tenure as secretary of the treasury has survived, providing insight into behind-the-scenes debates over U.S. policy during critical times. Known as the Morgenthau diaries, the materials amount to eight hundred volumes and are housed in the Franklin D. Roosevelt Library in Hyde Park, New York. Three volumes covering the years 1959 to 1967 were published in *From the Morgenthau Diaries* by John M. Blum.

For More Information

Blum, John M. *From the Morgenthau Diaries*. Boston, MA: Houghton Mifflin, 1959–67.

Blum, John M. *Roosevelt and Morgenthau*. Boston, MA: Houghton Mifflin, 1970.

Kesaris, Paul, ed. *The Presidential Diaries of Henry Morgenthau, Jr.* Frederick, MD: University Publications of America, 1981.

Morgenthau, Henry, III. *Mostly Morgenthaus: A Family History*. New York, NY: Ticknor & Fields, 1991.

Frances Perkins

Born April 10, 1880
Boston, Massachusetts

Died May 14, 1965
New York, New York

Secretary of labor

Frances Perkins. *AP/Wide World Photo. Reproduced by permission.*

Trained as a teacher, Frances Perkins became an advocate for the working classes, children, women, and the poor. As a social worker and reformer, she combined a practical approach, which she attributed to her New England common sense, with an energy and focus that allowed her to get things done in politically difficult situations. In a male-dominated workplace, Perkins overcame prejudices and restrictions to establish herself as an outstanding federal government official who significantly improved the lives of Americans. She shaped much of the basic labor legislation of the United States. She also authored two books: *People at Work* (1934) and *The Roosevelt I Knew* (1946).

Young Fannie

Fannie Coralie Perkins (later adopting the first name of Frances in her adult life) was born April 10, 1880, to Frederick W. and Susie E. Perkins in Boston, Massachusetts. The Perkins family descended from prominent British colonists who settled in New England in 1620. As an adult, Frances delighted in relating stories of her ancestors that expressed her own zeal for living. A favorite story concerned her spry ninety-nine-year-old great-grandfather who marched down from the hill where he lived and ordered a fine pair of leather boots. Certain the elderly gentleman would never live to wear out such an extravagant pair of boots, the boot maker was reluctant to accept the order. Dismissing the boot maker's concern, Fannie's great-grandfather stated that he most certainly could live to wear out the boots, because statistics plainly showed that very few people died after ninety-nine. The spunk, energy, courage, and intellectual talent of her ancestors flowed through Francis as she lived out her remarkable life.

When Fannie was two years old, her father moved the family to Worcester in central Massachusetts. He owned a shop offering cards and writing materials, a business that provided a comfortable living. Although not formally educated, Frederick Perkins was quite well-read and, as Frances recalled, knowledgeable about such topics as the law and the ancient Greeks. Frances believed her love of knowledge came from her father and her lifelong interest in art from her mother. She also owed her preference for wearing tricorn, or three-cornered, hats to her mother. Susie Perkins took twelve-year-old Fannie to a fine hat shop in Boston and placed a tricorn hat on her daughter's head. She instructed Fannie to always wear a hat that was wider than her cheekbones. Fannie complied, and the tricorn hat became her trademark in later years.

Student leader

As a teenager Fannie never thought of herself as especially bright, but she nevertheless easily completed her years at Worcester Classical High School in 1898. At a time when few women went on to college, Fannie was accepted into a prestigious women's college, Mount Holyoke in western Massachusetts. Her interests were history, art, and literature, but much to her dismay she was also required to take chemistry. Although the chemistry class under Professor Nellie Esther Goldthwaite proved very difficult, as the year progressed, Fannie proved to herself that she could indeed pass the course. For the first time she thought of herself as bright. By her senior year Fannie, known as "Perk," had become a popular class leader.

During her senior year at Mount Holyoke Fannie took a class that set her on her career path of promoting social justice. Taught by Professor Annah May Soule, the American economic history class required students to visit local factories and write about what they found. The dreadful factory conditions Fannie witnessed changed her forever. She became passionate about improving working conditions in factories, where so many Americans, including women, labored. She saw how job loss and poverty could result from industrial accidents such as loss of a limb or loss of eyesight. Together with other students from Professor Soule's class, Fannie helped form a chapter of the National Consumers' League on campus. This organization used consumer pressure to try to change factory conditions. Its members urged people not to buy products made in unsafe factories.

Teacher and budding social worker

After graduation in 1902 Perkins taught briefly at an academy in Connecticut and then at academies in Massachusetts, including in Worcester. All the while, she maintained her interest in improving the lives of American workers. She turned her interest into action in Worcester by running a girls' club for fourteen- to sixteen-year-olds who were already working in factories.

In 1904 Perkins took a job teaching physics and biology at a boarding school for wealthy girls, Ferry Hall, in Lake Forest, Illinois. Her free time was spent at Chicago Commons and Hull House, settlement houses in Chicago. Settlement houses were located in poor areas of cities and attempted to help the underprivileged with social services such as shelter, food, clothing, and job searching. Perkins often took on the most difficult tasks for the houses. For example, with intelligence, courage, and her piercing dark eyes, she visited employers who had failed to pay workers (generally immigrant workers) and convinced them to hand over the wages owed.

While teaching in Lake Forest, Perkins joined the Episcopal Church on June 11, 1905, using the name Frances C. Perkins (rather than her given name Fannie). Shortly thereafter she dropped the C and from that time on was known as Frances Perkins. Convinced that her future lay in social work rather than teaching, Perkins, after three years at Ferry Hall, moved to Philadelphia, Pennsylvania, in 1907. There she took a position as executive secretary of the Philadelphia Research and Protective Association. The association helped immigrant girls as well as blacks just venturing north from southern states and researched the situations they were subjected to, such as long hours of work in dirty and unsafe factory conditions. Perkins also took classes in the graduate school at the University of Pennsylvania, where economics professor Simon N. Patten taught her to attack problems with practical solutions. Recognizing her brilliance, Patten helped Perkins obtain a graduate school fellowship (grant of money to attend school) beginning in September 1909 at Columbia University in New York City.

In New York City

Perkins completed her master's thesis at Columbia in 1910. Her thesis was an investigation of undernourished children at Public School 51 in the crime-ridden, poverty-stricken area known as Hell's Kitchen, where Perkins herself briefly lived. In dramatic contrast to her time in Hell's Kitchen, Perkins managed to keep up a social life in the city. At a tea dance in 1910 she met a tall, handsome young man, **Franklin D. Roosevelt** (1882–1945; served 1933–45; see entry), the future president. Not particularly impressed, she remembered him only because he was a distant cousin of former president Theodore Roosevelt (1858–1919; served 1901–09).

During the time she worked on her master's thesis, Perkins also worked as the executive secretary of the New York City Consumers' League, a chapter like the one she and college friends had established at Mount Holyoke. Perkins successfully lobbied the New York legislature for the 54-Hour Bill. This piece of legislation prohibited males under eighteen years of age and females of any age from working more than fifty-four hours per week in factories. Perkins also undertook studies of factory fire safety and of filthy conditions in the many basement bakeries in New York City.

On March 25, 1911, by coincidence Perkins witnessed firsthand the Triangle Shirtwaist Company fire just east of Washington Square Park in New York City. Fire broke out on

Factory Working Conditions in the 1930s

In the 1930s, factory workers, including women, children, and immigrants, commonly worked twelve to fourteen hours a day, six days a week. Children as young as five or six worked as farm laborers. Children also worked in mines. Women earned less than half of men's salaries for the same work. In textile industries workers were typically paid by the piecework system; that is, they were paid by the number of goods they produced. This system often caused employees to work to the point of exhaustion, in the hopes of earning a little extra money.

A worker's job was always in jeopardy. Being late for work, working too slow, or questioning a supervisor were causes for firing. Workers could not afford to refuse the demands of employers, because there were always other people eager for their jobs. If business dropped off, the workers were simply laid off.

Workers were exposed to many dangers in the workplace: high temperatures, poisonous gases, and the loss of fingers and limbs in accidents involving large machinery. Working environments were stiflingly hot in summer and frequently not heated in winter. Work areas were overcrowded, poorly ventilated, and poorly lit, and breaks were rarely allowed.

---

the eighth floor of the Asch Building, trapping six hundred young garment workers, mostly immigrant girls. Perkins had been attending a tea nearby and upon hearing the sirens went to the site just as girls started jumping to their death to escape the flames.

Inspector Perkins

Following the tragedy, New York City leaders organized the Committee on Safety, and the state legislature formed the New York State Factory Investigation Commission on June 30, 1911. State senator Robert Wagner (1877–1953), who would be elected to the U.S. Senate in 1926, was chairman of the commission; assemblyman Alfred Smith (1873–1944), who would be elected governor of New York in 1918, was vice chairman; and Perkins became an inspector for the commission. Soon she was in charge of investigations, organizing trip after trip into an array of factories and making sure that Wagner and Smith personally saw the filth and dangerous conditions.

In 1913 Perkins married Paul Caldwell Wilson, an economist from the University of Chicago who had come to New York City to work in the mayor's office. She kept her maiden name, Perkins, to save Wilson and the mayor's office any embarrassment about the fiery speeches she made around the state to promote social justice for workers.

Highest-paid female state employee

For the next five years Perkins continued writing legislation. She also started a family. Her first child died shortly after birth in 1915, but in December 1916 she gave birth to a healthy baby girl, Susanna Winslow Wilson. Ready to settle into a more domestic life, Perkins foresaw the rest of her life as a mother, volunteer, and adviser on social justice issues. Yet an unexpected turn of events jolted her back into the need of paid employment. Her husband began to develop mental health problems, which she described as "ups and downs." He never recovered and until his death in 1952 needed periodic hospitalization. Perkins's friend from the New York legislature, Al Smith, was elected governor in November 1918. Because women were close to gaining the right to vote, Smith believed the time was right to appoint a woman to a high-level position. Besides, he had a commission that needed reorganizing. Knowing he had just the person for the job, he appointed Perkins as a member of the Industrial Commission of the Department of Labor of the state of New York. She accepted the position, which paid $8,000 a year, or about $90,000 in 1998 dollars. With this appointment Perkins became the highest-paid female state employee in the United States. Perkins was a fast learner, so fast that when trouble broke out among copper laborers and management in Rome, New York, Governor Smith sent Perkins. Her courage, self-assurance and ability to find practical solutions made her instrumental in settling the dangerous dispute.

Industrial commissioner

Governor Smith lost his reelection bid in 1920 but regained his position in the 1922 election. During Smith's terms as governor, Perkins continued her vigorous factory inspection work and skillfully helped straighten out the Industrial Commission's workmen's compensation department. She dealt with employees, employers, and insurance companies with intelligence, honesty, and fairness. During this time Perkins had also become good friends with **Eleanor Roosevelt** (1884–1962; see entry), whose husband, the former state senator Franklin Roosevelt, was recovering after being struck with polio. During his illness Eleanor and Perkins kept him in touch with labor leaders and organizations so that his period of recuperation would be productive. So constructive were those years that Roosevelt won the election for governor of New York in 1928, succeeding Governor Smith. Roosevelt immediately appointed Perkins industrial commissioner of the Department of Labor of the state of New York. She was the first woman ever to hold such a high-level state position. As head of the commission she continued to focus on workmen's compensation and factory inspection but also worked to further reduce the workweek (from fifty-four to forty-eight hours), prohibit child labor, and set a minimum standard wage.

At a speech in New York's Hotel Astor in February 1929, Perkins commented that it was good to be labor commissioner during such prosperous economic times. However, Perkins was aware of troubling undercurrents within her state. Both farmers and the textile industry had been struggling for some time. Then on October 24, 1929, Black Thursday, the stock market crashed. Overnight, Americans who had invested in the market lost most of their money. This crash signaled the start of the Great Depression, the worst economic crisis in U.S. history.

Onset of the Great Depression

Perkins's own words best describe what happened next. In a famous speech, "The Roots of Social Security," delivered on October 23, 1962, when she was eighty-two, Perkins explained: "Since 1929 we had experienced the short, sudden drop of everything. The total economy had gone to pieces; just shook to pieces under us, beginning, of course, with the market crash. A banking crisis followed it. A manufacturing crisis followed it. Everybody felt it. In less than a year it was a terror.... Everything was down. Nobody could get a job."

Perkins soon became disillusioned with President **Herbert Hoover's** (1874–1964; served 1929–33; see entry) attempt to rescue the economy. In late January 1930 Perkins read a report from President Hoover in the *New York Times* that there was a rise in employment and that the economy would soon swing upward. Perkins knew Hoover had not checked his sources and that the figures were false. This so angered Perkins that she held a press conference the next day to show how Hoover's figures were wrong. She had forgotten to ask Governor Roosevelt if he minded her rebuking the president of the United States. Nevertheless, Roosevelt completely supported what she had done. From that time on, newspapers, state officials, and labor leaders checked with Perkins whenever President Hoover issued employment figures.

Secretary of labor

President Hoover, unable to turn around the deepening crisis, was voted out of office on November 8, 1932; Democrat Franklin D. Roosevelt won a landslide victory. On February 28, 1933, Roosevelt announced his choice of Frances Perkins as secretary of labor. Perkins, by then in her early fifties, had accumulated roughly thirty years of experience to bring to the department. With her sixteen-year-old daughter, Susanna, Perkins left New York City by train for Roosevelt's inauguration on March 4, 1933. Perkins began her service that evening. The first woman in a U.S. president's cabinet, she stayed at the post until July 1, 1945, shortly after Roosevelt's death.

In his book *The Coming of the New Deal* (1958) historian Arthur Schlesinger Jr. describes what Perkins had gotten herself into at the Department of Labor:

> Frances Perkins had a keen sense of responsibility about being the first woman member of the cabinet. She had been incongruously given [it was ironic, or surprising, that she had been appointed to] that most masculine of departments, the Department of Labor, redolent [evoking images] of big men with cigars in their mouths and feet on the desk; but she took over with her usual quick competence.

> When subordinates asked her how she should be addressed, she replied, 'Call me Madam Secretary.'... From the beginning she was treated as an equal.

A First for Women

When Frances Perkins became the first woman to serve in the cabinet of a U.S. president, reporters asked the newly appointed secretary of labor if being a woman was a handicap. "Only in climbing trees," she replied. Perkins served at that post for twelve years and four months—longer than any other secretary of labor. Perkins came to Washington, D.C., from New York, where she had been the first woman to serve as industrial commissioner of the Department of Labor.

"Madam Secretary" set about making sure that all of President Roosevelt's early actions moved the administration toward social responsibility. For the next twelve years she remained his closest adviser on social legislation.

A time of action

Perkins's first major role in Washington was with the Civilian Conservation Corps (CCC), a relief program created by the Roosevelt administration to address unemployment. The CCC put unemployed young men to work on public works projects such as soil conservation, planting trees, building small reservoir dams, maintaining roads and trails, and fighting forest fires. Secretary of Labor Perkins was in charge of enrolling men for the program.

Perkins played the lead role in passage of the Social Security Act of 1935. The act was the premier legislation of Roosevelt's presidential years, and it was Perkins's proudest achievement. In June 1934 Roosevelt had created the Committee on Economic Security to make recommendations to him about unemployment insurance and old-age insurance. Perkins headed the committee and provided leadership until Congress passed the Social Security Act. President Roosevelt signed the act in August 1935. Over the next two years Perkins played an important role in developing a package of fair wages and hours. After many legislative battles Congress passed the Fair Labor Standards Act of 1938.

Perkins was responsible for persuading President Roosevelt to make the United States a member of the International Labor Organization. She increasingly gained the respect of union leaders and constantly worked to mediate labor difficulties between workers and management. (A union is an organized group of workers joined together for a common cause, such as negotiating with management for better work-

Frances Perkins, the first woman member of a presidential cabinet, leans in to talk to her close friend President Franklin D. Roosevelt.
©*Bettmann/CORBIS. Reproduced by permission.*

ing conditions or higher wages. If negotiations failed, unions could call strikes, in which the members would cease working for a time.) Perkins worked especially hard for the rights of women workers. She also cleaned up corruption in the U.S. Immigration Service and expanded the activities of the Bureau of Labor Statistics.

Perkins's service as secretary of labor included many rocky and controversial times. Her involvement in the 1934 Pacific Coast longshoremen's strike affected her office through the rest of the 1930s. (Longshoremen load and unload cargo for docked ships.) Several years before the strike Harry Bridges, a native of Australia and leader of the longshoremen, had affiliated himself for a few months with the Communist Party. (Communism is a theory that calls for the elimination of private property so that all goods are common property and available to all the people. Communism is incompatible with the economic system favored by the United States, capitalism, which embraces private ownership.) Communists had come into power in Russia in 1917. The Communist Party USA attempted, in general unsuccessfully, to organize new unions and infiltrate older ones. Many people believed Perkins should have had Bridges deported for his earlier communist ties. Perkins refused. Rumors abounded that Perkins herself was a communist. Ultimately, in 1939, the House Judiciary Committee considered a resolution that Perkins be impeached (removed from office). After conducting an investigation, the committee rejected the resolution.

Life of service continues

Perkins remained the secretary of labor until July 1, 1945, a few months after President Roosevelt's death. President Harry Truman (1884–1972; served 1945–53) called Perkins back into government service the following year. He appointed her as one of the three civil service commissioners who oversee all government employees. Perkins held this post until 1952 when her husband died.

Perkins continued to teach and lecture on labor and industry topics. In the mid-1950s she accepted a visiting professorship at Cornell University, where she taught until shortly before her death in New York City in 1965.

In the last decade of her life Perkins constantly challenged young people to work for the betterment of humankind. In *Frances Perkins: "That Woman in FDR's Cabinet,"* Lillian Holmen Mohr quotes Perkins as Perkins addresses students on the topic of social justice for all: "It is not something to be accomplished before breakfast. It will take years, and the enthusiasm and courage of youth can do much.... It is up to you to contribute some small part to a program of human betterment for all time."

For More Information

Books

Martin, George. *Madam Secretary: Frances Perkins*. Boston, MA: Houghton Mifflin, 1976.

Mohr, Lillian Holmen. *Frances Perkins: "That Woman in FDR's Cabinet."* Croton-on-Hudson, NY: North River Press, 1979.

Pasachoff, Naomi E. *Frances Perkins: Champion of the New Deal*. New York, NY: Oxford University Press, 1999.

Perkins, Frances. *People at Work.* New York, NY: John Day, 1934.

Perkins, Frances. *The Roosevelt I Knew.* New York, NY: Viking Press, 1946.

Schlesinger, Arthur, Jr. *The Coming of the New Deal.* Reprint. Boston, MA: Houghton-Mifflin. 1988.

Severn, Bill. *Frances Perkins: A Member of the Cabinet.* New York, NY: Hawthorne Books, 1976.

Web Sites

Perkins, Frances. "The Roots of Social Security." *Social Security Administration.* http://www.ssa.gov/history/perkins5.html (accessed on September 9, 2002).

United States Department of Labor. http://www.dol.gov/asp/programs/history/perkins.htm (accessed on September 9, 2002).

A. Philip Randolph

Born April 15, 1889
Crescent City, Florida

Died May 16, 1979
New York, New York

Labor and civil rights leader

"As a youngster, Randolph listened to his father's parishioners [church members] complain about the problems of racial prejudice. This exposure, combined with the experience of growing up in segregated Jacksonville [Florida]...raised his consciousness."

Paula F. Pfeffer in A. Philip Randolph: Pioneer of the Civil Rights Movement

A. Philip Randolph. *Courtesy of the Library of Congress.*

A. Philip Randolph was one of the most important black labor leaders of the twentieth century and was highly influential in the civil rights movement of the 1950s and 1960s. Unlike many other black leaders, Randolph sought social justice for black Americans primarily through increased economic opportunities. He formed a number of organizations to raise public awareness of the lack of opportunities in business and education for black Americans. He also organized groups to pressure presidential administrations to improve the situation of blacks. Most notable was the Brotherhood of Sleeping Car Porters union, organized in 1925.

The stock market crash in late 1929 devastated the American economy, triggering an economic crisis known as the Great Depression (1929–41) that lasted throughout the 1930s. Black Americans were severely affected. Jobs traditionally held by blacks were given to desperate unemployed whites, and the unemployment rate of black Americans soared as high as 80 percent in some cities. Throughout the 1930s Randolph worked to improve labor conditions for his fellow black Americans. In 1935 the Brotherhood of Sleeping Car

Porters became the first black union to be recognized as a legal bargaining unit (could negotiate working conditions and wages with company management). In the 1940s Randolph was the main force behind ending segregation in the military. While continuing his efforts on behalf of black workers, Randolph became a key figure in the civil rights movement of the 1950s and 1960s. At the massive black freedom march on August 28, 1963, in Washington, D.C., Randolph spoke just before Dr. Martin Luther King Jr. (1929–1968), who on that day delivered his famed "I Have a Dream" speech.

Early life

Randolph was the second of two sons born to a poor black family in Florida. His father was a minister who traveled to various small, poor churches and also worked as a tailor to make ends meet. The family focused on religion and education. Randolph entered a Methodist school for young black men, Cookman Institute, in 1903 and excelled. He showed particular skill at drama, public speaking, singing, and literature. Randolph was also a good athlete. He graduated in 1907 at the top of his class. While working at minor jobs around Jacksonville, Florida, following graduation, he also gave public readings, sang, and acted in plays. Ready for a new start away from the South's strict segregation, Randolph headed to Harlem in New York City in April 1911. There he held various jobs, working as a waiter, a porter, and an elevator operator, and he began participating in a theater club. Tackling difficult Shakespearean plays, Randolph developed public speaking skills that he used for much of his life. Randolph met his future wife while participating in the theater group, and they married in November 1914. They did not have children.

Under pressure from his parents, Randolph gave up his pursuit of an acting career and enrolled in City College of New York, which offered a free education for those who were considered financially or intellectually deserving. At the college, Randolph became interested in politics. He organized his own political action group, the Independent Political Council.

A shift into politics

While a student in New York City Randolph became close friends with Chandler Owen, a student at Columbia

Law School. They were intrigued and influenced by the Industrial Workers of the World (IWW), a labor union that fought hard in the early twentieth century for more-humane working conditions such as a forty-hour workweek, considered an extreme idea in the 1910s. Randolph and Owen both joined the Socialist Party in late 1916. Members of the Socialist Party advocate social reform supporting the rights of individual citizens over the interests of big business. Unafraid to speak out about their beliefs, the youthful Randolph and Owen often stood on the street corner of Lenox Avenue and 135th Street promoting the ideas of socialism and calling for blacks to join unions. But to most blacks socialism represented a white man's idea with no practical application. Many black Americans were actually antiunion, because they needed the jobs the striking workers left open. In 1917 Randolph organized a union of elevator operators. Also, through much of that year Randolph and Owen were hired to publish *Hotel Messenger,* a newsletter for the Headwaiters and Sidewaiters Society of Greater New York. After eight months Randolph was fired from his publication duties when black Americans lost control of the organization. Randolph and Owen then created their own magazine called simply the *Messenger,* in November 1917. The *Messenger* became a highly respected black journal and was published until 1928. Its peak of circulation was in 1919 with 26,000 readers. The publication expressed many controversial views, including criticism of black leaders for their cooperation with and reliance on white leaders. Randolph and Owen were arrested and briefly jailed for their antiwar views in 1918 during World War I (1914–18). They also organized the first socialist club in Harlem, the Friends of Negro Freedom, and both unsuccessfully ran for public offices.

By the mid-1920s Randolph's enterprises had lost steam. He had tried organizing black workers but without great success. Then in 1925 Randolph was invited to speak to a group of porters about trade unions. The porters were employed by the Pullman Company to assist railroad passengers with luggage, provide food service, and other conveniences for the travelers. A short while later the porters asked Randolph to organize a union for them; he accepted. On August 25, 1925, Randolph introduced the Brotherhood of Sleeping Car Porters at a mass meeting.

Union leader

Heading the Brotherhood, Randolph proved skillful in working with various groups of people. By 1928 the Brotherhood had joined the American Federation of Labor (AFL), a federation of labor unions representing various types of skilled craftspeople. With the onset of the Great Depression the union had difficulty achieving its goals, such as higher wages and better working conditions. Then in 1933 the newly elected president, **Franklin Roosevelt** (1882–1945; served 1933–45; see entry), introduced a policy under the National Industrial Recovery Act (NIRA) that recognized unions as formal, legal groups. Finally, in the summer of 1935 the Brotherhood gained recognition as the legal bargaining agent for Pullman's porters. It was the first black union to gain such recognition by an industry. However, it would take two more years of negotiation between the Brotherhood and Pullman before agreement on working conditions was achieved on August 25, 1937. The agreement was a major victory, bringing

A. Philip Randolph, right, and other officials of the Pullman Porter's and Conductor's Union in the 1939 Labor Day parade in New York City. *©Joseph Schwartz Collection/CORBIS. Reproduced by permission.*

an additional $2 million in wages to the porters. This victory greatly increased Randolph's prestige.

Despite his union victories, Randolph maintained an even broader vision of social change for black Americans. He continued to stress that blacks could only achieve social and racial equality after making substantial economic progress. In 1935 Howard University in Washington, D.C., hosted a conference on the economic condition of black America. Out of the conference emerged the National Negro Congress (NNC), an organization bringing together all existing black political groups to press for economic recovery. Randolph was its first president. Randolph remained a leader in the NNC until 1940 when, believing the Communist Party had gained too much influence in the organization, he resigned.

Increased economic opportunities

By 1940 as the United States got closer to entering World War II (1939–45), American factories increasingly shifted from the production of domestic goods to production of war materials. This wartime industry created many new jobs and began to rapidly pull white Americans out of the economic troubles of the Depression. However, black Americans were not benefiting from the new job growth, and many remained on unemployment relief rolls. Racial discrimination in employment and housing was pronounced, and the armed forces were segregated. To protest the lack of access to jobs in the defense industries, Randolph formed a coalition of black organizations to march on Washington, D.C., in the summer of 1941. Not relishing the prospect of a hundred thousand protesters converging on the capital, President Roosevelt tried to convince Randolph to call off the event. But Randolph held fast that black Americans must get better economic opportunities. Finally, in late June, Roosevelt relented and issued a presidential order prohibiting discrimination in defense industries. The order also created the Fair Employment Practices Committee (FEPC) to oversee progress in black employment and to hold hearings when complaints surfaced. Although the order did not end segregation in the armed forces, it did convince Randolph to call off the march. Randolph's coalition staged a number of mass rallies around the nation the following summer, further promoting black economic opportunities.

Fair Employment Practices Committee

One of A. Philip Randolph's key accomplishments during his long career was pressing President Franklin D. Roosevelt to establish an official policy that would prohibit racial discrimination in some industries and create an agency to investigate discrimination complaints. Discouraged and angered by the lack of jobs for blacks in the rapidly growing war industries in 1940 and early 1941, Randolph began organizing a major protest march on the nation's capital; the march was scheduled for the summer of 1941. Roosevelt wanted to avoid a potential crowd of one hundred thousand black American protesters descending on a highly racially segregated Washington, D.C. The president was trying to build strong unity in the nation to support the upcoming war effort. Therefore, Roosevelt desperately tried to convince Randolph to cancel his plans. An unrelenting Randolph only intensified his demands for better opportunities for black Americans in industry and the military. President Roosevelt finally issued a formal presidential order on June 25, 1941, prohibiting racial discrimination in employment in defense industries and creating the Fair Employment Practices Committee (FEPC).

Given little funding, few actual powers, and a small staff, the FEPC was primarily formed to hold public hearings on complaints about discrimination in defense industries and to develop policies for Roosevelt and Congress to consider. The FEPC could only use persuasion and publicity to pressure defense contractors to comply with the presidential order. Roosevelt gave the committee little public support, for fear of antagonizing Southern political leaders. After a June 1942 FEPC hearing in Birmingham, Alabama, Southerners became so angry with the FEPC that Roosevelt assigned the committee to the War Manpower Commission. As part of a regularly funded agency, Congress now had greater control over FEPC activities and, in particular, the funding to sustain it. Overwhelmed with continuing controversy, by 1943 the FEPC was no longer functional. Later that year Roosevelt replaced the FEPC with the Committee on Fair Employment Practices. The committee had greater powers and a larger staff than the FEPC had had. Roosevelt also banned discrimination by all government contractors, not just the defense industry. The new committee lasted another two years before being disbanded.

After the war Randolph renewed the campaign to end segregation in the armed forces. He formed the League for Nonviolent Civil Disobedience Against Military Segregation, and he applied pressure to President Harry Truman (1884–1972; served 1945–53), who needed the black vote in the upcoming presidential election. In July 1948 Truman signed a presidential order ending racial segregation in the military. It was another milestone for Randolph.

However, progress toward further increasing black influence in the labor movement was very slow. In the 1950s the American Federation of Labor (AFL) member unions finally began accepting black members. When the AFL and the Congress of Industrial Organizations (CIO) joined together in 1955, they forged a much more progressive position on black participation. Randolph became one of two blacks on the new AFL-CIO Executive Council.

Elder statesman

Randolph was recognized as an elder statesman of black America and had a direct influence on the growing postwar civil rights movement. One of the proudest moments in Randolph's career came in August 1963. He was the national director in charge of organizing a march on Washington, D.C. Over two hundred thousand Americans—blacks and whites—would participate, seeking an end to discrimination in the United States. At this gathering in front of the Lincoln Memorial on August 28, 1963, Randolph delivered his last major public speech. He was followed at the podium by Dr. Martin Luther King Jr. who delivered his epic "I Have a Dream" civil rights speech. Just as President Roosevelt had done in 1941, President John F. Kennedy (1917–1963; served 1961–63) had tried to convince Randolph to call off the event. But this time Randolph had decided the march needed to take place.

By the mid-1960s the AFL-CIO became a strong supporter of the civil rights movement and legislation prohibiting racial discrimination in the workplace. The labor organization also became a key sponsor of the A. Philip Randolph Institute, established by Randolph in 1964. The institute was charged with keeping an eye on black affairs in labor and with improving ties between labor and civil rights organizations.

After being mugged outside his Harlem apartment building in the summer of 1968, Randolph's health deteriorated through the late 1960s and 1970s. In 1968 he resigned as president of the Brotherhood and from the AFL-CIO Executive Council. Randolph received an honorary degree from

Harvard University in 1971. He died at the age of ninety in New York City in May 1979.

In 1989 the U.S. Postal Service issued a stamp for Black Heritage Month with Randolph's likeness on it. Randolph followed a unique path in his career. While most black leaders climbed to prominence as religious leaders or educators, Randolph first gained recognition for his work on behalf of black Americans in the labor movement. Randolph is remembered as a man of great integrity by both blacks and whites.

For More Information

Anderson, Jervis. *A. Philip Randolph: A Biographical Portrait.* New York, NY: Harcourt Brace Jovanovich, 1973.

Davis, Daniel S. *Mr. Black Labor: The Story of A. Philip Randolph, Father of the Civil Rights Movement.* New York, NY: E. P. Dutton, 1972.

Pfeffer, Paula F. *A. Philip Randolph: Pioneer of the Civil Rights Movement.* Baton Rouge, LA: Louisiana State University Press, 1990.

Will Rogers

Born November 4, 1879
Oologah, Oklahoma Indian Territory

Died August 15, 1935
Point Barrow, Alaska

Entertainer, social commentator

"Will Rogers had the general demeanor of a common man, self-elected representative of the world's underdogs. He was an 'Aw shucks' guy."

Ray Robinson in American Original: A Life of Will Rogers

Will Rogers.
©Bettmann/CORBIS.
Reproduced by permission.

Will Rogers was a national voice of the common person between 1929 and 1935 during the harshest period of the Great Depression, the worst economic crisis in U.S. history. Rogers conquered most of the media available at the time. He seemed equally at home on stage and on the movie screen, in print, and on the radio. He starred in Wild West shows, vaudeville, silent and talking movies, and radio programs, and he wrote a regular newspaper column. Vaudeville was a popular form of stage entertainment in the United States from the late nineteenth century to the mid-1920s with each show featuring a collection of various acts including dancing, singing, comedy, and acting. More than anyone else in American history, Rogers popularized Western cowboy humor. Though quite literate and well-read, Rogers put on a lesser-educated country image, exaggerating his Southwestern accent and using bad grammar. Rogers was not associated with any political party during most of his career. However, he liked President **Franklin D. Roosevelt** (1882–1945; served 1933–45; see entry), and through his public commentary Rogers supported many of the federal programs Roosevelt designed to help the United States recover economically.

Rogers's life was tragically cut short in a plane crash in Alaska. With his death Americans lost a voice of support and optimism during a time of national crisis.

A born cowboy

William Penn Adair Rogers was born in 1879 in Indian Territory, which in 1907 would become the state of Oklahoma. He was one-quarter Cherokee. His mother was Mary America Schrimsher and his father Clement Vann Rogers. Both were forty years old when Will, the last of eight children, was born. Will's father, known as "Uncle Clem," was a judge and banker and was prominent in Oklahoma politics. He was fairly well-to-do with five thousand head of cattle and many horses on his ranch near the rural town of Oologah. Rogers County, Oklahoma, was named after him. Young Will began riding at a very early age. Through his father, Will was well exposed to local and national politics. However, he was closest to his mother, inheriting her friendliness, gentle manner, and good sense of humor. Mary died of dysentery, an infectious intestinal disease, at age fifty-one in 1890, leaving eleven-year-old Will with a lasting feeling of loss.

Even though young Will was an above average student and had a particular interest in history, he had a strong dislike for structured education and was always restless. He attended high school at a private boarding school called Scarritt College. Known as the campus cutup, Will often got himself into trouble with poor grades and clowning behavior, and he left school without graduating. When he was fourteen, his father took him to the Chicago World's Fair. There he saw Buffalo Bill's Wild West Show and was particularly taken with a Mexican performer billed as the "greatest roper in the world." This experience significantly influenced his later life.

Will's family sent him to Kemper Military School in Missouri to finish his schooling. Not surprisingly, Will was a bad fit for a military school, never dressing properly, always late, and often amusing his classmates by his irreverence toward staff. After two years at Kemper, he ran away in 1898 and began working as a cowboy on a ranch near Higgins, Texas, breaking horses and rounding up cattle. After a brief period, Rogers returned home to manage cattle on the family ranch, but he was soon restless again. Looking for something more adventuresome, in 1902 Rogers left for Argentina, South America, where he briefly tried the cowboy life again. However, he found the wages too low. Seeing an announcement for jobs with a Wild West show in South Africa, Rogers caught a ship and made the long journey. In South Africa he began his entertainment career by performing as the "Cherokee Kid" in the traveling Texas Jack's Wild West Show. Rogers rode horses and performed roping feats with a lariat, or lasso. From South Africa he followed the Wild West Show to Australia and New Zealand. Rogers represented the youthful American frontier spirit to these overseas audiences.

Upon returning home in 1904, Rogers traveled to the St. Louis World's Fair and then on to New York City looking for performing jobs. He found jobs with various Wild West shows and became a quick hit with New York audiences. However, the popularity of Wild West shows was declining, while interest in American vaudeville acts—which combined singing, dancing, and comedy—was increasing. By 1907 Rogers began performing regularly for the Ziegfeld Follies, a popular vaudeville act in New York City. For the first eight years he would perform in a secondary stage group for Ziegfeld. With a steady job, in 1908 Rogers married Betty Blake, his sweetheart of the past decade. They had three sons, one of whom died in infancy, and one daughter.

Beyond rope tricks

While doing his rope tricks with the Ziegfeld Follies, Rogers began chatting to the audience. He found that his Southwestern accent captivated people and brought unexpected laughter. By 1916 Rogers had moved up into the main Ziegfeld Follies stage group and transformed his act into a talking act. He became a favorite of the Follies. Before long he started making pointed comments about politicians and public figures. A major turning point came in a Baltimore, Maryland, performance. Rogers decided to make some humorous comments about the U.S. policy toward Mexico. His comments were well received by the audience, including one especially important person—President Woodrow Wilson

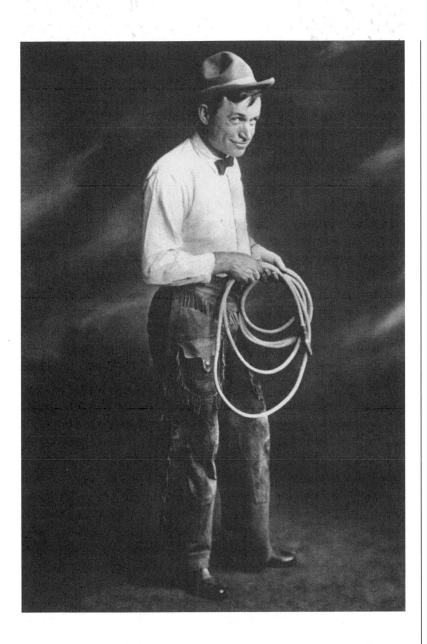

(1856–1924; served 1913–21). Rogers's career as a social commentator had begun in earnest. He continued to perfect his act, posing as a cowboy straight off the range, detached from the newly emerging modern U.S. city values. He freely commented on what he observed firsthand and what he read in the newspapers. With his storytelling and commentary, Rogers further cemented his position as the star attraction of the Follies.

Rogers's stage popularity led him to starring roles in motion pictures in 1918, when Goldwyn Pictures signed him for Hollywood silent movies. By 1929 Rogers had made forty-eight silent movies, mostly comedies and travel films. None was considered particularly memorable, but by 1924 his annual income was $160,000. When talking movies arrived, Rogers's career took off. Signed by Fox Studios, he first appeared in *They Had to See Paris,* a talkie released in September 1929. Many of his best movies through the early 1930s were directed by the legendary John Ford (1895–1973). Rogers routinely ignored scripts and improvised; he refused makeup and props. His popularity soared, and one reviewer commented in 1933, "He is what Americans think other Americans are like." By 1933 Rogers ranked ninth on the list of box-office stars earning $200,000 per movie. As the Depression deepened, many credited Rogers and child actress Shirley Temple (1928–) with saving Fox from bankruptcy.

Rogers's writing career began in 1919 when Harper Brothers published two short books of his observations. In 1920 Rogers added journalism to his activities when a news syndicate hired him to cover the political party conventions that year. By 1922 Rogers began writing a newspaper column titled "Will Rogers Says," which became a daily feature in 1926. Forty million readers faithfully followed his column. Rogers would often sit in the backseat of his car with his typewriter, writing his column. He was so popular that in December 1926 he was made honorary mayor of Beverly Hills, California, the first mayor for that community.

Other writing jobs came along. The *Saturday Evening Post* sent Rogers abroad on special assignments to Europe and Russia in 1927 and to the Far East in 1934. Continuing his stage performances with the Follies, Rogers also took to the lecture circuit and even starred in a Broadway play. The play, *Three Cheers,* ran from late 1928 through June 1929 and was a big hit. For his lectures he received $1,500 per appearance, including one at Carnegie Hall. He would typically stroll around the stage while talking, occasionally sitting on the edge of a stool placed to one side.

One more communication medium was left to conquer: radio. In the early 1930s Rogers began broadcasting on the radio and quickly became a popular radio personality. Be-

Rogers on Roosevelt

Will Rogers expressed a liking for Franklin D. Roosevelt as early as 1928, when Roosevelt was running for governor of New York. As Roosevelt progressed toward the presidency, Rogers became increasingly political. He missed few opportunities to praise Roosevelt, carefully balancing the needling in his act with positive comments. Late in Roosevelt's first presidential campaign, on September 23, 1932, Rogers made the following comment while introducing Roosevelt to a crowd at the Hollywood Bowl in California: "I'm wasting no oratory [speech] on you tonight. You're just a mere prospect. Come back when you are president and I'll do better."

Following Roosevelt's election victory several weeks later on November 8, Rogers advised Roosevelt, "Don't worry too much—and don't forget that a smile will look like a meal to us." This comment was a reference to Roosevelt's characteristic big, optimistic smiles, which were a welcome contrast to the more reserved, stern expressions of then-President Herbert Hoover. Rogers had grown to greatly dislike President Hoover's limited response to the country's economic problems. After Roosevelt's inauguration on March 4, 1933, Rogers commented, "The whole country is with him. Even if what he does is wrong, they are with him, just as long as he does something. If he burned down the Capitol, they would cheer and say, 'Well, at least he got a fire started, anyhow!'" Several days later on March 13, while Roosevelt was working on solving the nation's banking crisis, Rogers commented on a key radio speech made by the new president: "Mr. Roosevelt stepped to the microphone last night and knocked another home run. His message was not only a great comfort to the people, but it pointed a lesson to all radio announcers and public speakers what to do with a big vocabulary—leave it at home in the dictionary." The Roosevelts greatly appreciated Rogers's support and invited Rogers and his wife and daughter for an evening at the White House in February 1934.

sides his regular network shows, he was hired by Gulf Oil Company to do seven additional shows between April 1933 and June 1935.

Rogers's public appeal

Will Rogers's popularity in so many mediums was astounding. He always preached the traditional values of being neighborly and treating everyone equally. In all the mediums he consistently came across as friendly and honest, and he al-

The Wisdom of Will Rogers

Will Rogers was noted for one-liner jokes during his commentaries and during interviews. Here is a small sample of some of the more famous comments.

"My epitaph: Here lies Will Rogers. Politicians turned honest and he starved to death." (Rogers made his living by making witty observations about political issues and dishonest politicians.)

"Spinnin' a rope's a lotta fun, providin' your neck ain't in it." (Rogers's first performing act included riding horses and doing rope tricks.)

"Americans are the most generous, kind-hearted people on earth as long as they're convinced not one dollar of it is going for taxes." (Rogers was referring to wealthy Americans who opposed President Roosevelt's government-funded relief programs.)

"We are the first nation in the history of the world to go to the poorhouse in an automobile." (In the United States the rise of the automobile occurred just as the nation plummeted into a deep economic crisis.)

"You can't say civilization don't advance because in every war they kill you in a new way."

"He [President Calvin Coolidge, a Republican who served from 1923 to 1929] didn't do anything, but that's what the people wanted done." (The Republican Party philosophy in the 1920s involved letting business operate free of regulation and providing little assistance to the struggling farm economy.)

ways made people laugh. He also proved very shrewd by focusing public attention on key national issues at opportune moments, such as Prohibition (the national ban on the sale and manufacture of alcoholic beverages; 1920–33) and foreign relations following World War I (1914–18). Rogers knew how far to push a joke before it would be considered in bad taste. Many Americans saw Rogers as a reassuring link to traditional America during a period of substantial social and economic change in the 1920s and then during the severe economic crisis of the 1930s Great Depression. Rogers was so popular that national figures often felt honored to be the subject of his comments.

When the Depression arrived, Rogers changed his tone and became less critical of government. He tried to provide more optimism to the millions of people hit hard by the Depression. Rogers had routinely stayed away from any alignment with a political party. However, as the Depression worsened, he became increasingly critical of President **Herbert Hoover's** (1874–1964; served 1929–33; see entry) limited response to the people's plight. After Franklin Roosevelt took over as president in March 1933, Rogers promoted some of Roosevelt's New Deal social and economic programs in his commentary. At the same time he enjoyed ridiculing the elitism of Roosevelt's small group of advisers, known as the **Brain Trust** (see entry), who wielded great political power under the president's guidance. In 1934 the Democrats urged the popular Rogers to run for governor of California, but he declined, claiming he would rather be a bad actor than a bad governor.

A career tragically ended

In August 1935 at the peak of Rogers's career, his life came to a sudden end. He had just signed a new contract with Fox Studios to star in ten movies for $1.1 million. He was killed in a small plane crash on Point Barrow, Alaska, while on his way to the Far East. His death was a tragedy felt by millions across the nation. He had made an enormous amount of money during the Great Depression but had contributed much to charities to help the poor. Soon after his death the State of Oklahoma built the Will Rogers Memorial Museum in Claremore. The museum opened in 1938, and it was expanded and remodeled by 1995. When Rogers's wife, Betty, died in 1944, his ranch in Santa Monica was donated to the State of California to become a state park. Betty's and Will's bodies were taken to Oklahoma, where they were buried together at the Claremore museum. A life-size bronze statue of Rogers was placed in Statutory Hall in the Capitol in Washington, D.C.

For More Information

Books

Day, Donald, ed. *The Autobiography of Will Rogers*. Boston, MA: Houghton Mifflin, 1949.

Gragert, Steven K., ed. *Radio Broadcasts of Will Rogers*. Stillwater, OK: Oklahoma State University, 1983.

Ketchum, Richard M. *Will Rogers: His Life and Times*. New York, NY: American Heritage, 1973.

Robinson, Ray. *American Original: A Life of Will Rogers*. New York, NY: Oxford University Press, 1996.

Rogers, Betty. *Will Rogers: His Wife's Story*. Norman, OK: University of Oklahoma Press, 1979.

Web Sites

The Will Rogers Homepage. http://www.willrogers.org (accessed on September 9, 2002).

Eleanor Roosevelt

Born October 11, 1884
New York, New York

Died November 7, 1962
Hyde Park, New York

First Lady of the United States,
social activist

Eleanor Roosevelt served as First Lady from March 1933 to April 1945, longer than any other president's wife. She was also one of the first First Ladies to work for social reforms both in the United States and worldwide. Checking on conditions throughout the nation, she was President **Franklin D. Roosevelt's** (1882–1945; served 1933–45; see entry) "eyes and ears." In the United States she promoted better working conditions for men and women, the elimination of child labor, and racial desegregation. Internationally, she challenged injustice and discrimination wherever she found them. Eleanor served as the first U.S. delegate to the United Nations from 1945 to 1951.

Privileged but lonely childhood

Anna Eleanor Roosevelt was born in New York City to Elliott Roosevelt and Anna Hall Roosevelt. Both of her parents came from wealthy families who were prominent in New York society. Elliott's family was less concerned with formal society than Anna's; they donated some of their wealth to help peo-

"I think I must have a good deal of my uncle Theodore Roosevelt in me because I enjoy a good fight and I could not at any age really be contented to take my place in a warm corner by the fireside and simply look on."

Eleanor Roosevelt in The Autobiography of Eleanor Roosevelt

Eleanor Roosevelt. *AP/Wide World Photo. Reproduced by permission.*

ple such as newsboys on the streets of New York and the handicapped being aided by pioneering medical doctors. Elliott was dashing, witty, and loved by all. He was indulged by his mother and sisters and used his inheritance to travel on exotic expeditions such as hunting in India. His older brother Theodore would become president of the United States in 1901. Elliott married Anna Hall, who belonged to the old, traditional, and self-important New York society circle. Anna was beautiful and charming and a star within the social world. She dined and danced with only the right people.

Anna Eleanor was born in October 1884, and as she herself puts it in her autobiography, she was a "more wrinkled and less attractive baby than the average." Elliott adored young Eleanor, but her mother was dismayed with her daughter's looks and often called her "granny," which greatly embarrassed Eleanor. For unexplained reasons, Elliott developed a drinking problem. With great anxiety the family unsuccessfully attempted to help Elliott recover; the drinking was destroying his health. In December 1892 Anna suddenly contracted diphtheria and died. Elliott arranged for Grandmother Hall to take in Eleanor and her two younger brothers, Elliott and Hall. The three children and a nurse moved into the West Thirty-seventh Street house in New York City. Another tragedy struck the family later the same winter. Little Elliott died of diphtheria, just as his mother had. Eight-year-old Eleanor lived for visits from her father and dreamed of the day when she and her brother and father could all live together again. But Elliott's drinking problem continued, and on August 14, 1894, when Eleanor was nine years old, her beloved father died.

Discipline was strict in Grandmother Hall's house, and as an adult Eleanor remembered being forever fearful of displeasing people. Her grandmother raised Eleanor more out of duty than out of love. From her childhood Eleanor learned she was unattractive and that love and approval were hard to come by and not likely to last. As an adult she would constantly have to overcome self-doubt and the fear that she would not measure up.

Accompanying various relatives on charity missions at Thanksgiving and Christmas, Eleanor became aware at an early age that there were many needy people in the community. Eleanor experienced great joy in helping others. It gave her a sense of purpose and usefulness.

In 1899 at the age of fifteen Eleanor sailed to England to enroll in Allenswood, a school close to London, England, and under the direction of French headmistress Marie Souvestre. Souvestre was a strong, liberal-minded woman, partial to Americans, and was perhaps the first to see the intellect and compassion of the tall, slender young Eleanor. She chose Eleanor to accompany her on travels through Europe during school breaks. Souvestre taught Eleanor about the world of art, encouraged her to think for herself, and stressed service to the less fortunate. In later life Eleanor often credited Souvestre as starting her down a road of increased self-confidence.

In 1902 Eleanor returned to New York because her family insisted she participate in the formal New York social scene. She also began work that winter in Junior League and for the first time worked at a house for the poor, Rivington Street Settlement House. During this time Eleanor's distant cousin Franklin Roosevelt began to court her. He attended occasional dances on the social circuit that winter, and Eleanor was invited to a party at his Hyde Park home. He was attracted by her intelligence and caring—and also, no doubt, by the fact that she was the niece of President Theodore Roosevelt (1858–1919; served 1901–09), a man he greatly admired. Franklin proposed in the fall of 1903, and they married on March 17, 1905, with President Theodore Roosevelt giving Eleanor away. The newly married couple first lived in a small apartment in a hotel in the West Forties of New York City while Franklin finished at Columbia Law School.

Mrs. Roosevelt

After traveling in Europe, Eleanor and Franklin returned to New York to a house at 125 East Fifty-sixth Street. Eleanor's mother-in-law, Sara Delano Roosevelt, had already hired their servants and decorated their house. Sara had a domineering personality, which Eleanor would begin to resent after a few years. Eleanor settled in as a young society matron dependent on others, with all decisions made for her. On May 3, 1906, Eleanor's first child, a baby girl named Anna Eleanor (1906–1975), was born. Eleanor and Franklin would have five more children. One died in infancy; the other four, all boys, were James (1907–), Elliott (1910–), Franklin Delano Jr. (1914–1988), and John (1916–1981).

Eleanor's first taste of politics came in 1910, when Franklin was elected to a seat in the New York State Senate. Then three years later he was appointed assistant secretary of the navy in President Woodrow Wilson's administration. Although she would always contend with shyness, Eleanor began to acquire some independence as she oversaw frequent travels involving the whole young family between Washington, D.C., Hyde Park, and her mother-in-law's vacation home on Campobello, an island near Eastport, Maine. Highly outgoing, Franklin enjoyed the Washington social life, but Eleanor found the endless string of teas, dinners, and parties meaningless and tiring.

On April 6, 1917, the United States entered into World War I (1914–18). For the first time since before her marriage, Eleanor began to do volunteer work again and was thankful that the formal teas and parties had stopped for the moment. She joined the Red Cross canteen, helped organize the Navy Red Cross, and, for the Navy League, distributed raw wool to be knit into clothing for the men in the services. The joy she had felt at a much younger age in helping others returned. She also learned she could quite capably manage groups of people working for a common cause. The war came to an end on November 11, 1918. However, an unhappy revelation in September had caused Eleanor's personal world to fall apart. Eleanor discovered that Franklin had fallen in love with her own young, beautiful, and capable personal secretary, Lucy Mercer. As was the social custom, Eleanor gave Franklin the option of divorce. Franklin declined a divorce and promised never to see Lucy again. Nevertheless, Eleanor's self-pride and confidence were severely tested. The old childhood insecurities about her unattractiveness and worthiness to be loved took over for a while. However, this personal marital crisis actually worked to set free a strong and determined woman who was ready to craft an independent public identity.

Her compassion for others and her management skills, together with the family name, launched Eleanor on a life path of social reform and political activism. During the 1920s Eleanor would become a leader in four New York groups: the League of Women Voters; the Women's City Club and the Women's Trade Union League, both groups seeking better working conditions for women; and the Women's Division of the New York State Democratic Committee.

Into the political spotlight

Franklin resigned his position as assistant secretary of the navy in the summer of 1920 to accept the Democratic nomination as the vice presidential candidate and running mate of presidential nominee James M. Cox (1870–1957). Franklin proved extremely popular with Democrats. The nomination put Eleanor in the national spotlight. Although both Eleanor and Franklin made numerous campaign trips, the election was lost to Warren G. Harding (1865–1923; served 1921–23). Franklin returned with his family to New York City and formed a law partnership with Grenville Emmet and Langdon Marvin.

In the summer of 1921 Franklin's life took a sudden dramatic turn. He was diagnosed with polio, a disease that caused paralysis of his legs. Franklin withdrew from public life to recuperate. For the next seven years Eleanor and his friend and adviser Louis Howe (1871–1936) kept him informed on issues until he could return to politics. Eleanor often said she was Franklin's "legs and eyes" during his years of healing.

As her association with the Women's City Club, the Women's Trade Union League, and the New York State Democratic Committee increased, Eleanor developed friendships with many women activists, including **Molly Dewson** (1874–1962; see entry), head of the newly formed Women's Division of the Democratic National Committee. When Franklin Roosevelt became president in 1933, Dewson and Eleanor were instrumental in getting women appointed to influential government posts.

In 1926 Franklin planned and had built for Eleanor a cottage, called Val-Kill, on the Hyde Park property. Eleanor spent much time there with Nancy Cook and Marion Dickerman, two friends who were leaders in Dewson's Women's Division. Cook and Dickerman both resided at Val-Kill. Together they operated an Early American furniture manufacturing

company. In addition, the threesome bought Todhunter School in New York City, a private school for girls from elementary grades through high school. Eleanor began teaching the older girls in 1927 in American history, English, literature, and current events. In the current events courses Eleanor took students into New York courtrooms and into tenements. She wanted students to see the city as a real place—alive—rather than just seeing it through textbooks. Eleanor began to make a few political speeches on her own. Louis Howe would sit in the back of the room and evaluate her effectiveness and advise her. Eleanor also reported back to the much improved Franklin what the public thinking was on various issues. Franklin would depend on her for input for the rest of his life.

Eleanor Roosevelt helps feed the unemployed at a New York City soup kitchen in December 1932. *AP/Wide World Photo. Reproduced by permission.*

In the spring of 1928 Franklin had recovered his health, but he could walk only with extreme difficulty, with the aid of heavy braces and a cane. Franklin ran and won the 1928 governor's race in New York, and the Roosevelts moved to Albany, New York's capital, on January 1, 1929. Eleanor's life was consumed with being a mother and a governor's wife, and with teaching, which she continued to do two and a half days a week by traveling to New York City during the first half of each week. Eleanor also learned to be an expert reporter, describing conditions and situations to her husband when his disability prevented him from going and seeing all himself. Eleanor explains in her autobiography, *The Autobiography of Eleanor Roosevelt:*

> Walking was so difficult for him that he could not go inside an institution and get a real idea of how it was being run from the point of view of overcrowding, staff, food, and medical care. I was asked to take over this part of the inspection, and at first my reports were highly unsatisfactory to him. I would tell him what was on the menu for the day and he would ask: "Did you look to see whether the inmates were ac-

tually getting that food?" I learned to look into the cooking pots on the stove and to find out if the contents corresponded to the menu.... Before the end of our years in Albany I had become a fairly expert reporter.

First Lady and role model

In 1932 Franklin ran as the Democratic presidential candidate and won handily over Republican president **Herbert Hoover** (1874–1964; served 1929–33; see entry). Franklin Roosevelt was inaugurated as the thirty-second president of the United States on March 4, 1933, when the nation was at the depth of the Great Depression. Beginning with the stock market crash in the fall of 1929, the Great Depression had become the worst economic crisis in U.S. history. Approximately 25 percent of the nation's workforce was unemployed, and many Americans did not have enough food.

Eleanor approached being the First Lady with great apprehension. She feared losing her hard-won independence as a teacher and political activist. However, Eleanor would soon set the standard for political and social involvement against which future First Ladies would be measured. Even further, she became a role model for women actively involved in their communities and nation.

One of Eleanor's early innovations was to hold a weekly press conference for women journalists only. This required the media organizations to keep women on staff in Washington, D.C., and ensured that some of the nation's news was written from a woman's point of view. Eleanor began holding the conferences at the suggestion of journalist **Lorena Hickok** (1893–1968; see entry), a close friend who also became a trusted adviser to Eleanor in the 1930s. The press conferences continued throughout Franklin Roosevelt's presidency.

Champion for youth, women, and minorities

Eleanor believed it was the government's responsibility to aid people struggling through the Depression. She traveled around the country to observe firsthand the predicament of the American people. Besides reporting her observations to

Eleanor Roosevelt felt it was important to have firsthand contact with the American people. Here, she distributes Christmas gifts to needy children on December 24, 1934. *AP/Wide World Photo. Reproduced by permission.*

her husband, she made sure that people who would not normally have access to the president gained his attention. Throughout Eleanor's time as First Lady thousands of individuals wrote personal letters to her about their troubles. She often passed requests on to the appropriate agency and answered many letters personally. Eleanor's energy and tireless work became legendary. She was determined that no group who needed New Deal projects would be left out. (The New Deal was the name given to the programs Roosevelt's administration designed to bring relief, recovery, and reform to the United States during the Depression.)

Eleanor supported appointments of women to government positions, and she was a strong voice in support of women's opportunities in general. She also promoted aid to young people, relief for miners trapped in some of the worst conditions of the Depression, and the civil rights of black Americans. Eleanor worked with others to ensure that programs for women were included in the New Deal's Works

Progress Administration (WPA), which created work projects for people on relief. Likewise, programs in the National Youth Administration (NYA) benefited from her input. She believed that young people had a right to be heard and to be assisted by Washington. Eleanor worked with officials from the National Association for the Advancement of Colored People (NAACP) and supported federal antilynching laws that her husband had failed to endorse for fear of losing Southern votes. And in 1937, in a famous action that proclaimed her support for black Americans, she resigned her membership in the Daughters of the American Revolution (DAR) when the group refused to allow black singer Marian Anderson (1897–1993) to perform in Constitution Hall in Washington, D.C. The concert later took place on the steps of the Lincoln Memorial, where thousands heard Anderson sing.

By late 1940, following President Roosevelt's election to a third term in office, the nation's focus had shifted to preparation for war. In late 1941 the United States entered World War II (1939–45), effectively ending the Depression with the creation of many war-related jobs—more jobs than could be filled. Eleanor received a steady line of foreign visitors at the White House. In her autobiography she noted, "All the royal families whose countries had been overrun sooner or later appeared, looking for assistance."

Eleanor soon undertook extensive trips abroad. She went first to England in 1942 at the invitation of Elizabeth (1900–2002), wife of King George VI (1895–1952), to see what work the women were doing in the war and to visit U.S. servicemen. In 1943 Eleanor traveled to the South Pacific islands, New Zealand, and Australia. Although conditions were dangerous, she visited troops on Guadalcanal. Walking many miles in hospital wards each day, Eleanor had to accept the bravery of the men and hide her emotions at the horror of how severely they were injured—both physically and mentally. In March 1944 Eleanor took a 13,000-mile trip, going to the islands of the Caribbean, where U.S. servicemen were stationed, and then to Central and South America.

Eleanor realized at Franklin's fourth inauguration in January 1945 that his health might be failing. Still, he insisted on having all of his thirteen grandchildren, ranging in age from three to sixteen, attend the ceremony and spend a few

Eleanor Roosevelt, Prolific Writer

Throughout Eleanor's time in the White House and in later years she was a prolific writer. When Eleanor first came to the White House, she was writing a weekly column for the *Women's Home Companion*. A bit bored with this column, she began writing "My Day" in January 1936, signing a five-year contract with United Feature Syndicate for the daily column. In her later life she continued writing the column, but only three days a week. "My Day" ran from 1936 until Eleanor's death in 1962. From June 1941 until spring 1949 she wrote a monthly question-and-answer column called "If You Ask Me" for *Ladies' Home Journal*. And from 1949 until her death she wrote a monthly column for *McCalls*. It is estimated that she wrote 2,500 newspaper columns and 299 magazine articles between 1933 and 1945, her years at the White House.

Eleanor Roosevelt's books include *This Is My Story* (1937), *This I Remember* (1949), *India and the Awakening East* (1953), *On My Own* (1958), *You Learn by Living* (1960), *The Autobiography of Eleanor Roosevelt* (1961), *Ladies of Courage* (1954) with Lorena Hickok, and *UN: Today and Tomorrow* (1953) with William DeWitt.

days at the White House. Franklin then insisted on making a trip in February to Yalta, on the Black Sea. There he met with other world leaders to chart what the course of the world would be after the war.

In April 1945 Franklin went to his retreat at Warm Springs, Georgia, for a rest. On the afternoon of April 12 Franklin collapsed from a cerebral hemorrhage (bleeding in the brain) and died. It was a time of shock and sorrow for the Roosevelt family. Eleanor quickly made plans to move from the White House. In *The Autobiography of Eleanor Roosevelt* she commented, "I was now on my own."

On her own

Although she felt a large void with the loss of her husband, Eleanor made the adjustments necessary to carry on and continue contributing. She commented that she had been making adjustments ever since Franklin first fell ill with polio. Eleanor made the necessary financial arrangements and enjoyed visits with friends and family at Hyde Park. She then turned the big house at Hyde Park over to the U.S. government for safekeeping but continued living at Val-Kill on the property. She also maintained an apartment overlooking Washington Square in New York City.

In 1946 President Harry Truman (1884–1972; served 1945–53) appointed Eleanor as a delegate to the United Nations (UN) General Assembly. Her appointment was confirmed by the U.S. Senate. She was elected chairperson of the UN Commission on Human Rights, and she helped author the Universal Declaration of Human Rights. Eleanor referred to her time at the UN as "one of the most wonderful and worthwhile experiences in my life." She served as a UN delegate until 1952. In 1952 Eleanor traveled throughout the world in support of humanitarian causes. First she visited the Arab countries and then Israel, Pakistan, and India. In 1953, as a volunteer for the American Association for the United Nations (AAUN), she traveled to Japan, Hong Kong, Turkey, Greece, and Yugoslavia.

In 1952 and again in 1956 Eleanor supported Democrat Adlai E. Stevenson (1900–1965) for president, but he lost to war hero Dwight Eisenhower (1890–1969), a Republican, in both elections. Eleanor was bitterly opposed to the anti-communist campaign of persecution led by Senator Joseph McCarthy (1908–1957) during the 1950s. McCarthy and his followers accused many loyal citizens of being communist sympathizers and would then conduct investigations that bordered on harassment.

Continuing to travel worldwide, Eleanor related that two of her most interesting trips were to the Soviet Union in 1957 and 1958. There she met with Soviet leader Nikita Khrushchev (1894–1971). As a result of these trips, during which Eleanor witnessed firsthand a communist political system in which all industry and property was government-owned (in opposition to the capitalist United States, where industry and property are owned by the people), she believed even more strongly that only in a democracy could people fully function.

Last years

Although Eleanor's family urged her to slow down, slowing down was not in her nature. In September 1960 she made her first trip to two cities in Poland, Warsaw and Kraków. She found the Poles full of optimistic energy and suggested they might be the people to help bring understanding between Western and Eastern nations.

Eleanor continued writing her regular newspaper column, but cut back to only three times a week rather than daily as she had been doing since 1935. She also wrote a monthly column for *McCalls* magazine. She also did radio and television work, lectured widely, and served as a volunteer member of the American Association of University Women (AAUW). Although she vowed not to actively campaign in the 1960 presidential election, by autumn she was on the campaign trail. She had supported Adlai Stevenson at the Democratic nominating convention, but the chosen candidate, John F. Kennedy (1917–1963), soon won her approval.

Eleanor loved to celebrate anniversaries, birthdays, and other special occasions, and she continued to enjoy these events at Hyde Park or at her apartment in New York City. A steady stream of dignitaries, family, and friends came and went at Hyde Park. Eleanor also enjoyed corresponding with President Kennedy and with Mrs. Kennedy, both of whom she thought were serving the country well. In February 1962 Eleanor made her last trip to Europe. Sensing her time was very limited, she began sending out checks months early for school tuition for godchildren, to friends, and to favorite organizations. She died on November 7, 1962, at Val-Kill.

For More Information

Beasley, Maurine H. *Eleanor Roosevelt and the Media: A Public Quest for Self-Fulfillment.* Urbana, IL: University of Illinois Press, 1987.

Hareven, Tamara R. *Eleanor Roosevelt: An American Conscience.* Chicago, IL: Quadrangle Books, 1968.

Hoff-Wilson, Joan, and Marjorie Lightman, eds. *Without Precedent: The Life and Career of Eleanor Roosevelt.* Bloomington, IN: Indiana University Press, 1984.

Lash, Joseph P. *Eleanor and Franklin.* New York, NY: New American Library, 1971.

Lash, Joseph P. *Eleanor: The Years Alone.* New York, NY: Norton, 1972.

Roosevelt, Eleanor. *The Autobiography of Eleanor Roosevelt.* New York, NY: Harper & Brothers Publishers, 1961.

Franklin D. Roosevelt

Born January 30, 1882
Hyde Park, New York

Died April 12, 1945
Warm Springs, Georgia

Thirty-second president
of the United States

Franklin D. Roosevelt, the thirty-second president of the United States and commonly referred to as FDR, is the only person in U.S. history to be elected president four times. After serving as New York's governor from 1929 to 1933, Roosevelt entered the White House in March 1933, during the worst economic crisis the nation had ever experienced, the Great Depression. With charm, an optimistic grin, and a willingness to surround himself with able advisers, Roosevelt brought hope to most Americans. He also brought a fundamental change in federal government by greatly expanding its powers. He then successfully guided the nation through World War II (1939–45). To many he was the savior of democracy and architect of the modern bureaucratic state. Roosevelt had an unusual ability to mobilize the nation in times of crisis and maintain a high level of public support.

"[Election] campaigns always stimulated Roosevelt enormously. He liked going around the country. He enjoyed the freedom and getting out among the people. His personal relationship with crowds was on a warm, simple level of a friendly, neighborly exchange of affection...."

Frances Perkins, in The Roosevelt I Knew

Franklin Roosevelt.
©Bettmann/CORBIS.
Reproduced by permission.

Life among the privileged

Franklin Roosevelt was an only child born to James Roosevelt and Sara Delano Roosevelt on the family's Hyde

Park estate in the Hudson River valley of Dutchess County, New York, in January 1882. The Roosevelts primarily lived off family wealth accumulated in the early nineteenth century from maritime trade. Young Franklin grew up in an affluent social environment of great security and comfort, detached from the larger world, which was increasingly dominated by industrial giants. Through his early school years he was privately tutored at home, and a tutor accompanied him during the family's frequent European travels. In 1891 when Franklin was just nine years old, his father had the first in a series of heart attacks that left him largely an invalid. Young Franklin learned to subdue his emotions and always present a calm and cheerful appearance to his frail father. Later in life as president, this practice would be one of his greatest assets, especially when addressing the American people in times of trouble.

In 1896, at age fourteen, Roosevelt left home to attend Groton Preparatory School, a Massachusetts boarding school. It was the first time he attended school with others, and he felt socially awkward. He was too slight of build to make his mark in athletics. But although he was a social outsider during his four years there, Roosevelt felt the influence of the Groton experience. The school further strengthened his Episcopal Christian values, which emphasized a civil duty to serve the less fortunate. Through Groton Roosevelt became involved in religious and charity work, including work at a boys' club in Boston, Massachusetts.

Raised in a genteel environment at home and educated at Groton, where controversies were few, young Roosevelt developed no strong political views, but rather remained open to varying ideas and philosophies. His inward reserve was masked by a cheerful personality and an outward self-assurance that gave him a persuasive manner with others. A future trademark of Roosevelt's public speaking was the genial greeting "My friends."

Roosevelt entered Harvard in 1900. During his first year of college, his father died and his mother moved to Boston to be near Franklin. At Harvard he proved quite adept at making friends; in fact, his social life often seemed to outweigh his academic studies. His many extracurricular activities included being editor of the student newspaper. While at Harvard, Roosevelt became very taken with the progressive politics of his distant cousin Theodore Roosevelt (1858–1919). Theodore, elected vice president in the 1900 presidential elections, advocated increased government involvement in the U.S. economy. Theodore Roosevelt became president in September 1901 when President William McKinley (1843–1901; served 1897–1901) was assassinated. Franklin was also taken with Theodore's niece, **Eleanor Roosevelt** (1884–1962; see entry), who was active in New York City charities serving the poor. Distant cousins, Franklin and Eleanor saw each other more and more frequently over the next few years, sometimes at White House events. Outwardly they seemed like opposite personalities, with Eleanor being very serious and reserved, but inwardly they shared many traits, including intelligence and compassion for others. Franklin graduated from Harvard in 1904 and married Eleanor in March 1905. Theodore Roosevelt gave Eleanor away at the wedding. Franklin and Eleanor Roosevelt would have four sons and a daughter.

Early politics and the navy

Roosevelt entered Columbia Law School in 1905. Though he did not receive a degree, he did pass New York's bar exam (a test, once passed, that allows a person to legally practice law in a particular U.S. state) and began work as a law clerk for a prestigious law firm in New York City. Greatly influenced by Theodore Roosevelt, young Franklin had a strong interest in public service. The Democratic Party leaders of Dutchess County, New York, invited him to run for the state senate in 1910. Surprisingly, at just twenty-eight years of age, Roosevelt won the election. He enthusiastically began building a political record based on representing the farming interests of upstate New York and aggressively opposing the big-city Democratic political machine (an organization that tightly controls a political party's activities in a particular city or region) known as Tammany Hall. Tammany Hall had great control of New York politics since the early nineteenth century and had been the subject of various scandals concerning corruption. Advocating an open and honest government, Roosevelt easily won reelection in 1912.

In early 1913 newly elected president Woodrow Wilson (1856–1924; served 1913–21) appointed Roosevelt assistant secretary of the navy, a position Theodore Roosevelt had held in his rise to the presidency. Relishing the Washington, D.C., atmosphere, Roosevelt performed well in the quickly expanding navy department. Making a name for himself, Roosevelt participated in naval shipyard labor issues involving unions and the navy's civilian workers. Active in the Democratic Party, Roosevelt unsuccessfully ran for the U.S. Senate in 1914. With the United States entering World War I (1914–18) in 1917, Roosevelt assumed important duties overseeing military operations in the North Atlantic.

Personal and political downturns

In 1918 the relationship between Eleanor and Franklin changed when she discovered a romantic relationship between her husband and her social secretary, Lucy Mercer. Though they remained married, Franklin and Eleanor's relationship became less intimate and based more on shared career goals and mutual respect for each other.

After seven years as assistant secretary of the navy, Roosevelt had attracted the attention of national Democratic Party leaders. In 1920 the party nominated him to run as the vice presidential candidate with presidential nominee James M. Cox (1870–1957), governor of Ohio. Roosevelt resigned his naval post for the campaign. Though they were soundly defeated by Republican candidate Warren G. Harding (1865–1923; served 1921–23), Roosevelt demonstrated strong campaigning skills and made many new influential friends.

Roosevelt's life took a dramatic turn in August 1921 when he contracted polio (a viral disease that can cause damage to the central nervous system resulting in paralysis or loss of muscle tissue). Within only a few days he had lost use of both legs. Told he would never walk again, Roosevelt retreated to his Hyde Park estate for the next seven years, relentlessly searching for a cure. During this time he tried various forms of therapy and became attracted to the spa-like baths in Warm Springs, Georgia. Roosevelt bought an old resort hotel there and made it into a center for treating polio victims. Roosevelt learned ways of concealing his paralysis from the public. When he was in public, he wore heavy leg braces and support-

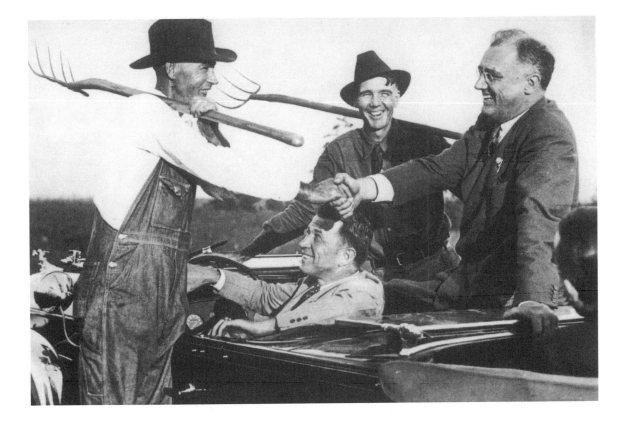

ed himself with a cane and the arm of another person, often one of his sons. Throughout the rest of Roosevelt's life the press very quietly cooperated in not reporting the condition. As a result, the public knew little of his condition, and most people were unaware that Roosevelt was confined to a wheelchair when not in public. Very few photographs were taken of him in a wheelchair. Though Roosevelt did not reveal his own suffering in public, his condition likely gave him great sympathy for others who suffered in life.

Franklin D. Roosevelt loved to campaign because it gave him a chance to interact with Americans across the country. *©HultonArchive/ Getty Images. Reproduced by permission.*

Triumphant rebound

During the years Franklin spent rebuilding his strength, Eleanor and his personal adviser, Louis M. Howe (1871–1936), kept the Roosevelt name alive in New York politics. They constantly updated Franklin on important issues. At Howe's direction Eleanor made many public appearances while Howe dealt with Franklin's correspondence. Roosevelt also

Louis M. Howe

Though he was little known to the public, Louis McHenry Howe (1871–1936) was the most influential political adviser to President Franklin Roosevelt during Roosevelt's sensational rise in the Democratic Party from 1911 to 1936. Howe was born in Indianapolis, Indiana, on January 14, 1871. His father owned the *Saratoga Sun* newspaper. Young Howe never went to college but began working as a reporter for his father's paper at age seventeen. He became coeditor at twenty-one years of age.

Throughout his youth Howe suffered from major health problems, including a presumed heart condition, asthma, and severe bronchitis attacks. In addition, a cycling accident left permanent black pitted scars on his face. He was barely 5 feet tall, gruff, and disheveled in appearance, often wearing the same clothes for several days. His sickly look was described as "ghoulish," and he was sometimes called a "gnome." He often joked about his own appearance.

As a reporter Howe was intrigued with politics and political power. He had a keen ability to interpret the actions of others and to sense the public's mood. Howe first met Roosevelt in 1911, when Roosevelt was still a first-term state senator. Roosevelt's fight against the prevailing Democratic political machine (an organization that tightly controls a political party's activities in a particular city or region), known as Tammany Hall, gained Howe's respect. Tammany Hall had held considerable influence in New York politics since the early nineteenth century and various scandals concerning corruption had tarnished its image with many voters. Immediately, Howe

maintained some physical presence in the party by making the nomination speeches for Alfred Smith (1873–1944) at the Democratic National Convention in 1924 and 1928. Ready for a return to public service, Roosevelt agreed to run for governor of New York in 1928. Conducting his typically energetic and upbeat campaign, Roosevelt easily won the election.

While he was governor, Roosevelt faced the difficult task of providing leadership during the early Great Depression years. Roosevelt was one of the first political leaders to take government action to relieve the economic suffering. Late in 1931 he established the Temporary Emergency Relief Administration to assist needy New York families. He also developed a public power company to deliver electricity at lower rates, and he reduced taxes for farmers. With his land-

thought the tall, charming, and ambitious Roosevelt was future president material. Howe offered to combine his skills and experience with Roosevelt's youthful enthusiasm and charisma. He became Roosevelt's personal adviser and, counseling him to shed his aristocratic mannerisms and his air of self-righteousness, helped Roosevelt expand his appeal to the American public. Howe directed Eleanor Roosevelt as well, urging her to become more visible to the public and influencing her public speeches. While Roosevelt served four years as New York governor (1929–33), Howe quietly worked behind the scenes, paving the path toward the presidency.

When Roosevelt won the presidential election of 1932, Howe moved into the White House along with the Roosevelts and advised the president daily. Though losing some influence to other advisers, Howe remained the one person who could bluntly challenge Roosevelt on issues. Howe was largely a mystery to both the press and the public. He was so private that no one knows how much he actually shaped the president's and the First Lady's decisions. However, given some critical political mistakes Roosevelt made after Howe's death in 1936, it is possible that Howe's influence was indeed large, and certainly it was sorely missed. Howe was labeled "kingmaker" by the news media for building Roosevelt's exceptionally high popularity and helping him maintain it for such a long period of time during such grave national crises. Howe received a state funeral in the White House.

slide reelection as governor in 1930, he became a potential Democratic nominee for president in 1932.

Roosevelt won a tough presidential nomination battle at the Democratic convention, held in Chicago in July 1932. Immediately flying to Chicago from New York, he was the first Democratic nominee to accept the nomination in person at the convention. In his acceptance speech Roosevelt promised "a new deal for the American people." The public welcomed Roosevelt's charm and broad grin, which contrasted with President **Herbert Hoover**'s (1874–1964; served 1929–33; see entry) stern, unsympathetic manner. Hoover was so unpopular that Roosevelt did not have to offer many details about what he proposed to do if he was elected president. However, with his distinct progressive philosophy, it was clear that he would make extensive use of the government to spur economic recovery. Relying on his personal adviser, Howe, and surrounded by great intellectual talent (including three technical advisers recruited from Columbia University, who were known as the **Brain Trust**; see entry), Roosevelt gradually revealed a plan for bringing recovery to various sectors of the nation's economy. Roosevelt easily won the presidential election over Hoover. In February 1933 in Miami, Florida, a lone gunman made an assassination attempt on the president-elect. The city's mayor was killed during the assault. Roosevelt's aides were awestruck by his calm and seemingly unperturbed manner through the whole ordeal, even with the mayor dying in his arms en route to the hospital.

Roosevelt entered the White House in March 1933 at the depth of the worst economic crisis in U.S. history. Most banks were closed, thirteen million workers were unemployed, and industrial production had fallen 44 percent from its 1929 levels. Despite the overwhelming national concerns, people could not help but notice the change of mood within the White House. Literally overnight the formal and sedate air of Hoover and his staff gave way to the lively and self-confident Roosevelt White House. In *The Autobiography of Eleanor Roosevelt* Eleanor described the sense of security Franklin conveyed to the troubled American people:

> I have never known a man who gave one a greater sense of security.... I never knew him to face life or any problem that came up with fear, and I have often wondered if that courageous attitude was not communicated to the people of the country.... He believed in the courage and ability of men, and they responded.

A popular national leader

Restoring calm to the worried nation, Roosevelt established one landmark program after another, reshaping the U.S. government through his New Deal programs. He also began a series of radio addresses, called "fireside chats," in which he informally spoke directly to the general public on important issues and explained why he was taking certain actions. He used a calm, reassuring, friendly voice and simple language.

Having been raised comfortably on inherited wealth, Roosevelt did not have a high regard for the importance of money and did not believe the business ethic should dominate society. Roosevelt was irritated by business's opposition to his programs, which he believed were saving the U.S. economy. In early 1935 the president charted a new legislative course emphasizing government regulation of business, increased taxation of the wealthy, and antitrust activity (breakup of business monopolies that restrict competition). The business community reacted strongly, accusing Roosevelt of promoting socialism (an economic system in which the government owns and operates the means of production). Business leaders argued that the programs undermined free market economics, unconstitutionally expanded government powers, and created a welfare state in which people became dependent on government handouts. Nonetheless, Roosevelt's popularity soared again. He was reelected in a landslide victory in 1936, and the Democratic majority increased in both houses of Congress. For the first time a broad coalition of various groups combined their support for the Democratic candidate. The coalition included black Americans, farmers, the poor, women, and the working class in addition to traditional liberals and progressives. Together these groups came to be known as the Democratic Coalition, and they would propel Democratic candidates for decades to come.

Glee over the resounding victory was short-lived. Supreme Court rulings in 1935 and 1936 struck down some key New Deal programs, greatly angering Roosevelt. With his strong reelection support, Roosevelt felt bold and introduced a radical plan to revise the Supreme Court by adding justices that he would appoint. Called the "court-packing" plan by the press and opponents, the proposal attracted enormous opposition. Even supporters feared that Roosevelt was grabbing for too much power. It was one of his first grave political mistakes following the death of his longtime personal adviser Louis Howe. The Court, under intense pressure, did become more favorable to Roosevelt's programs in its rulings. Roosevelt was also able to fill seven vacancies on the Court between 1937 and 1941. However, the damage was done, and valuable support was lost. Southern Democrats formed a coalition with Republicans that would strongly influence the 1938 congressional elections. In addition, a new economic recession hit in August 1937, discouraging the general public, who had thought the Depression was ending. (Roosevelt carefully used the term "recession," another word for economic depression, when addressing the public in late 1937 so as not to rouse the raw emotions associated with the word "depression.") Roosevelt was able to resurrect government spending for relief, and the economy rebounded once again. However, conservative Republicans and Southern Democrats in Congress would try to block any further progressive reform legislation proposed by Roosevelt.

Saving democracy

By 1939 foreign issues were gaining greater attention. With the rise of dictatorships in Germany, Japan, and Italy and the growth of communism in the Soviet Union, the threat of radical politics and war was steadily growing. The U.S. public and Congress had maintained a strong isolationist perspective (opposition to involvement in any foreign affairs) since World War I. Roosevelt therefore had to act cautiously through the 1930s in dealing with foreign issues. Following Germany's invasion of Poland in September 1939, Britain and France declared war on Germany. World War II (1939–45) had begun. While officially taking a neutral position, Roosevelt was clearly sympathetic toward Britain and its allies. When Germany launched attacks into Western Europe in early 1940, eventually capturing Paris, France, the American public's support for U.S. action increased. Following an unprecedented reelection to a third term as president in November 1940, Roosevelt became much bolder in mobilizing the United States to support Britain in the war.

On December 7, 1941, Japanese forces made a surprise bombing attack on U.S. military bases at Pearl Harbor, Hawaii, killing over two thousand American military personnel and destroying many military ships and airplanes. Within the next few days the United States plunged into war on two fronts, Europe and the Pacific. For the next several years Roosevelt provided firm, steady, inspirational leadership to the nation while leaving the detailed orchestration of war to a group of highly capable military and corporate leaders. Roosevelt ended any further efforts at domestic reform legislation and put up little

Fala, the Presidential Dog

Murray of Falahill ("Fala"), a black Scottish terrier, was born on September 9, 1940, and was trained by Margaret (Daisy) Suckley. Fala moved into the White House in November 1940 to become the faithful and much loved companion of President Franklin Roosevelt. Fala slept on a chair in the president's bedroom. A typical Scottie, Fala would always find a way to get his exercise; he could be seen and heard racing up and down White House stairs and in and out of rooms. Every day before placing Fala's dinner bowl on the floor, Roosevelt asked Fala to do his "Supper Act," which included sitting up and rolling over. Fala loved to go for rides with the president in his open car. Fala brought joy and laughter not only to the president but to Americans dealing with the trials of World War II.

Accompanying the president on many trips throughout the world, Fala performed for dignitaries such as England's Winston Churchill. Fala sailed on the presidential yacht and on the battle cruiser *Tuscaloosa*. He was even the subject of a rumor: As the story was told, Fala was accidentally left in the Aleutian Islands, and the president sent a destroyer to pick him up—at the cost of two to three million taxpayer dollars. The president turned the false rumor into a political asset by saying in a campaign speech before his 1944 reelection that even his little dog was slandered by political opponents. According to Roosevelt, Fala's "Scotch soul was furious."

When Franklin Roosevelt died in 1945, Fala attended the funeral with almost a human presence. Eleanor Roosevelt said that Fala never adjusted to his master being gone. Living with Eleanor at Hyde Park, Fala never stopped waiting for his master to return. His legs would straighten and his ears perked up when sirens of a police escort approached the house, announcing important visitors. Fala perhaps hoped to see the president coming down the drive as he had so often. Fala died in 1952 and was buried next to President Roosevelt at Hyde Park. Fala is the first pet to be honored with a statue at a presidential memorial, the Franklin Delano Roosevelt Memorial in Washington, D.C.

---

resistance in 1943 when Congress ended several New Deal programs. The massive U.S. wartime spending essentially ended the Great Depression and brought full employment.

By mid-1944, with victory on the horizon, Roosevelt began focusing more on the nature of the world following the war. In July 1944 he hosted a forty-four-nation conference at Bretton Woods, New Hampshire, to plan for the postwar monetary systems. Still believing that government had a responsibility to protect the economic security of American citizens, Roosevelt promoted the Servicemen's Readjustment Act of 1944, more commonly known as the G.I. Bill. The bill provided generous housing, education, and other benefits to war veterans.

Roosevelt won reelection again in November 1944, securing a fourth term as president. However, his health was clearly fading; he suffered from advanced heart disease. In February 1945 Roosevelt met with British leader Winston Churchill (1874–1965) and Soviet leader Joseph Stalin (1879– 1953) at the Yalta Conference to determine postwar occupation of Germany and to discuss creation of the United Nations to help avoid future wars. Roosevelt appeared to be in very poor health at the meetings. In April 1945 Roosevelt traveled to his retreat in Warm Springs, Georgia, for a much needed rest. On April 12, while an artist painted his portrait, Roosevelt suddenly collapsed from a massive cerebral hemorrhage (bleeding in the brain). He died only a few hours later. The nation was plunged into profound grief; one of its most beloved leaders had passed away.

A giant figure

Franklin Roosevelt is recognized as one of the great figures of the twentieth century. He served an unprecedented twelve years as president of the United States, leading the nation through the major crises of the Great Depression and World War II. Through his New Deal programs, Roosevelt established a new perspective—that government should provide an economic safety net for its citizens in times of trouble—and laid the foundation for liberal social reform in the 1960s, including the Great Society programs of President Lyndon Johnson (1908–1973; served 1963–69). Roosevelt is not without his critics. Some historians argue that he was foremost a politician, too ready to satisfy the short-term desires of the voting public rather than working for the long-term goals of the nation. For example, important civil rights issues received little attention. Racial discrimination continued largely unchallenged, including in the armed forces, which remained racially segregated through World War II. Also during World War II, thousands of Japanese Americans were forced from their homes and confined to internment camps for two years, from 1942 to 1944, despite lack of any evidence of their disloyalty to the United States. The United States also made minimal efforts to assist European Jews trying to flee from the oppression of Nazi Germany. Nonetheless, Roosevelt immediately stopped the dramatic decline of the national economy in early 1933, successfully guided the nation through a massive and complex world war, and laid the foundation for the postwar international order that led to the formation of the United Nations.

Numerous tributes to Roosevelt have been made. The Franklin Delano Roosevelt Presidential Library was built near his home at Hyde Park, New York. His image appears on the dime in U.S. currency and the Franklin Delano Roosevelt Memorial was dedicated in Washington, D.C., in 1997.

For More Information

Books

Freidel, Frank. *Franklin D. Roosevelt: A Rendezvous with Destiny.* Boston, MA: Little, Brown, 1990.

Graham, Otis L., Jr., and Meghan R. Wander, eds. *Franklin D. Roosevelt: His Life and Times, An Encyclopedic View.* Boston, MA: G. K. Hall, 1985.

Lash, Joseph P. *Eleanor and Franklin.* New York, NY: New American Library, 1971.

Perkins, Frances. *The Roosevelt I Knew.* New York, NY: Viking Press, 1946.

Rollins, Alfred B., Jr. *Roosevelt and Howe.* New York, NY: Knopf, 1962.

Roosevelt, Eleanor. *The Autobiography of Eleanor Roosevelt.* New York, NY: Harper & Brothers Publishers, 1961.

Roosevelt, Eleanor. *This I Remember.* New York, NY: Harper, 1949.

Roosevelt, Franklin D. *The Public Papers and Addresses of Franklin D. Roosevelt.* 5 vols. New York, NY: Random House, 1938–50.

Web Sites

Franklin D. Roosevelt Library and Museum. http://www.fdrlibrary.marist.edu (accessed on September 10, 2002).

The New Deal Network. http://newdeal.feri.org (accessed on September 10, 2002).

Roosevelt University - Center for New Deal Studies. http://www.roosevelt.edu (accessed on September 10, 2002).

Roy Stryker

Born May 11, 1893
Great Bend, Kansas

Died September 26, 1975
Grand Junction, Colorado

Pictorial historian, documentarian

"We introduced Americans to America. The reason we could do this, I think…was that all of us [FSA photographers] in the unit, were so personally involved in the times, and the times were so peculiarly what they were."

Roy Stryker

Roy Stryker.
©Bettmann/CORBIS.
Reproduced by permission.

Roy Stryker was not a photographer, but he understood that pictures spoke louder than words. His talent was recognizing great photographs that told a story, then compiling and organizing those photographs. In doing so Stryker played a key role in introducing documentary photography to the people of the United States. Documentary photographs tell so much about a subject that they can serve as historical documents. They record and mirror the social and political scene of a particular time, providing images of work, play, family, church, clubs, political organizations, and war.

Stryker moved to Washington, D.C., in 1935 to head the Historical Section of the Resettlement Administration (RA), which was later absorbed into the Department of Agriculture and renamed the Farm Security Administration (FSA). He had been hired to increase public awareness of Great Depression conditions through still photographs—and thereby win support for New Deal programs. The New Deal programs had been introduced by President **Franklin D. Roosevelt** (1882–1945; served 1933–45; see entry) beginning in 1933. They were designed to bring relief, recovery, and reform to Depression-weary America. (The Great Depression was the worst economic crisis in U.S. history.) Eventually Stryker's goal was to amass a collection of photographs that would provide a historical record of American life from the 1930s to the early 1940s.

Early years

Roy Emerson Stryker was born on May 11, 1893, in Great Bend, Kansas, to George and Ellen Stryker. George, a rancher, moved his family to Montrose, Colorado, when Roy was three years old. Roy later described his dad, who was a Civil War (1861–65) veteran, as a strong populist, always ready for a hearty political discussion. (Populists believe in promoting the rights and interests of the common people.) George also loved to try new things and did so with gusto. The family home was full of books, and the Stryker children were urged to thoughtfully and thoroughly pursue educational opportunities.

Roy graduated from Montrose High School, attended Colorado School of Mines for one year (1912–13), and then started his own cattle ranch with his brother. Entering the armed services during World War I (1914–18), Roy was assigned to the infantry in France. Upon returning to the United States, with the cattle business in a slump, he went back to Colorado School of Mines in 1920. After one year, Stryker's curiosity about the eastern United States he had glimpsed while traveling to and from the war got the best of him. He married Alice Frasier, and they headed for New York City, where he enrolled in Columbia University. Experiences in New York City began to deepen Stryker's social awareness. For example, having very little money, the newly married couple lived in a tenement (a run-down apartment building) and saw up close poverty-stricken people who seemed to have lost hope.

The college experience

Roy was excited about his classes at Columbia and chose to major in economics. He wanted to know why some Americans were so poor and how the geography of the United States affected economic conditions. He soon struck up a friendship with economics professor **Rexford Guy Tugwell** (1891–1979; see Brain Trust entry). Stryker also became aware of and studied the work of two photographers, Lewis Hine (1874–1940) and Jacob Riis (1849–1914), who had recorded life in the New York slums with their cameras. Stryker completed his bachelor's degree and was appointed in 1924 as an assistant in the economics department at Columbia. Stryker often tried new ways of teaching his students. Instead of lecturing his economics classes, he took them on field trips throughout the city to let students experience for themselves factories, slums, museums, and banks. He used photographs to show students various conditions and aspects of American life.

Aware of Stryker's interest in and knowledge of photography, Professor Tugwell asked Stryker to help him gather the pictures for a book titled *American Economic Life and the Means of Its Improvement,* which Tugwell published in 1925. This was Stryker's first experience in organizing illustrations for a specific topic. Stryker toyed with the idea of producing his own book; he hoped to present the history of agriculture in pictures. He started logically collecting and organizing photographs for the project so he would be ready if he ever got the chance to carry through with his idea. For the next ten years Stryker continued teaching his unconventional classes for Columbia and continued collecting photographs for books he never produced. Meanwhile, Professor Tugwell had become one of President Roosevelt's closest advisers and was serving as an assistant secretary of agriculture. In 1935 Roosevelt appointed Tugwell as chief administrator of the newly established Resettlement Administration (RA), whose goal was to assist the rural poor. Soon Stryker, Tugwell's former student assistant, would also head to Washington, D.C.

Historical Section of the RA/FSA/OWI

Rex Tugwell knew that if the RA program was to be successful, he would first have to educate the American public about the conditions the rural poor were facing in the 1930s. So Tugwell created the Historical Section within the RA's Division of Information and, with the power of photographs in mind, named Roy Stryker to administer the section. Tugwell defended the section from members of Congress who were determined that no pictures would come out of their districts; he allowed Stryker the freedom to run the

Resettlement Administration, Farm Security Administration, and Office of War Information

One of the key purposes of the New Deal programs of the 1930s was to give economic aid to American farmers. The Resettlement Administration (RA), established in 1935, directed its efforts toward helping small farmers, who had largely been overlooked by the major New Deal farm agency, the Agricultural Adjustment Administration. The purpose of the RA was to provide low-cost loans to impoverished farmers, relocate farmers on productive land, and allow them to eventually buy the land. The RA sponsored temporary camps for migrant farmworkers and planned model communities of self-sufficient communal farms where certain needy families could be relocated. The RA also assisted poor farmers by providing farm machinery for temporary use and government-purchased seed. The RA aided efforts to reclaim eroded land, clean up polluted rivers, and control potential flooding.

In July 1937 the Bankhead-Jones Farm Tenancy Act became law. After President Roosevelt signed the measure, he established the Farm Security Administration (FSA) within the Department of Agriculture. The FSA's purpose was to carry out the act's provisions of aiding tenant farmers (farmers who rented the land they worked) with loans and with conservation programs for eroded and otherwise damaged land. The RA was absorbed into the FSA, and Roy Stryker's Historical Section of the RA simply moved intact into the FSA. Stryker's photographers became commonly known as the FSA photographers.

By 1941 the United States was gearing up to enter World War II (1939–45). The Office of War Information (OWI) was created in 1942, and Stryker and several of his photographers were moved into the OWI to photograph the nation's preparations for war. Hence the FSA collection of photographs became known as the FSA/OWI collection.

section. Although Stryker never became a photographer himself, he was acutely aware that a camera could be a device for recording history.

Stryker's first duty at the Historical Section was to gather a staff of photographers. He did not seek out famous photographers; he simply looked for talent and idealism. These men and women photographers of the Historical Section would eventually take 270,000 pictures that set the standard for modern-day visual (pictorial) history. At first Stryker was not sure exactly how the project would go. He explains in

Shot by a FSA photographer in 1935, this photo of a family on the road from the Dust Bowl region to California communicated the plight of the rural poor to Americans across the nation. *Courtesy of the Franklin D. Roosevelt Library.*

"The FSA Collection of Photographs," published in *In This Proud Land:*

> I had no idea what was going to happen. I expected competence. I did not expect to be shocked at what began to come across my desk. The first three men who went out—Carl Mydans, Walker Evans and Ben Shahn—began sending in some astounding stuff that first fall, about the same time that I saw the great work **Dorothea Lange** *[1895–1965; see entry]* was doing in California and decided to hire her. Then Arthur Rothstein, who had set up the lab, started taking pictures. Every day was for me an education and a revelation. I could hardly wait to get to the mail in the morning.

Stryker received negatives in the mail, had them developed, and took the pictures home each night to pore over them. Then the next morning he would let the photographers know how they were doing. Before the photographers went out on assignments, which often lasted months at a time, Stryker demanded that they thoroughly understand the situation of the area they were going to document. He delighted in teaching them important information about the areas and often gave the photographers pep talks just before they left. Stryker also sent them with "shooting scripts," outlining the kinds of pictures he needed. However, he made it clear that photographers had the freedom to shoot anything that seemed important. At first the photographers focused on rural poverty, and their photos helped increase the public's awareness of those in need. Congress was compelled to act to relieve the suffering. Later the photographs reflected every aspect of small-town and rural life, and the entire collection became a national treasure documenting the 1930s.

By 1941 the FSA budget was slashed as the United States prepared to enter World War II (1939–45). The Historical Section was transferred to the Office of War Information (OWI) in 1942. Stryker continued to head the section and took a few FSA photographers with him. The OWI was charged with photographing America's war preparation, showing the positive side of America's industrial might. Aircraft factories, shipyards, oil refineries, and women in the labor force were all subjects. Stryker liked to show the role of factory workers, but his bosses at the OWI did not always select the pictures he would have chosen. By 1943 Stryker was ready to leave the OWI. For a time the fate of the RA/FSA/OWI negatives and photographs was in question. Some in Congress wanted the entire collection destroyed. Archibald MacLeish (1892–1982), then head of the Library of Congress, rescued the collection and had it brought to the library. At the start of the twenty-first century, most Americans base their images of 1930s America on the remarkable collection of RA/FSA/OWI photographs.

Photographs On-Line

Many of the photographs made by the Historical Section photographers of the Resettlement Administration (RA), Farm Security Administration (FSA), and Office of War Information (OWI) can be viewed on the Library of Congress web site. The collection is part of the library's American Memory program. In all, about 270,000 RA/FSA/OWI exposures were made. Roy Stryker, who led the project, punched holes in up to 100,000 negatives that he felt were inferior. Therefore, the main part of the collection includes approximately 164,000 black-and-white negatives and 1,600 color negatives, the latter taken during the last days of the project. Color photography became widespread late in the 1930s with the development of Kodachrome and other color films. The FSA/OWI photographers secured a limited number of color images near the end of the Great Depression. In 2001 over 112,000 of the black-and-white and color images were available online. The images may be found at http://memory.loc.gov/ammem/fsowhome.html.

Standard Oil of New Jersey

On October 4, 1943, Stryker left the OWI to work full-time for the Standard Oil Company of New Jersey. Between 1943 and 1950 Standard Oil sponsored a documentary project to compile a photographic record of the oil industry. Stryker was hired to head the project, which was patterned after the FSA project. As he had done with the FSA, Stryker hired a diverse group of talented photographers, who documented not only the complex oil industry but also much of small-town America in the 1940s. Sixty-seven thousand black-and-white photos and one thousand color photos were produced by 1950. Money for the project was cut back starting in 1948, and Stryker resigned in 1950. From July 1950 through 1951 Stryker was director of the Pittsburgh Photographic Project, an ambitious project designed to create a collection of photographs about the city of Pittsburgh and its people during a time of dramatic change for the community. By the time Stryker left, his staff had produced over 18,000 photographs. From 1952 to 1958 he directed a photographic project documenting steel production for Jones and Laughlin Steel Corporation. Stryker then moved back to Colorado and occasionally took consulting jobs.

In 1962 the Museum of Modern Art in New York presented two hundred of the FSA photographs in an exhibition titled *The Bitter Years*. The exhibition set off a round of books and articles and more exhibitions of the FSA photographs. In 1972 while living in Grand Junction, Colorado, Stryker chose about two hundred photos that he considered the essence of the FSA project. That was less than one-tenth of 1 percent of the 270,000 photos taken. He published the selected photos in 1973 in his book *In This Proud Land*. Stryker died two years later at the age of eighty-two.

For More Information

Books

Garver, Thomas H. *Just Before the War: Urban America from 1935 to 1941 As Seen by Photographers of the Farm Security Administration.* New York, NY: October House, 1968.

Hurley, F. Jack. *Portrait of a Decade: Roy Stryker and the Development of Documentary Photography in the Thirties.* Baton Rouge, LA: Louisiana State University Press, 1972.

O'Neal, Hank. *A Vision Shared: A Classic Portrait of America and Its People, 1935–1943*. New York, NY: St. Martin's Press, 1976.

Plattner, Steven W. *Roy Stryker: U.S.A., 1943–1950*. Austin, TX: University of Texas Press, 1983.

Stryker, Roy E., and Nancy Wood, eds. *In This Proud Land: America 1935–1943 As Seen in the FSA Photographs*. Greenwich, CT: New York Graphic Society, 1973.

Web Sites

"America from the Great Depression to World War II: Photographs from the FSA-OWI, 1935–1945." *Library of Congress*. http://memory.loc.gov/ammem/fsowhome.html (accessed on September 10, 2002).

Robert F. Wagner

Born June 8, 1877
Nastätten, Germany

Died May 4, 1953
New York, New York

U.S. senator

"He is one of the most approachable men in the Senate. He is 'Bob' to his friends, and those who know and admire him refer to him in this manner."

From Senator Robert F. Wagner and the Rise of Urban Liberalism

Robert F. Wagner.
©Bettmann/CORBIS.
Reproduced by permission.

A German immigrant, U.S. senator Robert F. Wagner was a political champion for the worker and common citizen in the United States. He embraced progressive politics, strongly believing that the government had a responsibility to help solve pressing social problems. (Progressive ideas gained support from a variety of groups in the United States in the early twentieth century.) In the Senate Wagner was one of the leading advocates of President **Franklin D. Roosevelt**'s (1882–1945; served 1933–45; see entry) New Deal in the 1930s and President Harry Truman's Fair Deal programs later on. (The New Deal was a collection of federal legislation and programs designed by the Roosevelt administration to aid those most affected by the Great Depression, America's worst economic crisis. The Fair Deal was Truman's proposed program to promote greater racial and economic equality in American society.) Throughout his career Wagner contended that in an industrial society, it is the government's role to provide economic security for the working class. To achieve this goal of economic security, Wagner sought a balance of power between business and labor and supported the workers' right to form labor unions. A spokesman for the disadvantaged, Wagner created legislation that had great influence for the remainder of the twentieth century. His numerous legislative victories included recognizing the rights of workers to organize into unions and creating public housing for the poor.

A gifted student

Robert F. Wagner was born in June 1877 in Nastätten, a small Rhineland village near Wiesbaden, Germany. He was one of the youngest of seven children in the family. His father, Reinhard Wagner, ran a local dyeing and printing business. Farmers and villagers brought their homespun woolens and other textiles to him for coloring. His mother, Magdalene, was a schoolteacher. Although they were reasonably comfortable financially, the Wagners decided to immigrate to the United States in 1886, when Robert was eight years old, to seek better economic opportunities for their children. They settled in New York's Upper East Side in Yorktown, a German immigrant colony. It was a tough area full of poverty and occupied mostly by lower-working-class immigrants. With industrialization in America well established, Reinhard found little demand for a craftsman dyer. Instead he worked as a janitor for various tenement houses, earning five dollars a week and receiving a basement apartment for the family. Magdalene did washing for money, and the children made additional money for the family by doing odd jobs. Even young Robert would sell newspapers and deliver groceries after school.

Robert's parents decided that at least one of their children should have a chance at a college education. Robert, who graduated at the top of his class in high school, was the chosen one. Readily meeting the relatively high academic standards of City College of New York, Robert enrolled in the tuition-free school. While attending college Robert worked as a bellhop at the New York Athletic Club, where he became acquainted with many of New York's wealthy residents. He was a well-rounded student, excelling in academics and the debate team as well as being quarterback and captain of the football team and shortstop on the baseball team. In 1896 with Robert established in school, Reinhard and Magdalene, tired after a decade of hard work making ends meet, returned to Germany. When Robert earned his degree in 1898, a close friend convinced him to seek a law degree. Wagner graduated from New York Law School with honors in 1900.

New York law and politics

Fresh out of school, Wagner began a New York law practice and became active in the Democratic Party. He first served as a local representative of the New York Democratic political machine (an organization that tightly controls a political party's activities in a particular city or region) known as Tammany Hall, which dominated the city's politics until 1933. He also joined other organizations and made many useful political and business contacts. Quickly showing aptitude in politics, Wagner won a seat in the New York State Assembly in 1904 and moved to the state's upper house in 1908. That same year he married an Irish American woman, Margaret Marie McTague. They had a son, Robert F. Wagner Jr. (1910–1991), who would later become mayor of New York City in the 1950s and 1960s.

With the rise of progressive politics in New York in the early 1900s, Wagner embraced progressive social reform goals, seeking to change society to better meet the needs of workers and the common citizen. As a young legislator he successfully sponsored a highly popular public transit bill that reduced fares for many working-class riders who commuted long distances. With his reputation rising, in 1910 at age thirty-three Wagner became the youngest legislator in New York history to assume the lead of the state senate. In all, he guided fifty-six reform bills through the New York legislature, addressing a wide range of labor and industrial concerns. One of his biggest successes was regulation of public utilities through the creation of the Public Service Commission, which had the task of overseeing the rates charged for gas, electricity, and public transportation. Regulation of these everyday expenses served to protect the average citizen's pocketbook. Wagner also established a workmen's compensation law to make payments to workers injured on the job. It was considered the most effective legislation of its kind in the nation at the time. After a tragic industrial fire in New York City killed almost 150 workers, Wagner played a critical role in the investigation. Using the findings to support his arguments, he pushed through labor laws that addressed workplace safety and sanitation, restricted child labor, and limited working hours for women. He was less successful sponsoring legislation designed to promote labor unions by legally protecting their activities.

In 1918 Wagner was elected to the New York State Supreme Court, one of the busiest judicial districts in the nation. As a justice he handed down a number of historic decisions, including rulings that protected the rights of striking workers and rulings that upheld laws controlling rent prices. He issued the first court order in U.S. legal history requiring an employer to honor an agreement with its workers. Reluctant to leave a stable position of influence, he nevertheless accepted the Democratic Party's call to run for the U.S. Senate in 1926. His campaign was successful, and he joined the Senate in 1927. Constantly supporting the underdog, he would serve in the Senate with sweeping popular support for twenty-two years.

Economic hard times

With the onset of the Great Depression in late 1929, Wagner sought to bring economic relief to the common person and worker. During President **Herbert Hoover's** (1874–1964; served 1929–33; see entry) term, Wagner pushed for improved gathering and tracking of labor statistics and for deficit government spending (spending more than received in revenues) to fund public works projects that would aid the unemployed. Public works projects funded by the government included construction of roads, public buildings, and parks; these projects created many new jobs. Wagner believed the jobs would increase public purchasing power, which would stimulate industrial recovery. After having had one public works bill vetoed by Hoover, Wagner pushed through the Emergency Relief and Construction Act, which Hoover reluctantly signed, in 1932.

In 1933 the Democrats, led by President Franklin D. Roosevelt, came into power. Wagner became a leading supporter and defender of Roosevelt's New Deal programs. He began as sponsor of the Federal Emergency Relief Act and the Civilian Conservation Corps (CCC) in 1933. Both provided jobs for the unemployed. Wagner played a leading role in drafting the key industrial recovery legislation, the National

The Wagner Act

Only five weeks after the U.S. Supreme Court ruled that the National Industrial Recovery Act (NIRA) was unconstitutional, Senator Robert Wagner successfully worked a new piece of labor legislation through Congress. On July 5, 1935, Congress passed the National Labor Relations Act (NLRA), reasserting the right of workers to organize into unions. The NLRA, more commonly called the Wagner Act after Senator Wagner, is the most important piece of labor legislation in U.S. history. The act prohibits employers from firing employees simply for joining a union. It also prohibits companies from engaging in certain unfair business practices, including interfering in union activities, refusing to bargain with a union, or gaining control over a labor organization. The act also bars unions from re-quiring workers to join a union. To enforce these provisions, the Wagner Act created the National Labor Relations Board (NLRB), whose members are appointed by the president for terms of five years. The NLRB holds considerable power to enforce the law. For example, when a company violates the act, the NLRB can issue a cease and desist order demanding that an employer halt questionable activities. If the company persists, the NLRB can go to the U.S. Court of Appeals for a ruling to force the company to stop unfair practices. The NLRB promotes unions by helping workers hold elections to decide whether to form a union and, if a union is formed, elections to determine their representatives. After passage of the Wagner Act, the number of unions in the United States rapidly increased.

Industrial Recovery Act (NIRA). He was particularly interested in three of its provisions: the right of workers to bargain collectively for improved working conditions through independent labor unions; establishment of industrial codes for minimum wages, maximum hours, and working conditions; and establishment of the Public Works Administration (PWA) to create jobs for the unemployed. The NIRA also created the National Labor Board (NLB) to settle labor disputes and make sure NIRA programs were carried out. Wagner was named head of the NLB. However, the board had insufficient power to be effective; many companies refused to recognize unions and defied the spirit of the act. Frustrated with the NLB, in March 1934 Wagner introduced the Labor Disputes bill, which was designed to give the NLB enforcement powers. However, the bill faced strong industry opposition and got nowhere in Congress.

When the U.S. Supreme Court ruled on May 27, 1935, that the NIRA was unconstitutional, Wagner already had a stronger new bill in the works. The bill, introduced in Congress on February 21, 1935, more effectively recognized the rights of workers. It was designed to strengthen certain aspects of the NIRA, such as enforcing workers' rights rather than simply settling labor disputes. Formally named the National Labor Relations Act (NLRA), but more commonly called the Wagner Act after Senator Wagner, it was passed on July 5, 1935. The landmark act prohibited certain unfair labor practices and created the National Labor Relations Board (NLRB) to oversee management-labor relations. Wagner also sponsored many other acts through the 1930s, including the Social Security Act of 1935 and the Wagner-Steagall Housing Act of 1937. The housing act established the U.S. Housing Authority and provided federal funds for low-income housing.

Other legislative efforts proved less successful. Wagner's concern for victims of racial discrimination led to his cospon-

Senator Robert F. Wagner, center, greets a group of supporters of his Wagner-Steagall Housing Act of 1937, which provided federal funds for low-income housing.
©Bettmann/CORBIS. Reproduced by permission.

soring an antilynching bill in the Senate. The bill was introduced in January 1934, but strong resistance from Southern members of Congress and the absence of Roosevelt's endorsement led to the bill's ultimate demise by February 1938. Wagner also actively supported unsuccessful bills prohibiting discriminatory voting laws. In foreign policy, Wagner joined Roosevelt in sounding early alarms about the rise of Adolf Hitler (1889–1945) and Nazism in Germany. He was also outspoken in favor of allowing an increased flow of Jewish refugees to enter the United States from Nazi Germany in the late 1930s.

Postwar period

After World War II (1939–45) Wagner became involved in a wide range of issues once again, including labor, Social Security, full employment (an economic condition where job opportunities are plentiful and unemployment rates are kept below 6 percent), housing, international economic assistance, the creation of a Jewish state in Palestine, and economic development of the St. Lawrence Seaway in the Northeast. Wagner had success with legislation promoting public housing and urban redevelopment, and the Jewish state, Israel, became a reality in 1948. With the strong support of President Harry Truman (1884–1972; served 1945–53) Wagner also promoted legislation for national health insurance and civil rights. However, the conservative Congress made Wagner's proposals increasingly difficult to pass. A major defeat came when Congress passed the Taft-Hartley Act over Truman's veto. The act revised the NLRA and reduced the power that Wagner had helped labor achieve in the previous decade.

With his health failing, Wagner quietly resigned from the Senate on June 28, 1949. In his retirement statement he proudly proclaimed that he could count more legislative victories than defeats in the battle for human rights. During his years of service Wagner had reflected the rise of progressive politics and the increased political power of immigrants. He died in New York City in May 1953 in the same neighborhood where he grew up as a young immigrant boy.

For More Information

Dubofsky, Melvyn. *The State and Labor in Modern America*. Chapel Hill, NC: University of North Carolina, 1994.

Huthmacher, J. Joseph. *Senator Robert F. Wagner and the Rise of Urban Liberalism*. New York, NY: Atheneum, 1968.

Martin, George. *Madam Secretary: Frances Perkins*. Boston, MA: Houghton Mifflin, 1976.

Tomlins, Christopher L. *The State and the Unions: Labor Relations, Law, and the Organized Labor Movement in America, 1880–1960*. Cambridge, NY: Cambridge University Press, 1985.

Henry Wallace

Born October 7, 1888
Orient, Iowa

Died November 18, 1965
Danbury, Connecticut

Secretary of agriculture, secretary of commerce, vice president of the United States

Henry Wallace. *Archive Photos. Reproduced by permission.*

Henry Wallace played several major roles in President Franklin D. Roosevelt's (1882–1945; served 1933–45; see entry) administrations. Wallace was secretary of agriculture from 1933 to 1940 during the Great Depression, then vice president from 1941 to 1945 during World War II (1939–45), and finally secretary of commerce in the early postwar years of 1945 and 1946. He is widely regarded as one of the most knowledgeable people ever to serve as secretary of agriculture. In the 1920s young Wallace earned an international reputation for scientific advances in plant breeding and for editing a highly respected agricultural magazine, *Wallaces' Farmer.* Believing in increased use of science and mechanization on farms, Wallace greatly influenced America's transition from small family-operated farms to large corporate farms. As secretary of agriculture, Wallace designed programs for government control of crop production and government price supports that continue to shape the U.S. agricultural industry into the twenty-first century. Outspoken on controversial subjects, Wallace gained criticism as well as praise.

The Wallaces of Iowa

Henry Agard Wallace was born to Henry Cantwell Wallace (1866–1924) and Mary Broadhead in late 1888 in a modest frame farmhouse—with no indoor toilet, running water, or electricity—near the rural town of Orient, Iowa. No doctor or midwife attended his birth, and he had no birth certificate until much later in life. His grandfather, a United Presbyterian minister turned farmer and editor, was known as "Uncle Henry" Wallace (1836–1916). Family farms struggled in the early 1890s because of a national economic downturn. To provide additional income Henry Cantwell Wallace took a professorship in agriculture at Iowa State College in 1892. He left that job in 1896 to help Uncle Henry run a new family publication, *Wallaces' Farmer*. Meanwhile, being the oldest of six children, young Henry Agard Wallace was responsible for most household and farm chores. By 1898, as the publication began doing well, family finances improved.

Following in the footsteps of his grandfather and father, who were highly respected in the corn-growing region of the Midwest, young Henry labored under the high expectations that came with the Henry Wallace name. While the younger children seemingly received preferential treatment from their dad, Henry worked hard to earn the approval of his father. As a result, he greatly respected his father but resented him for not being close. His mother, an avid gardener, perhaps provided greater influence with her love of plants and strict thriftiness. Uncle Henry provided his grandson with an intellectual and strong religious outlook, teaching young Henry to worship God through service to other people. From the combination of these strong family influences, Henry A. Wallace became an independent loner who suppressed his need for affection and strove for perfection in personal achievement.

In his youth Wallace was fascinated with the scientific study of plants and by sixteen was conducting experiments in breeding seed corn. In 1910 Wallace graduated from Iowa State College with honors and began working as assistant editor for the family magazine. In 1912 his father sent him on an agricultural tour of Europe to visit various agricultural experiment stations. Full of new ideas, Wallace began experimenting in earnest with crossbreeding different strains of corn he had collected on his travels. Also at this time, Wallace met Ilo

New Deal Agricultural Programs

U.S. secretary of agriculture Henry Wallace held strong beliefs on how the nation's agricultural industry should be structured and the role government should play in that structure. President **Herbert Hoover**'s (1874–1964; served 1929–33; see entry) policies of modest government support for private farmer cooperatives (organizations of farmers striving for economic cooperation by coordinating the production and marketing of their produce) and for voluntary production controls had proved ineffective in solving the severe economic problems of U.S. farming. After Roosevelt's election to the presidency, the newly appointed Wallace pushed several programs through Congress in 1933. The Agricultural Adjustment Act created the Agricultural Adjustment Administration (AAA), which paid farmers to cut back their production of major crops such as wheat, corn, and cotton in order to raise the market prices. The AAA also promoted the controversial practice of destroying existing crops and produce, such as plowing up 10 million acres of cotton fields and killing six million young pigs. The Commodity Credit Corporation made loans to farmers who cooperated with the AAA and stored surplus crops until better prices appeared. The Farm Credit Administration (FCA) provided low-interest loans to help farmers avoid bankruptcy and established a banking system to support farm cooperatives. In 1935 the Soil Conservation Service (SCS) was established to help farmers take better care of their land and make it more productive. Also in 1935 the Resettlement Administration (RA) was formed to assist needy small farmers and help some of them move to more productive lands. The RA was absorbed into the Farm Security Administration (FSA) in 1937.

Browne of Indianola, Iowa, and they married in May 1914. They would have two sons and a daughter. To supplement the modest income from his editing job, Wallace also farmed 40 acres near Des Moines, Iowa. He would often rise at 4:00 A.M. to milk the cattle, then work in his office through the day, and complete his farmwork well into the evening.

In 1921 President Warren Harding (1865–1923; served 1921–23) appointed Wallace's father as secretary of agriculture. Young Wallace took over as lead editor of the family magazine. He also gained international recognition in plant genetics by successfully developing a hybrid seed corn that would increase the productivity of corn farmers. Just as family fortunes seemed high, Henry Cantwell Wallace died sud-

Electrification of rural America was another important part of New Deal farm policy. Creation of the Tennessee Valley Authority (TVA) and the Electric Home and Farm Authority (EHFA) in 1933 brought electric power and inexpensive electric appliances to farms in the Southeast for the first time. The Rural Electrification Administration (REA) was formed in 1935 to expand farm electrification efforts nationwide.

When the U.S. Supreme Court found the 1933 Agricultural Adjustment Act unconstitutional, Congress quickly passed the Soil Conservation and Domestic Allotment Act of 1936. Under this act the government paid farmers for planting soil-conserving crops like soybeans instead of soil-depleting crops like corn, cotton, and wheat. A more comprehensive farmer support program came with the Agricultural Adjustment Act of 1938. This legislation continued the soil conservation payment program, introduced certain controls on the market, encouraged crop storage during times of abundance, and provided for price support loans (guaranteeing a minimum price for crops by providing low interest loans to farmers when prices are down) to farmers. Complete economic recovery for farmers did not come until World War II (1939–45), when European demand for farm products sharply increased. However, the New Deal programs greatly contributed to modernizing the American farm. The programs also saved thousands of farmers from bankruptcy and made it possible for U.S. agriculture to support the massive American war effort of the 1940s.

denly in 1924. His father's premature death profoundly affected Wallace. More driven than ever, Wallace established the nation's first hybrid seed company, the Hi-Bred Seed Company, in 1926 to produce the new hybrid corn. The breed of corn was very popular and brought Wallace increased wealth and praise. Later, in 1934, Iowa State College awarded Wallace with an honorary doctor of science degree in recognition of his scientific achievements.

Farm politics

During the 1920s U.S. farmers faced difficult economic times. The international demand for their produce had significantly declined following World War I (1914–18), and competition from other countries, such as Australia, had increased. Many farmers were going bankrupt, and small rural banks across the country were going out of business. The farmers' fight to raise produce prices was proving ineffective. Wallace could not understand how the government could allow hardworking farmers to go broke while they were providing the nation an abundance of produce. He promoted programs that increased crop storage and controlled farm prices through reduction in farmed acreage. The theory was that if less produce was available in the marketplace, prices for produce should increase. Yet these ideas directly contradicted the prevailing Republican philosophy that business should be free of government regulation and interference. By 1928 Wallace had grown dissatisfied with the Republicans and shifted his support to the Democrats, voting for Al Smith (1873–1944) for president in 1928 and Franklin D. Roosevelt in 1932. Wallace even had a private meeting with Roosevelt during the campaign. Roosevelt was so impressed with Wallace's ideas that he appointed him as secretary of agriculture in March 1933. It was the first time in the nation's history that a father and son had been appointed to the same secretarial post.

In Washington, D.C., Wallace was quite unlike other government leaders and not well understood. Many found Wallace's personality too unique for Washington and uncomfortable to be around. Wallace was an intellectual with a strong interest in science, which made him popular with intellectuals, businessmen, and New Dealers for his great technical knowledge and analytical thinking. Everyday politicians, however, found Wallace aloof and unwilling to follow normal informal lines of communication on Capitol Hill.

The newly appointed Wallace was determined to restructure American agriculture with government playing a significant role. He wanted to make farming as profitable as it had been before World War I. Wallace guided the development and passage of the Agricultural Adjustment Act in March 1933, which created the Agricultural Adjustment Administration (AAA). AAA paid farmers not to plant all their acreage; the goal was to reduce the availability of farm products in order to raise prices. Serving as the cornerstone of the New Deal farm program, AAA was the first step in govern-

ment oversight of farm production. The program saw some modest success by the mid-1930s: Crop prices had risen, and farmers' debt was down.

Wallace was both praised and condemned for the AAA. He came under criticism for focusing on large farm operations and not helping farmworkers, sharecroppers, or small farmers, all of whom were most vulnerable to the effects of the Great Depression, the worst economic crisis in U.S. history. However, Wallace firmly believed that U.S. agriculture was moving away from the traditional small family farm to large corporate farms. Therefore, he believed giving aid to small farmers would only prolong a lifestyle no longer economically important to the nation.

Wallace responded to the criticism by showing that his interests went beyond agricultural production. In 1936 while considering bringing the Resettlement Administration into the Department of Agriculture, Wallace took a trip to the

Henry Wallace, right, worked closely with President Franklin D. Roosevelt to institute several New Deal programs, such as the Agricultural Adjustment Administration and the Farm Credit Administration, to help farming and agriculture. *©Bettmann/CORBIS. Reproduced by permission.*

South to see the conditions in which poor farmers were living. He came away greatly affected by the high degree of rural poverty and rampant racial discrimination he witnessed. Wallace supported the Food Stamp program and school lunch program. He was also chairman of the Special Committee on Farm Tenancy. Proposals from the committee eventually led to the Bankhead-Jones Farm Tenancy Act of 1937. The act established the Farm Security Administration (FSA) to help small farmers modernize their operations and increase the size of their farms. The FSA also helped farmers on poor lands move to more productive lands and helped tenant farmers become landowners.

New roles

In 1940 a new political role arrived for Wallace as President Roosevelt selected him to be his vice presidential running mate. With Wallace being from Iowa, the choice was made in part to counter the popularity of Republican Wendell Willkie (1892–1944) in the critical Midwest part of the nation. Roosevelt was elected to an unprecedented third presidential term, so Wallace took on the job of vice president in January 1941 and served in that role through much of World War II. Wallace proclaimed a new era—the "Century of the Common Man"—and introduced an initiative that promoted domestic social and economic reform, defeat of foreign dictatorships, decreased trade restrictions, and establishment of strong international organizations. Wallace was chairman of the Board of Economic Warfare (BEW), which was responsible for acquiring a supply of essential raw materials for the war industry.

Through the war years Wallace became increasingly concerned about the growing influence big business and the military had on legislation and the operation of various agencies. Also, after witnessing the suffering of the poor during the Great Depression, he believed a general spiritual revolution was coming. His antagonism toward big business and mystical outlook was too much for Democratic Party leaders. By 1944 Roosevelt's health was declining, and many believed the next vice president might likely become president. Therefore, they persuaded Roosevelt to drop Wallace and adopt

Senator Harry Truman (1884–1972) of Missouri as a running mate in the 1944 election campaign. Following his reelection, Roosevelt appointed Wallace as secretary of commerce. After Roosevelt's sudden death in April 1945, Truman kept Wallace in that role because Wallace was popular with some elements of the party. However, Wallace and Truman clashed over U.S. foreign policy. Wallace accused Truman of being too militarily aggressive against the Soviet Union and blamed Truman for starting the cold war (an intense political and economic rivalry from 1945 to 1991 between the United States and the Union of Soviet Socialist Republics falling just short of military conflict). Wallace argued for a more cooperative position with the Soviets, built around trade relations. Wallace continued to speak out publicly against Truman's foreign policies, and as a result, Truman dismissed Wallace from his cabinet position in late September 1946.

In earlier years a number of influential Democrats had seen Wallace as Roosevelt's successor to the White House. But by late 1947 Wallace saw no hope of gaining the Democratic nomination for president for the 1948 campaign. Instead, he became the candidate of a third party known as the Progressive Party. Strongly opposed to Truman's policies of militarily containing the spread of communism in the world, Wallace gained the active support of some Communists in the United States. This support scared away many of his other supporters as the campaign progressed. In addition, organized labor, a longtime friend of Wallace, chose not to break away from the Democratic Coalition, a diverse group of voters that had formed in the 1930s to successfully support Democratic candidates. Wallace gained less than 3 percent of the vote in November 1948, coming in fourth behind another third-party candidate, Strom Thurmond (1902–) of the Dixiecrats. It was a strong rejection of Wallace's political ideas. His public life was over.

Back to science

Wallace returned to scientific experiments in plant and animal genetics on his farm. In 1964 Wallace was diagnosed with amyotrophic lateral sclerosis, a degenerative disease that leads to loss of muscle control and eventually leads to death. In November 1965 he died at age seventy-seven.

For More Information

Culver, John C., and John Hyde. *American Dreamer: The Life and Times of Henry A. Wallace*. New York, NY: Norton, 2000.

Lord, Russell. *The Wallaces of Iowa*. Boston, MA: Houghton Mifflin, 1947.

Markowitz, Norman D. *The Rise and Fall of the People's Century: Henry A. Wallace and American Liberalism, 1945–1948*. New York, NY: Free Press, 1973.

Schapsmeier, Edward L., and Frederick H. Schapsmeier. *Henry A. Wallace of Iowa: The Agrarian Years, 1910–1940*. Ames, IA: Iowa State University Press, 1968.

Schapsmeier, Edward L., and Frederick H. Schapsmeier. *Prophet in Politics: Henry A. Wallace and the War Years, 1940–1946*. Ames, IA: Iowa State University Press, 1970.

Walton, Richard J. *Henry Wallace, Harry Truman, and the Cold War*. New York, NY: Viking, 1976.

White, Graham J., and John Maze. *Henry A. Wallace: His Search for a New World Order*. Chapel Hill, NC: University of North Carolina Press, 1995.

Ellen Woodward

Born July 11, 1887
Oxford, Mississippi

Died September 23, 1971
Washington, D.C.

Administrator

Ellen Woodward's energetic work on behalf of women and children spanned several decades, from 1925 to 1953. Many consider Woodward one of the most important women in the New Deal, second only to Secretary of Labor **Frances Perkins** (1882–1965; see entry). The New Deal was a collection of legislation passed during President **Franklin D. Roosevelt**'s (1882–1945; served 1933–45; see entry) administration. The legislation established programs that were designed to bring economic relief to those most affected by the Great Depression, the worst economic slump in U.S. history. One of Woodward's key goals during the Depression was to provide jobs for women who were heads of households. As the head of women's relief programs for several federal agencies, Woodward provided jobs for women in every state, often using state organizations largely staffed and operated by women. Woodward also pushed for equality for women in society, including pay equal to men's salaries for equal work. From the 1930s to the 1950s she was director of the women's divisions of the Federal Emergency Relief Administration (FERA), the Civil Works Administration (CWA), and the Works Progress Administration (WPA); a presidential ap-

"Woodward's grassroots approach to the administration of programs to promote economic security and social betterment brought significant change to the lives of many women."

From Ellen S. Woodward: New Deal Advocate for Women

Ellen Woodward. *AP/Wide World Photo. Reproduced by permission.*

pointee to the Social Security Board; and an administrator for the Office of Inter-Agency and International Relations of the Federal Security Agency.

Early influences of politics

Ellen Sullivan was born in Oxford, Mississippi, in July 1887. Her father, William Van Amberg Sullivan, was an attorney who was active in politics. Ellen's mother, Nancy Murray, died of tuberculosis in 1895 when Ellen was almost eight years old. The family had a distinguished past with several generations of political and military leaders, including a governor and several U.S. senators. Her father's involvement in politics through the 1890s introduced Ellen at a young age to public issues and political debate. Her father served in the U.S. House of Representatives from 1897 to 1898 and in the U.S. Senate from 1898 to 1901. During this time Ellen's interest in public affairs continued to grow. After her father's senate term expired, they stayed in Washington, D.C., where William reestablished a law practice. Ellen attended a private school in Washington, D.C., and then Sans Souci Female Academy in Greenville, South Carolina, from 1901 to 1902. When Ellen reached age fifteen, her education ended. Even though Ellen wanted to go on to college, she returned to Oxford. Her father believed that higher education was not proper for a young woman, a common perspective at that time. In 1906 Ellen married Albert Woodward, a practicing attorney in Oxford, Mississippi, and they had one son.

During her early years of marriage Woodward was active in various community organizations in Oxford, becoming president of the Methodist Women's Missionary Society and state leader in the Mississippi Federation of Women's Clubs. By the 1920s she had become a leader in community activities. Increasingly her involvement took her beyond local groups to broader circles concerned with child welfare, education, economic opportunities for women, and community development. In 1924 Woodward was appointed a trustee for a state hospital, her first public agency role.

Woodward's husband also had an active public life. After first serving as mayor, he successfully ran for a judge position and later a seat in the Mississippi House of Representatives.

Women in Work Relief

Ellen Woodward, who headed the women's divisions in the Federal Emergency Relief Administration (FERA), the Civil Works Administration (CWA), and the Works Progress Administration (WPA), had several major challenges to overcome in establishing work programs for women. Women had a difficult time qualifying for and receiving work relief under the WPA. First, many women did not have a work history. Therefore, they were not considered part of the labor force and did not qualify for relief. Secondly, many women had children at home and could not work full-time. Thirdly, the administrators of the relief agencies were primarily men, and they placed strict limitations on what jobs women could do. Lastly, Southern states, due to their generally more conservative views, were particularly hesitant about employing women in the WPA, especially black American women. Segregation policies (laws that required separation of whites and blacks in public places) meant that women's projects had to be duplicated in separate facilities, one for white women and one for black women (segregation rules were especially strict for indoor activities). This made the projects much more costly to run. In addition, many Southerners objected to employment programs that would take black American women out of domestic service jobs, where many worked for low wages as maids and cooks in white people's homes.

Woodward proposed two hundred and fifty job categories that she considered appropriate for women. However, WPA administrators rejected almost all of them. Little was left but sewing. As a result, 56 percent of the women in the WPA worked on sewing projects; nine thousand sewing centers were established around the country. Nevertheless, through determination and persistent effort Woodward was also able to create some training and employment programs in mattress making, bookbinding, domestic service, canning of relief foods, school lunch preparation, and child care. She also pushed for more professional jobs for women, including positions as stenographers and office workers. In 1938, the peak year for women's involvement in the WPA, six hundred thousand women were employed. Unfortunately, that number fell far short of the need, leaving more than three million women unemployed. Nevertheless, the relief programs of the FERA, CWA, and WPA were significant in that they provided many women an entrance into the workforce.

His sudden death by heart attack in 1925 led Ellen at thirty-eight years of age directly into politics; she took her husband's seat in a special election, becoming the second woman to serve in Mississippi's House. However, she refused to run for reelection. Instead, she took the position of director of the women's division of the Mississippi State Board of Development (MSBD) in 1926. The MSBD was an agency designed to promote educational and economic development in the state. By 1929 Woodward had become the executive director of the MSBD. She remained with the MSBD until 1933. During this period her club and civic work brought her substantial recognition.

Arrival of the Great Depression

When the Great Depression (1929–41) worsened in 1931 and 1932, President **Herbert Hoover** (1874–1964; served 1929–33; see entry) established a federal program making funds available to state relief programs. Woodward, having great familiarity with living conditions throughout Mississippi, became a member of the state's Board of Public Welfare to help direct the available funds within Mississippi. For Woodward this proved an important experience in dealing with the unemployed. In the 1932 presidential election, Woodward actively campaigned for Franklin Roosevelt. As a result, when Roosevelt was elected, the new administration appointed Woodward, who was already experienced in relief work, director of the Women's Division of the Federal Emergency Relief Administration (FERA) in 1933. The agency provided grant money to states to support their relief efforts. Shortly after Woodward began her job as director, **Eleanor Roosevelt** (1884–1962; see entry) held the White House Conference on the Emergency Needs of Women on November 20, 1933. At the conference Woodward and others generated ideas on how to meet the needs and abilities of women and created a network of organizations to support women's relief programs.

Late that same year, under the Civil Works Administration (CWA), Woodward provided temporary jobs for 375,000 unemployed women during the winter of 1933–34. However, that was a small number out of the four million workers employed by the CWA. By 1935 women made up 12 percent of FERA workers thanks largely to the efforts of Woodward. Woodward proved fairly effective in battling with male administrators, who continually resisted providing relief jobs to women because many of the projects involved heavy construction work.

In 1935 Woodward was appointed assistant administrator for a massive new agency, Works Progress Adminis-

tration (WPA). Unlike the FERA, which primarily provided money to states for the states to administer, the WPA directly operated federal relief programs. Through the Women's and Professional Projects Division of the WPA, Woodward provided jobs for 450,000 unemployed women. Jobs included sewing, gardening, nursing, housekeeping, and museum and library research work, as well as positions in public health, emergency nursery schools, school lunchrooms, and canning centers. Woodward was also appointed administrator for Federal One, part of the WPA, which provided jobs in the arts (including music, art, theater, and writing) for some 750,000 people. Though Woodward was the administrator, many of the policy decisions were made by directors of the various units of Federal One. Federal One attracted the wrath of conservative congressional committees, who accused the program of spreading communist propaganda. In late 1938, with the WPA past its peak of activity and facing funding cutbacks, Woodward left to tackle new challenges.

Ellen Woodward, assistant administrator of the Works Progress Administration, testifies at an un-American activities hearing on December 5, 1938, to deny that communism has spread into the Federal Theatre Project of the WPA. *AP/Wide World Photo. Reproduced by permission.*

Woodward was next appointed to the Social Security Board, replacing **Molly Dewson** (1874–1962; see entry), who had resigned. The board oversaw the main elements of Social Security, including old-age payments, unemployment compensation, and public assistance to the needy. The board provided Woodward another opportunity to promote greater economic security for American women. As a board member, Woodward represented the interests of housewives and working women. A key role of Woodward's was to educate wives and mothers about benefits available to them under Social Security. However, many women worked in positions not covered by Social Security, including those who were self-employed or working for nonprofit and educational organizations and those working in health care. Therefore, Woodward fought to broaden Social Security coverage from individual workers to entire families, including the wives of workers, and to extend coverage to a broader range of workers, such as domestic workers. Woodward also fought for and defended the hiring of women in Social Security offices.

Life after the New Deal

In the 1940s Woodward became more involved in international relief issues. From 1943 to 1946 Woodward was an adviser to U.S. delegations attending the United Nations Relief and Rehabilitation Administration (UNRRA). Woodward worked on getting relief to European victims of war. She also joined the Committee on Women's World Affairs, a coalition of women's activist groups. Her reputation as an effective administrator continued to grow, and in 1945 Woodward was listed in "Washington's Ten Most Influential Women" list. After the Social Security Board was abolished in 1946, Woodward was appointed director of the Federal Security Agency's Office of Inter-Agency and International Relations. She was able to continue lobbying for an international children's fund as she had done earlier through the United Nations organization. In 1947 the Women's College of the University of North Carolina awarded Woodward an honorary degree in recognition of her dedication to public welfare in Mississippi, social security in the nation, and domestic and international relief efforts.

In December 1953 Woodward retired at age sixty-six. She remained active for another decade in women's organizations, the Democratic Party, and various charities. After a long battle with heart disease, Woodward died in 1971 in Washington, D.C. In 1976 Woodward was named to the Mississippi Hall of Fame, and her portrait hangs in the Old Capitol building in Jackson, Mississippi.

For More Information

Books
Swain, Martha H. *Ellen S. Woodward: New Deal Advocate for Women.* Jackson, MS: University Press of Mississippi, 1995.

Ware, Susan. *Beyond Suffrage: Women and the New Deal.* Cambridge, MA: Harvard University Press, 1981.

Periodicals
Swain, Martha H. "'The Forgotten Woman': Ellen S Woodward and Women's Relief in the New Deal." *Prologue* (winter 1983).

Where to Learn More

Books

Badger, Anthony J. *The New Deal: The Depression Years, 1933–1940*. New York: Hill and Wang, 1989.

Bowen, Ezra. *The Fabulous Century: 1930–1940*. New York: Time-Life Books, 1969.

Britton, Loretta, and Sarah Brash, eds. *Hard Times: The 30s*. Alexandria, VA: Time-Life Books, 1998.

Buhite, Russell D., and David W. Levy, eds. *FDR's Fireside Chats*. Norman: University of Oklahoma Press, 1992.

Burns, James McGregor. *Roosevelt: The Lion and the Fox*. Norwalk, CT: Eaton Press, 1989.

Cochran, Thomas C. *The Great Depression and World War II, 1929–1945*. Glenview, IL: Scott, Foresman, and Company, 1968.

Federal Writers Project. *These Are Our Lives*. New York: W.W. Norton & Company, Inc., 1939.

Horan, James D. *The Desperate Years: A Pictorial History of the Thirties*. New York: Bonanza Books, 1962.

Kennedy, David M. *Freedom From Fear: The American People in Depression and War, 1929–1945*. New York: Oxford University Press, 1999.

Leuchtenberg, William E. *Franklin D. Roosevelt and the New Deal, 1932–1940*. New York: Harper & Row, 1963.

Martin, George. *Madam Secretary: Frances Perkins.* Boston: Houghton Mifflin, 1976.

McElvaine, Robert S. *The Depression and the New Deal: A History in Documents.* New York: Oxford University Press, 2000.

McElvaine, Robert S. *The Great Depression: America, 1929–1941.* New York: Times Books, 1993.

Meltzer, Milton. *Brother, Can You Spare a Dime? The Great Depression, 1929–1933.* New York: New American Library, 1977.

Pasachoff, Naomi E. *Frances Perkins: Champion of the New Deal.* New York: Oxford University Press, 1999.

Perkins, Frances. *The Roosevelt I Knew.* New York: The Viking Press, 1946.

Phillips, Cabell. *From the Crash to the Blitz, 1929–1939.* New York: Macmillan, 1969.

Rogers, Agnes. *I Remember Distinctly: A Family Album of the American People, 1918–1941.* New York: Harper & Brothers Publishers, 1947.

Roosevelt, Eleanor. *The Autobiography of Eleanor Roosevelt.* New York: Da Capo Press, 2000.

Roosevelt, Franklin D. *The Public Papers and Addresses of Franklin D. Roosevelt.* 5 vols. New York: Random House, 1938–1950.

Schlesinger, Arthur M., Jr. *The Age of Roosevelt.* 3 volumes. Boston: Houghton Mifflin Company, 1957–1960.

Schlesinger, Arthur M., Jr. *The Coming of the New Deal: The Age of Roosevelt.* Boston: Houghton Mifflin Company, 1988.

Terkel, Studs. *Hard Times: An Oral History of the Great Depression.* New York: Pantheon Books, 1986.

Thompson, Kathleen, and Hilary MacAustin, eds. *Children of the Depression.* Bloomington: Indiana University Press, 2001.

Washburne, Carolyn Kott. *America in the 20th Century, 1930–1939.* North Bellmore, NY: Marshall Cavendish Corp., 1995.

Watkins, T. H. *The Great Depression: America in the 1930s.* Boston: Little, Brown, & Co., 1993.

Watkins, T. H. *The Hungry Years: A Narrative History of the Great Depression in America.* New York: Henry Holt and Company, 1999.

Winslow, Susan. *Brother, Can You Spare a Dime? America From the Wall Street Crash to Pearl Harbor: An Illustrated Documentary.* New York: Paddington Press, 1976.

Web Sites

Franklin D. Roosevelt Library and Museum. http://www.fdrlibrary.marist.edu

Library of Congress. American Memory. http://memory.loc.gov/ammem/fsowhome.html

New Deal Network. http://newdeal.feri.org

Index

**Bold type indicates
main entries and their
page numbers.**

**Illustrations are marked
by (ill.).**

R

S

Y

Z